How to Avoid Digital Slavery

Stories and Advice From 40 Authors

The White Rose UK

How to Avoid Digital Slavery

Stories and Advice From 40 Authors

Take back control and live a healthy life in freedom.

The White Rose UK

Copyright © 2023 by The White Rose UK
All rights reserved

Published in July 2023

thewhiterose.uk

Contents

	Introduction	8
1	Get Behind Me, and I Will Protect You (Cherry)	10
2	Strengthen Your Mind (Randall Bachman)	13
3	A Lot of Hot Air (Gail Foster)	18
4	Acts of Resistance (Fran Walker)	23
5	The Escape (Connie Lamb)	34
6	How Things Will Turn Out Good In the End (Teresa Bacon)	42
7	The Brigadoon Inn (Andy Thomas)	51
8	Built on Rock (Eileen Coyne)	62
9	Controlled by Technology (Alyssa R. Mills)	67
10	Don't Succumb to Fear (Stephen McMurray)	73
11	My Week In Southern Turkey (Fiona Cullen-Skowronski)	79
12	The Scrabble Group (Maronica)	84
13	The Warning (Nicole Katie Sedlak)	96

14	Technology Detox (Daniel Greene)	101
15	I Never Thought About It Like That (Stephen James Gray)	112
16	Always Make a Fuss (Radical Nan)	123
17	August 2025 (Moira M. Malcolm)	126
18	The Overbearing Octopus (E Mc M)	129
19	The Party Is Over (and It's All Our Fault) (Dee)	134
20	Seek (Jeanne G Dust)	137
21	Slavery (Mev Berwick)	142
22	Survival of the Smartest—A Beginner's Guide (Tony Zhang)	146
23	The Enemy In Your Pocket (Harry Hopkins)	152
24	The New Resistance (Ray Wilson)	156
25	The Scamdemic (Ryta C Y N Lyndley)	163
26	The Wake-Up Call (Wayne More)	166
27	Children (Tim Bragg)	170
28	The Exhibition (Tim and Annie Bragg)	181
29	Walkies Fido—Now How About It, Mr Prime Minister? (Tim Haselup)	193
30	I Don't Have a So-Called Smart Phone ... Imagine That! (Willie Fi Fife)	207
31	You Decide (Stephen James Gray)	219
32	There Is Reason to Be Optimistic (David Sheppard)	232
33	Moving Forward (New Fan of Sophie Scholl)	236

34	Digital Identity—The Final Lock Down in the Final Countdown (Simon of the family Shields)	239
35	Time Traveller (Ruth Reins)	246
36	Davos Speech Codes—The Grammar of Digital Slavery (Dominic Berry)	250
37	Where We Are and How to Resist and Fight Back (David Lawrenson)	260
38	Box Clever (U Canrun)	269
39	Steps Towards a Brighter Future (Alan Kay)	273
40	God Knew (Lily)	276
41	Human Flourishing in a Digital World (Dylan Roberts)	279
42	Region One (Stephen James Gray)	287

Introduction

Welcome to this collection of intriguing, entertaining, amusing and thought-provoking essays, written by no less than forty authors. Each piece reminds us of the threat of a digital enslavement and encourages us to resist and win back our lives. The contents range from practical advice and critical observations to personal experiences and futuristic fiction. The essays differ in style and content—some are light-hearted, some charming, some may be classified as literary gems. They are all written by genuine authors who are driven by a desire for the truth. One of my favourites (and there are quite a few) is 'You Decide'—a kind of game story with various outcomes.

Since there is no particular order the way the essays are lined up, you may begin reading this book at any chapter.

We have received even more essays than are presented here. But not all of them could make it into the book. A number of essays that are missing here, can be found on our website (use the tags 'essays' and 'how to avoid digital slavery' in the search field on thewhiterose.uk).

In case you have lost trust in humanity over the past three years, I hope that by reading this book, your trust will be restored. Not all is lost. There are wonderful, intelligent, wise and courageous people out there. You are not alone. We are many; and the awakened crowd is growing.

If you have enjoyed reading this book, don't forget sharing it with colleagues, friends and family.

Veronica Finch, May 2023

1

Get Behind Me, and I Will Protect You

By Cherry

I think we could all agree that we are living in chaotic times, those of us who are awake know this to be true, and live with that knowledge every day. Those who are awake have a bond and a connection with each other and share the immediacy of the danger in the current situation.

I think we are acutely aware that tough times await us and there will be fights aplenty in the coming months and years; there is much in the pipeline that we know the Government and its minions will try to gaslight and scare us with. Expect there to be new 'viral' threats, new energy crises, new vaccines 'to keep us all safe', oh yes, make no mistake, there is all this and much, much more in store.

So we need to dig deep, find our inner strength and push back like our lives depended on it. Resist, resist, resist. Object to plans that curtail our freedoms, such as the '15-minute cities', make representations, disagree, disrupt. Keep using cash, if you can, grow some vegetables, use small businesses who contribute to the fight for our independence, and in all decisions, aim to promote and support your right to be a sovereign individual, for there is no other way.

When we feel that the fight is too hard, and in times of doubt, we all look to draw strength where we can. For some this will be their God or whatever is dear to them, to gain the courage to get them through.

I seek strength so that I can face each day, and like so many, I personally have experienced something in this last year that has shown me that there is some greater love. I was never religious, I never considered myself to be Christian, and I have openly proclaimed my atheism. I can't say exactly what happened to me on a couple of occasions in the last year, but I do know that it moved me to tears and was unexplainable. Why did this happen to me? I have no idea, I only know that I needed something at the time. I think others have experienced similar happenings and I have heard this reported on many forums.

My children and my grandchild are exceedingly precious to me and I don't want to see them come to harm. I will do what I need to do to protect them.

For everybody else, I hope they have their protectors too.

When we think of the predicament that we are in, we have heard told that 'we are the many and they are the few', so it would seem easy to overthrow those that seek to do us harm the problem is that even though they are in the minority, they tend to occupy those key positions: in local government, in the judiciary, in the police force, they are, in most cases, what we would call 'jobs-worths'. They are, in the most part, bent to a particular ilk, by the belief that their role affords them power and has importance far above what we, 'the little people' need in order to make progress in our lives. We are, as a collective, seen as unimportant and, frankly, an irritant to the implementation of the plan for the 'greater good'. These individuals do not realise that they are eminently dispensable, and will be dispensed with after they have served their purpose.

My family, and in particular, my children and grandchild, are the most important humans that I know. I have a duty to protect them from harm, and to warn them when harm is near. This is not always easy. Who really wants to be told that their government and health service wish them to 'be gone', who wants to hear that the food and drink supply is contaminated, that the education system has been corrupted, that they could be accused and convicted of 'wrong think', if they don't follow the doctrine of the day? This is the reality we live with now, in the 21st century.

Unless we can stop this, our future looks bleak. Who wants to hear that, as a young person, embarking on their life's journey? I wouldn't have wanted to hear it. I am pretty sure it would have scared me witless. I was a teenager in the 80ss and I remember the fear I felt about possible nuclear war and the adverts for 'protect and survive' on the television. But this is worse. And regardless of the fear, I have no choice but to tell them that there are plans in place to curtail all semblance of what anyone would expect as a normal healthy life. That they are, in effect, in a battle for their very survival.

So, I have to be there, and when the chips are down, I must tell them to 'get behind me', and let me keep them as safe as I can for as long as I can. And those who face me, should I find myself in that situation, will rue the day.

2

Strengthen Your Mind

By Randall Bachman

Introduction

Tools from the beginning have been mankind's key object for carrying out the Dominion Mandate of Genesis. Whether it be clothing, a knife, a plow, plough or jumbo jet. Each tool has a function and purpose.

In these latter days we have seen the growth of new types of tools. No longer are they fit for purpose to perform an action; now the tools are complete environments, immersive, and ultimately enslaving. So is the digital age no longer a tool, but a new faux Garden of Eden.

As we have seen in the 20th Century the enemy of our souls has been permitted by the Almighty to use the precursors to digital technology: surveillance cameras, audio recording devices, surveillance video, and tracking devices, to enhance tyrants' abilities to control and subjugate men and women. We saw this in Nazi Germany, but perhaps more so in East Germany under the Soviet regime.

In tyranny the one thing you always have, and short of death, will always have, is your mind. If you are confined or tortured you still have your mind. Pain and suffering may empty you of all dignity, but if what you have in your memory is yours, it cannot be taken away. Your memory is the most important thing you possess, and that is the one thing the digital tyrants want most to capture.

Surveillance

We know that surveillance works, works against those bearing God's Image, and in favour of those belonging to the father of lies. We know this. We can see it. It is growing daily with each app, each new phone feature, each new law enforcement 'tool'. Ultimately, God decides how far the wicked are allowed to go. It is foolish to assume God will stop them before it gets out of hand. He has used such wicked people in the past to punish sinful nations, to temper and try the godly, and to bring Himself glory. There is no reason to presume, and it is a presumption, that He will not do it again.

What do we do? The answer is the same as it was in the Garden at the beginning, the same as what Christ did when he battled His and our enemy in the desert, the same as it was when Peter and the Apostles faced down the rulers of their day: Speak the Words of God. The answer always begins with: 'God hath said'.

Preparing

In preparation for the already growing tyranny, and the already growing subjugation (varies by country, but the flight path is the same), is to *memorise Scripture*. Be ready in season and out of season, at work, at school, and even in the police station under questioning, to give an answer; to quote Scripture.

Pagans and the weak often see Scriptures as magic words, and incantations of sorts. This is not the case. Scripture is the God-Breathed Word of God, the words of our Creator, the words of the one Sovereign over all the universe. What He says matters, it matters acutely, His words are the most important words that exist. Most of you agree, most of you could say these things even better than I can. But is this belief present in your life? Do you find it easier to recite rock-n-roll lyrics than passages from the Bible?

Preparation is necessary for the coming digital-powered tyranny. I am not prophesying that there will be a digital-powered tyranny, but I am recommending that preparing for that possibility is prudent. Unlike a lot of preparations, this one has no downside. The Word of God in your heart will always be used by the Holy Spirit to build you up and to bring others into the Kingdom, both when times are good and when they are not.

Memorisation

There are numerous plans for memorising, numerous suggested lists of verses to memorise, and techniques to improve and enhance the memorising process. I will not go into these. They are easy enough to find on the internet, at the moment. My thoughts are more recommendations on the Memorising Project itself.

1. Decide to make Memorisation a major priority in your life. 'Major?' Maybe 'Most Important'.

2. Identify specific actions to take to open up reliable daily space and time for memorising (e.g. less TV, less social media, etc.).

3. Decide on an approach. Here are some suggestions to consider. Take your time before committing to one, but do take the time, and do decide.

　　1. Flash cards (3x5 or UK equivalent, or cut them in half) to carry with you.

　　2. Memory app on your phone (I use BibleMemory.com) but there are others. I tried 4 or 5 before settling on BibleMemory. And yes, the enemy may see what you are

memorising. So what?

3. Cheat sheet (single sheet with verses written on them, carrying them with you for reference wherever you go.)

4. Record your voice or snip the verse from a prerecording and use it on your phone or device for audio memorising

4. Set a couple of simple goals.

1. Time spent daily in memorising: pick a small but measurable number to track: 15 or 20 minutes to start

2. A number of verses to review daily: 2 to 5 is a good start. Test to see if the number fits the time you apportioned in [NB: I do not recommend setting goals for number of verses to memorise daily/weekly etc. You are not in a competition. Better to spend a time daily and review a number of verses daily. These things are easy to track and to do]

5. Make a list of verses you already partially know to a lesser or greater extent: John 3:16, The Lord's Prayer, Psalm 23. Make these the first verses you nail down.

6. Make a running list of candidates you want to memorise at some point. When you hear or read a verse, or its used in your liturgy, and it struck you as important, put it on the list for later.

7. Make a list of hymn lyrics or simple songs (there are a lot of simple songs that are only a verse or two). Some may object to non-scripture hymns. I will explain below.

8. Add three long-passage memorisation items: The Lord's Prayer; The Ten Commandments; The Apostles Creed. Some may object to the Creed, I will explain below.

Errata

I would include a few of your favourite hymns, particularly if they are theologically rich. Avoid the modern pop-songs masquerading as spiritual. Remember, when the Apostles were jailed, chained up, tied down—they sang hymns. These expressions of praise to God can be done under the most extreme tyrannies. And if in your head, they cannot be taken away except by death.

I have included the Creed for a specific reason. It is not Scripture. However, it is the closest thing Believers have globally, to cite to each other as a pass-code. I do not support many communions over doctrinal matters, but in times of tyranny and incarceration, I will gladly join with others confessing the Creed in worshiping and praying. It is the closest thing we have to a universal membership card.

A final word concerning confessions and catechisms

Many of you are members of a communion with a defined Confession of Faith, and a catechism. Things to consider: A confession is helpful when witnessing to others of your faith in a non-combatant situation. A catechism is helpful in more challenging but non-life threatening circumstance. A catechism is also helpful in schooling others in the faith. So, in a prison or concentration camp, a catechism may find great utility in instructing others who are new to the faith, or to young people stripped from their families and churches. I value my catechism and have committed it to memory. But I did so after I had built a solid catalogue of Scripture. These important memory projects should be second to the core Scriptures.

If you want suggested lists of Scripture to memorize, feel free to contact me at rbachman@protonmail.com

3

A Lot of Hot Air

By Gail Foster

'Oh phew Murphy!' I buried my head in my T-shirt and covered my nose.

'Sara, have you fed Murphy sardines again?'

'No, his breath is getting worse.'

'He could peel paint,' said Peter as he emptied the kitchen rubbish bin.

'I reckon we could market him as a COVID cure,' I suggested. 'No self-respecting virus would mix with that foul smell.'

'Too true,' agreed Peter.

'Well, I'm not sending him to the vet,' declared Sara. 'I don't want him to be a walking mRNA factory. I don't even want them to know he's alive. They'll track and trace him, then decide he has dog 'flu and that'll be the end of him.'

'It sounds far-fetched but look what they are doing to the cows.'

'Our Minister for Agriculture, Fisheries, Forestry and Emergency Management, Murray Watt agrees with the United Nations push to reduce methane emissions by 30% by 2030,' I read from the local rag.

'Let me guess,' said Sara. 'It's climate change.'

'You've got it Sa. Minimising methane emissions, will prevent climate chaos.'

'Oh well, we better rush right in then.'

'Haven't we always had cows and herd animals?' asked Peter.

'I'm thinking so. There are a lot of ancient bible verses about milk and honey and I am thinking it is not referring to soy beans.'

'Fair point,' agreed Peter as he poured soy milk into his morning coffee.

'And He owns the cattle on a thousand hills... (Psalm 50). I have been reading my bible, Mum.'

'Don't some cultures count wealth in cows?' asked Peter.

'Yes, hence the term, cash cow.' I replied.

'Cash cow... I think we're on to something here, Mum. How does our Minister for Agriculture, Fisheries, Forestry and Emergency Management, propose to reduce methane emissions?'

'Good question, in Holland their government want to reduce the numbers of cows by one third. There are riots in the streets. Here, they propose feeding cows, seaweed.'

'Seaweed, weeds of the sea, sea-grass?' asked Sara.

'We can't feed cows grass from the land but we can feed them grass from the sea?' asked Peter.

'What exactly are the qualifications of our Agriculture Minister, Mum?

'I'm glad you asked, Sa. Murray Watt has qualifications as a lawyer and experience as a public servant, a judge's associate and a political adviser.'

'Obviously, he knows all about bovine digestive processes.'

'If seaweed is so good for cows why hasn't it been used before?'

'Another excellent question, Sa.'

'Some companies are making seaweed-based, livestock feed additives to reduce methane by up to 98%.'

'I wonder if Minister Watt has a financial interest in said companies?'

'Such cynicism, Sa. It does make you wonder who is benefiting from 'de-carbonised energy solutions'.

'What's that?' asked Peter.

'It is the raison d' être of the Environmental Defence Fund.'

'Oh, so where are the funds coming from?'

'Now Peter, should we be asking so many questions? It is so obviously safe and effective. The EDF is going to save us and the environment.

'Oh.'

'I wonder if seaweed would help Murphy emissions?' Sa pondered.

Murphy padded to his blue plastic food bowl and looked mournfully at his cold porridge. He looked hopefully at the fridge as Peter opened the door.

'They'll probably market it to dogs next,' I said.

'Of course, it's vegan isn't it?' Sara agreed.

'Then they will need pills for the inevitable digestive problems … which will be diagnosed as dog flue…'

'So he will need a needle for that,' I suggested.

'And then he will get really sick.' Sara picked up Murphy and rubbed his ears affectionately.

'He'll need pills for that,' said Sara.

'And more pills for the side effects,' I added.

'And then, he will be offered euthanasia,' Peter concluded.

'And a little plot in a pet cemetery.'

'A merciful end,' said Peter as he washed the coffee pot.

'Eternal repose,' said Sara.

Murphy growled. Sara released her hold and Murphy padded back to his station at his food bowl.

'Fido's finish,' I said. Murphy slurped dejectedly at his water bowl.

'May he rest in peace.' I looked sadly at Murphy. Murphy looked sadly at his food bowl.

'That is so depressing, I think he needs some yoghurt in his porridge,' I suggested.

'Good idea,' agreed Peter. Peter took the pot of yoghurt from the fridge, pulled off the lid and filled a rounded dessertspoon with creamy, white yumminess. He added the yoghurt to the congealed porridge and cut with the spoon to disperse it through the cereal. Murphy was not slow to notice this nutritional amendment.

'That took about 30 seconds.' Peter shook his head in amazement.

'Let's add this up. We are feeding Murphy with porridge, sardines, yoghurt and leftovers, taking him for daily walks and giving him cuddles which costs very little.'

On a seaweed or bought dog food we would be paying for packaged food, vitamins, vet visits, pills and potions, injections and a cemetery plot.'

'Phew, that'd add up,' said Peter. 'You would need pet insurance.'

'Why are they taxing methane from cows and not possums?' I wondered.

'Why aren't they taxing cabbage and beans?' asked Peter.

'What is stopping them taxing people?' asked Sara. 'They'll do a study soon on human flatulence and climate change.'

'You mean fart facts?' I asked.

'There would be a vaccine for that,' said Peter.

'Of course Peter, it's probably caused by Covid,' I agreed.

'We have a few voices of sense. Malcolm Roberts of One Nation says that a grass fed cow produces 1,597 times more protein than it consumes and that methane is part of a biogenic carbon cycle. Methane plus oxygen produces water and carbon dioxide which is reabsorbed into pasture through photosynthesis and produces plant growth,' I said.

'You can't mean it mum. You mean cow farts are not a threat to life as we know it?'

'No, but our politicians are,' said Peter.

'Oh well, Mr Albanese said the targets are aspirational and non-binding.'

'I suggest, Sa, they are more inspirational, to profit making corporations. I fear, also there will definitely be binding if we feed cows seaweed.'

'Climate change Mum, climate change.'

Murphy sprawled on his pillow in the sun and snored contentedly.

4
Acts of Resistance

By Fran Walker

'Emergencies' have always been the pretext on which the safeguards of individual liberty have been eroded.
(Friedrich August von Hayek)

Introduction
(Historical context)

For many of us, faith in the government and mainstream media has been destroyed over the last few years as increasingly, yesterday's conspiracy theories become today's reality. Agents of the state, for example the heads of the BBC and the NHS have been gathered into the dystopian fold along with the banking elite to be brought into obedient alignment toward the aims of Agendas 2020-30.

Alternative scientists, health officials and other dissidents who have tried to offer opposing views to the mainstream narrative with their truths and concerns about all things 'COVID' have been cruelly de-platformed and cancelled without democratic redress.

Free speech has been gagged or re-branded as dangerous

rhetoric. Alternative opinions are quickly ordained as mis-information or rendered surplus to requirement. We have silently arrived at the beginning of a 'New World Order.' Orwellian 'Newspeak' has been kidnapped and transported from 1984 to the present day. For those of us who are 'awake' (not to be confused with those who are 'woke'), loyalty to the establishment is under scrutiny and suspension.

'All animals are equal, but some animals are more equal than others.' (George Orwell, Animal Farm)

At first, it may seem more comfortable to discredit the conspiracy theorists: Ostensibly, it feels more palatable to deny 'back channel' warnings of impending doom in practically every area of our lives as merely the fictional imaginings of conspiracy nuts. We reason that everything that has been uncomfortable and difficult in the last three years has been for our greater good. Examples of normal life being suspended include being mandated and coerced into accepting experimental gene therapy jabs in order to keep jobs. Citizens were told that in an exchange for taking the 'vaccine' and wearing masks they would be rewarded with a return to freedom of movement, to the erstwhile life we naively took for granted as a human right.

Furthermore, the endurance of punitive lockdowns and dubious social distancing rules were imposed upon us all lest we become ill with 'COVID' and become a selfish burden to our already failing NHS. Moreover, school and church closures and not being able to get an appointment at one's local GP surgery has all been considered necessary for our safety. It has also become the norm for many who were instructed to work from home during the height of the 'pandemic' to carry on doing so.

Worryingly, it has been made the norm to live one's life

through the use of home internet. For example, the relentless media drive to get everyone to download apps for everything from banking and buying insurance to listening to music and socialising. Our phones are now to be a further source by which government can warn us of impending doom. We are told that it is cheaper and safer to purchase our white goods and even the weekly food shop online. Even dance classes, meditation and work meetings are encouraged through the use of zoom on one's own computer or smartphone paid for presumably by Joe Public. Perhaps; it is somewhat convenient to use the internet but it is not free (subscriptions and gadgetry are required).

But more than this, by living life digitally, we are losing our grasp on the old life and our ability to make offline choices. Many of us have unwittingly transferred bodily autonomy and digital control to the State. The high street has inevitably been shunned in favour of purchasing goods and services online. We are losing the freedom to choose how we do life. It's time to 'wake up' and realise where this is leading.

Curiously, there is little need to leave your home for very much at all. After all, it seems life is being *delivered to us* rather than sought out by us.

If the state succeeds in containing us in 'smart' neighbourhoods, everyone will be under scrutiny via the installation of *potentially* criminalising camera surveillance. Thus our sovereignty ebbs away and we become less spontaneous, less free. As the State organises life for us our behaviour becomes more robotic and aligned with a set of approved protocols as posited by remote un-elected oligarchs. Of course, they may say that this is necessary to keep us 'safe'—an undertaking we are constantly being led to believe is something we cannot achieve for ourselves anymore.

'You will own nothing and be happy.' (The Great Reset)

However, like a child naively hiding behind the sofa so as not to be traumatised by a scary television programme, we cannot remain in our 'comfort zone' indefinitely. If we do not come out from behind the sofa, we cannot hope to challenge the status quo with our dissidence and so will fail to save the future for those who are yet to come. Together though, we can restore hope as we engineer mass change by applying our individual efforts simultaneously.

The impending digital nightmare that is the Great Reset can be challenged and indeed defeated if we pull together against the elitist minority. The elite may be disgustingly rich but they do not have a patent just yet on our free will. We can upset their plans to silently roll out fifteen-minute-cities in the name of un-realistic net zero goals. We can also veto the digital IDs and challenge the mass installation of the untested 5G as well as the oligarchs' plans to eradicate cash by imposing digital currency. It is thought that digital currency, once installed will seamlessly be linked into a citizen's digital ID and social credit score and processed according to elitist ideals: A citizen's ability to access their funds will be assessed externally by an approved agent of the State, probably Artificial Intelligence (AI). At this point we will have truly departed from anything resembling human democracy and instead will be living in a world of totalitarian rule. Do you want to be a digital slave?

'A man convinced against his will is of the same opinion still'
(unknown)

Let's rewind. For now, we continue to hang onto our remaining freedoms and our children's future by a fragile thread. Although at times, there seems to be such a mood of dreaded inevitability about the future, I believe that we owe it to ourselves, to future generations and to God to 'do the right thing' which is of course to challenge digital slavery.

Most have busy lives full of various commitments and for many the Cost of Living Crisis keeps us 'down at heel' as we try to achieve the basic business of getting through the week, the day or even the hour. But the inconvenient work of resistance should be peacefully taken up by *us all* if we are to triumph.

Individually, we can all do practical things to defend our human rights, to re-establish our way of life, imperfect as it may be. Together, we can restore our eroding democracy and disappearing freedoms. Victory against the tyrannical aims of the godless oligarchs with their nefarious agenda against the global masses can be usurped and justice served.

'*Cometh the hour, cometh the man.*' (John 4:23)

Here is an accessible pick and mix list of useful strategies that we can all employ to resist impending digital slavery:

Get offline!

Consider deleting online customer accounts with those big corporations that are affiliated with or invested in the Great Reset. Use the high street to buy goods and services as much as you can. It will help to keep physical shops open. Also, ask for a printed receipt instead of divulging your personal e-mail address or phone number to strangers who may well sell or share your data.

Using cash does not incur bank charges or stoke political intervention. Cash is inclusive and it protects your privacy and current location. Using cash will also help to justify keeping the banks and Post Offices open. If you have to use your bank card to pay for goods and services, use chip and pin instead of wirelessly tapping or using your phone to pay. Many dissenters still use cheques wherever possible. If a shop won't accept cash, politely tell them that you won't be using them anymore. If everyone did this, the problems of a cashless society would fade away.

Tip: Good to know—Cash can be drawn out from your local Post Office as well as from ATMs and banks. Equally, cash can be paid into your bank account via the Post Office and cheques too can be paid into your bank via your local Post Office. Many utility bills and store card payments can be completed at your local Post Office—use it or lose it as the saying goes.

Have your say

Give customer feedback whenever you can to businesses. Businesses and the Public Sector often ask customers to fill in surveys and consultations so take the opportunity to give customer feedback. For example, politely and clearly express your concerns; explain that due to health and safety concerns (particularly around the untested 5G) that you are trying to reduce your usage of the internet. Say that you would prefer to assess goods in a shop rather than buying online. At least express your need for there to be a choice to shop offline.

Another way of having your views heard is to sign petitions, lobby your local MP. Challenge the mainstream media and Ofcom. There are various ways of getting in touch. If everyone took the time to do this, it would make a difference.

Note: Many adults with special educational needs, some disabled folk, poorer people and many elderly folk cannot use the online world for a variety of reasons including lack of the required 'know-how', inability to afford the internet or gadgetry required to use it as well as genuine security/vulnerability issues. Businesses and banks need to respect people's need for payment choice and accessibility to services. Businesses and shops should not be manoeuvring us into a 'one-world-option'.

Shun the digital health appointments

Do you remember when you could simply walk into your local GP Surgery or ring up to get an appointment? It usually took mere minutes and for the most part worked rather well. Alas, the NHS has rolled out a digital system to 'process' patients remotely. Obtaining a traditional routine appointment has become something of a struggle; it is no longer a given outcome. For example, patients are now led to use e-consults to contact their doctor in the first instance. Offline face to face appointments are, we are told, in short supply or unnecessary. If you do ring your doctor's surgery you will notice that you have to listen to a lot of automated 'right speak' about how to safely proceed to the next level which means waiting in a long queue of other patients.

If you manage to get through to a receptionist she will ascertain whether you may progress to the next stage: For example, the receptionist will decide if your medical concerns (which she will have extracted from you by now) are indeed worthy of a call back from a doctor or a face to face appointment.

You may also be directed to seek pharmaceutical advice from a chemist or told that various links will be sent to your phone for your convenience. It is hoped that you have not run out of phone credit or breath whilst you wait for all of these stages to come to an end.

If you dislike this digital approach then consider challenging it. Simply tell the receptionist that you don't have access to the internet or that you are not willing to upload photographs of bodily parts online for safety and privacy reasons.

If told that you can have an online appointment, explain that you do not have a smartphone or zoom applications. The receptionist will have little option left but to offer you a face to face appointment. You may wish to write to NHS England

and or your local MP and give them your criticisms on these digital requirements. The more people that challenge the status quo, the more the public sector will have to listen.

Wear a regular watch

They have been helping us keep time for centuries and are arguably more attractive than 'Fitbits' and other digital monitors. A regular watch is not going to chastise you because you ate a Curly Wurly instead of going to the gym today. In fact, it will not process you at all, how refreshing. We don't need a gadget linked to the internet to manage our fitness and health. Most people can use their God-given common sense if allowed to do so.

Social media

Consider ditching your social media accounts such as Facebook or as I call it Facecrook. Despite reassurances to the contrary, your information is not private nor is it safe from scrutiny. Companies such as Facebook use software designed to remove your posts if they do not comply with their strict view of the world. Free speech seems to have been re-branded as hate speech so if you don't 'comply' with the agreed narrative, 'Big Brother' has the power to suspend your account or you may be cancelled altogether. Why give these globalists the opportunity to censor you? Why line their pockets with your support? If everyone ditched them, they would lose their easy revenue and more importantly their power to adjudicate over the masses. Instead communicate with your friends directly. People are often delighted to receive a hand-written letter in the post. Better still, meet up in person and enjoy a private conversation by taking a walk with a friend or by visiting your local coffee shop.

Challenge the mainstream narrative when you can

Obviously, it is unwise to get into physical fights or arguments with others, you will only turn them off from what you have to say and you may lose their friendship and/or support permanently and face being criminalised as has sadly happened with public lawful protesters.

The last few years have been tough for everyone and some people feel that they have been doing the right thing by getting vaccinated, using contactless payment methods and staying six feet away from family and friends. People who've followed government guidelines without engaging critical thinking may also assume that the need to achieve 'net zero' is based on science not on the State's plan to control us. Obeying instructions from the government and the NHS means unwittingly obeying other organisations placed higher up in the hierarchy such as the WHO (World Health Organisation) and the WEF (World Economic Forum).

You may need to be very patient with people who have fallen in with this encroaching regime. I find that people take note better when you first listen to their reasoning for following the mainstream narrative. I sympathise with them as to how they gave their trust over to the 'powers that be' thinking that we were still living in a democratic system that had one's best interests at heart. When people feel listened to, they are more likely to consider your viewpoint.

The mainstream narrative has been executed with such military-style efficiency that it is not easy for many people to 'hear' a different opinion or to believe that something more sinister is afoot. It is a massive ask for us to expect the masses to comprehend the deliberate manipulation of the global population in one conversation. Many will need to adjust to the planned dystopian nightmare that the rest of us have been silently screaming about for so long and many more will not realise the truth until it is directly affecting them. For example, when there is no bank left on any high street for them to use, or when the only option left to access their life lies in submitting to the digitalisation of everything and everybody.

Deliver the truth

If you feel unable to speak with family and friends directly there are still other ways in which you can help to awaken people.

You can become involved in distributing 'wake up' or action leaflets. See the White Rose Website for details and indeed David Clews at UNN. Also, there is a newspaper called the Light Paper that carries lots of political and medical information that is well referenced throughout.

Get involved in your local 'Stand In The Park' (STIP) or form your own group of like-minded people. Tune in to Unity News Network. Use alternative social media networks such as Brand New Tube and open a window to world events on the Telegram App. You can access GB News on your television and radio. GB News allows democratic debate by engaging the opinions of a wide variety of presenters, guest speakers and other bastions of knowledge and ambassadors for free speech and common sense.

Whatever you decide, please do your own research and apply critical thinking before accepting the status quo. We are supposed to be sovereign beings. Do not blindly believe that something is for your own good even if the person or agent telling you has previously seemed trustworthy and is placed in a position of authority.

As Shakespeare warns in the Tempest...

Acts of Resistance

'Hell is empty, and all the devils are here.'

Now is the time to choose which side of history you want to belong to.
I pray for courage, I pray for you and for all mankind.

References:

Josh Jones, 'George Orwell Explains How "Newspeak" Works, the Official Language of His Totalitarian Dystopia in 1984', 25 January 2017, *Open Culture* [website], <https://openculture.com/2017/01/george-orwell-explains-how-newspeak-works.html> | George Orwell, *Animal Farm*, Harcourt Brace & Co, 1945 | George Orwell, *1984*, Secker and Warburg, London, 1949 | Friedrich August von Hayek, '"Emergencies" have always been the pretext on which the safeguards of individual liberty have been eroded.', *Brainy Quote* [website], <https://brainyquote.com/quotes/friedrich_august_von_haye_185957?src=t_freedom> | 'The Great Reset, Davos Agenda 2021—"You'll Own Nothing And Be Happy"', 21 February 2021, *Alex Hickman* [website], <https://alexhickman.co.uk/the-great-reset-2> | 'Prof. Klaus Schwab on Digital Inclusion', *World Economic Forum* [website], <https://weforum.org/videos/ksc-on-the-digital-inclusion> | *World Economic Forum* [website], <https://weforum.org/events/world-economic-forum-annual-meeting-2023> | *The White Rose* [website], <https://thewhiterose.uk> | *A Stand In The Park* [website], <https://astandinthepark.org> | *The Light / The Uncensored Truth* [website] <https://thelightpaper.co.uk> | *Unity News Network* [website], <https://unitynewsnetwork.co.uk> | GB News live on TV Virgin 604, Freesat 216, SKY 512, Freeview 236 and DAB+Radio | *Stop World Control* [webstite], <https://stopworldcontrol.com> | 'MPs and Lords', *UK Parliament* [website], <https://members.parliament.uk/FindYourMP> | 'Contact Ofcom', *Ofcom* [website], <https://ofcom.org.uk/about-ofcom/contact-us> | Henry Grabar, 'Is the tiny little neighborhood the city of the future?', 25 January 2023, *The Guardian* [website], <https://theguardian.com/us-news/2023/jan/25/15-minute-city-urban-planning-future-us-cities> | 'Mass leafleting in Oxford against 15-minute cities', 11 January 2023, *YouTube* [website], <https://youtube.com/watch?v=XypqPNHLl2U> | 'Do You Have Doubts About the Science Behind This Global Pandemic?' [file], <https://thewhiterose.uk/freedom/uploads/2021/05/Flyer-The-White-Rose-UK-Resistance_02.pdf> | *Free Speech Union* [website], <https://freespeechunion.org> | 'A man convinced against his will is of the same opinion still', *Quotation Celebration* [website], <https://quotationcelebration.wordpress.com/2017/02/20/a-man-convinced-against-his-will-is-of-the-same-opinion-still-unknown> | *All Great Quotes* [website], <https://allgreatquotes.com/the-tempest-quotes-51>

All websites or files accessed on 10 May 2023.

5

The Escape

By Connie Lamb

Jane couldn't believe her eyes. Emerging in front of her was a tight log fence enclosing, what seemed like a whole village. Thatched and slate roofs loomed over the fence. From one or two buildings smoke rose up into the hot summer sky. A short stone tower stuck out in the centre, probably a chapel. So this is where the bell ringing came from, she thought.

Behind her lay the wilderness through which she had staggered for days, aimless and desperate. She was weak and hungry. Her dark long hair, tied at the back, shone of grease. Her jeans and lumberjack blouse were scruffy. She was dirty and smelly. But most of all, lonely. Up to now, the only buildings she had come across had been abandoned farms, overgrown with weeds and ivy. Young trees breaking up the masonry, brick walls crumbling and roofs collapsing. Full of hazards. But the atmosphere they emanated was worse: cold and ... creepy. She avoided abandoned buildings as the devil avoids holy water. The fields that had once been used for growing crops, such as wheat, barley and oats, were now overgrown with dark-leafed bitter docks, and endless thorns, which made it impossible to cross through. After that came the big forest which provided some comfort. It was good for hiding, and she found food. Very little of course, not enough to last for long, but it had kept her alive over the past ten days. Raspberries, blackberries, a couple of apples, spring water. Hunger driven, she had had to learn on the spot, how to hunt, butcher and roast rabbit over a small fire.

In her pocket she kept a lighter, a pocket knife, a few photos and a hair comb. She had dumped her smart phone in the depths of the river, as soon as she was out of reach of all face recognition cameras. That stopped them from tracking her movements. Since she had not been eligible to leave the city for more than forty-five minutes, she had had to make sure nothing looked suspicious. She had left without a rucksack, without a bag. Not even a bottle or a sandwich. Now she hadn't changed her clothes for ten days. Nights had been cold and rough, days scorching hot.

Jane didn't regret running away. Everything had become too much in the city. Half of her relatives and acquaintances had passed away due to the depopulation shots received—when was it?—already 18 years ago—and the other half was lost to the mindless stupidity of cyber-controlled New Normal. She had been forced out of her job as a reporter after artificial intelligence had taken over. All she had been doing in that position, was copy-pasting and reciting scripts filled with lies, lies, lies. She had hated it. But unemployment wasn't better. The highlight of a usual day was the lab food delivery by drone to the front door of her shared flat. Her boyfriend, whom she had intended to marry, was one of the few (like her) who hadn't had the depopulation shot. But he was nevertheless poisoned by mRNA injected beef, as he refused to eat the synthetic meat, produced by Big Cooperation. This was how they singled out refusers, and she knew, she too, was on the hit-list. She had heard of other refusers running away from the controlled city, surviving in the wilderness. Everyone knew that escapees existed, but no one talked about them, much less, saw them in the news. It took her a year of inner struggling (following his death), until she was ready to leave. She was in her late twenties, and nothing held her back. If she'd die out there, in the wilderness, so be it. Could anything be worse than living like a zombie with 24/7 surveillance?

She stepped along the thick fence and soon found an entrance to the village. The tall wooden gate stood open. She peered inside, not yet daring to go any further. There were dozens of stone and wooden houses, small barns and stables, inbetween grass and fenced gardens. No wires, no antennas, no cameras, no roads, no cars, not even a bike in sight. A couple of speckled hens strutted across the grass and the foot-trodden path, pecking occasionally from the ground as they went along. An open shelter with an anvil and bellows lying next to it on the ground—seemed to be the smithy. Not far from that stood a large stone oven, a thin line of white smoke rose out of the chimney. The smell of baking bread. To the right she saw a fountain with sparkling water running into a long grey stone basin. Wooden buckets and clay jugs stood next to it, ready for carrying water away. She pinched herself twice to make sure this wasn't a dream. Could she be hallucinating? No, she thought. After all, she hadn't ate any mushrooms when roaming through the forest (she couldn't distinguish between edible and poisonous ones).

Jane touched the fence. The wood felt real. She took a deep breath and walked through the porch.

Just as she wondered if anyone was there, a strongly built, middle-aged man wearing a leather apron jumped up from a stool in the shade, an invisible question mark written across his face. The sudden appearance made her blood rush into her face. He must be the smithy, she thought.

The Escape

'Hello, I'm an escapee,' she stuttered, hoping he wouldn't refuse her access to the village.

He nodded and stroked his thick, greying beard. 'That's how it looks,' he said before he beckoned her over.

'You look hungry and exhausted.'

'That's what I am!' she answered. It was good to hear another humanly voice—not only after days of solitude, but also after living in the city.

'We'll soon have something ready for you!'

'That's kind,' she mumbled and followed him through the village. Everything around her looked like in the olden days, how it must have been hundreds of years ago. Every building was made of stone or wood, some were quite new, as the wood was still light and fresh. There were more open shelters, like the smithy. One was filled with wicker baskets of all sizes, some of them not finished yet. They passed gardens with vegetables and herbs, groups of berry bushes, plum trees, a goat tied to a long rope, pigs grunting in their pen and single dogs and cats lazing in the shade. To the back of the village, dozens of thin fields ran down the slope with plenty of grain swaying in the breeze. In the meadow sheep, cattle and a few horses were grazing in the sun and resting in the shade of apple and pear trees with ripening fruit on.

'The grain fields ... how do you farm them?' She hadn't seen any machines or tractors.

'With horse, ox and plow,' he answered quite naturally.

It was quiet in the village, apart from the buzzing bees hovering over lavender bushes in full blossom and the occasional animal sound, and she wondered where everyone was.

'Where are the people who live here? Do they go elsewhere to work?'

He shook his head and chuckled. 'No, they're at Mass.'

He pointed at the chapel—a stone building with tower and a bell hanging in an open niche. 'There's Mass everyday,' he added.

'It's my duty to be doorkeeper, today,' he said. 'We don't really expect intruders. But years back, we were far more anxious. Now out of habit, we stick to guarding the village entrance during Mass.'

They came near the chapel, so close that she could hear a male voice through the open window, speaking words in a language she didn't recognise.

'What language?'

'Latin.'

'Why?'

'We celebrate Mass in the old rite. That's how it used to be in every church across the country—up to five hundred years ago. We've gone back to how it was in those days, before the state took over the church and all.'

'A lot here seems to be as it was five hundred years ago,' she said grinning.

The door swung open and bearded men, women in long dresses and giggling children swarmed out. The villagers all looked somewhat weatherbeaten, yet strong and healthy. Those who noticed Jane stopped shortly to glance at her, others smiled and greeted her with a nod before heading off home or back to work in the fields, stables and workshops.

'Are they obliged to take part in this Mass?'

'No, of course no one's forced to. But most do—it gives us a kind of balance ... a refreshment between all the hard work, if you get what I mean. There's lots of work, you see. But it's good, the way it is.'

The man brought her to a wooden hut with a thatched roof. The entrance was decorated with carved swirly patterns painted in red, green and yellow and there was a doorbell with a rope dangling down. Inside it was dim and cool. There was only a single window with a wood shutter. She sat down at a long table surrounded by benches and stools. As her eyes got accustomed to the dim, she discovered bunches of dried herbs hanging from the ceiling, jars of honey, pickles and other conserves lined up on shelves along the wall and leather stretched out on frames. A mixed scent of spice, animal skins, smoke and straw filled the air.

'I'm John, by the way,' he said as he brought her tea from a cauldron hanging over the fire place. 'I'm the smithy of the village.'

'Oh, I thought so!' she said, accepting the drink. 'Thanks, I'm Jane.' Before taking a sip, she held up the mug in front of her. 'A familiar face,' she exclaimed. The mug depicted the coronation of King Charles III. 'It doesn't match to the rest of the house, though…'

'Oh, it came with us, when we moved away,' he answered. 'Yes, a relic from the olden days.' They both chuckled.

The tea was tepid and sweet.

'What kind of tea?'

'You guess!'

'Peppermint?'

'Almost! Home-grown lemon balm.'

'With sugar?'

He shook his head. 'I've added a bit of honey to it. My brother in-law is a bee-keeper,' he answered while piling up a plate with cookies, two crusty bread rolls, a slice of butter and a chunk of cheese.

'These were baked in our stone oven outside,' he said, pointing at the baked goods. He sounded proud and meek at the same time. 'My daughter bakes a lot. Butter and cheese are from my friend's sheep's milk.'

Jane never tasted anything so good. She ate and drank greedily. He smiled and topped up.

'How did you get here?' he asked when she was full.

She told him how she had escaped the city, crossed through former farm estates and roamed the forest in search of other escapees. She felt safe to talk about it now, these village people had left everything behind.

'How did you manage to build this up, and remain unnoticed?' she asked in awe.

'Around sixteen years ago, some of us decided to go off-grid. We were five families at the beginning. As the idea spread underground, more and more joined us. By the time we moved, there were dozens. That was when the authorities spoke about creating 15-minute cities. You'd only be able to exit and enter if you were connected to the digital system. As things were getting tighter, it was "now or never". Leaving meant a lot of sacrifices: no comfort, no electricity, no modern way of transport, no internet, no phones... But it was all worth the while.'

John leaned back against the wall and stretched his legs.

'I knew the system was wrong, years before, but hadn't found the courage to step out until that point. All people were going to be forced to work, live, and move and breathe within the 15-minute ghetto, and only a few would be allowed out with special permission, but who am I to tell this to you...'

'That's how it was,' Jane confirmed.

'After the first groups moved up here to build the village, smaller groups followed, and later single people—they didn't really move, the way we did—we came with suitcases, bags, rucksacks and trollies loaded with stuff: tools, clothes, books, kitchen utensils, seeds, plants and animals. People who escaped later, turned up with hardly anything at all. We villagers only learnt bit by bit what was going on in the city when new people arrived. I've never returned to the city in all these years.'

Jane nodded. 'The restrictions only got tighter from when

you left, however, people's mental and physical health went down rapidly. And...' she paused. There was a lot more to say, but she wasn't ready yet to talk about all the troubles she had experienced.

'Don't worry,' he said, as if he knew what was going on in her head. 'It will take you a few weeks to settle in ... and to process your past.'

'You will accept me then?'

'There's no other choice,' he said chuckling.

Later that day, Jane was introduced to some other villagers; two women who showed Jane where to bath. The hot water came from a large cauldron and they mixed in cold water. They gave her clean clothes and a piece of lavender soap.

'Homemade?' she asked.

'Yep!' came the answer.

They showed her a place where she could rest—the log cabin of John's sister, Mary, who lived here with her husband. Their children were grown-up and they had a spare bed behind a large weaving loom and baskets filled with yarn. The wood-framed bed was low to the ground. The mattress was stuffed with straw and covered with sheepskin. A striped blanket lay folded at the foot of the bed. She took it in her hands and inhaled the pleasant scent of real wool. (When was the last time she had touched and smelled sheep's wool? It must have been in her early childhood, when visiting one of the last working farms with Dad). She stretched out. It surprised her how comfortable the bed was. Her last thoughts were: 'home at last', before drifting off to sleep with the steady thumping sounds of Mary's weaving loom and the distant tune of a fiddle playing to tap dance in the background.

6

How Things Will Turn Out Good In the End

By Teresa Bacon

So how can we avoid digital slavery and how will things turn out good, when it seems that those who assume so much power over us no longer hide their wish to stamp out the very essence of humanity? It can only be because we will use the power invested in us by our Creator, to overcome their evil intentions. As more and more people become aware of the crimes being perpetrated under guise of being 'for our own good' or for 'saving the planet', it may help us to draw inspiration from past and present defenders of truth and freedom.

In 1373 Julian, Anchoress of Norwich, struggled to understand why the bad things and evil doings of her day were allowed to occur. This was perhaps similar to our own present-day bewilderment, as digitisation[1] confronts us with the loss of an authentic sense of who we really are—alongside the

---

1 *Digitisation*—'the process of converting information from a physical format into a digital one', David Burkett, 19 December 2017, *WorkingMouse* [website] <https://workingmouse.com.au/innovation/digitisation-digitalisation-digital-transformation>, accessed 4 May 2023.

threat of our demise through 'climate change', 'the war on terror', multiple 'pandemics' etc. Julian was given an answer which must count as the greatest validation and reassurance for us as God's children, in all English literature:

> 'And thus, in my folly, afore this time often I wondered why by the great foreseeing wisdom of God the beginning of sin was not letted: for then, methought, all should have been well. This stirring [of mind] was much to be forsaken, but nevertheless mourning and sorrow I made therefor, without reason and discretion.
> But Jesus, who in this Vision informed me of all that is needful to me, answered by this word and said: It behoved that there should be sin; but all shall be well, and all shall be well, and all manner of thing shall be well.'[2]

Julian also explains her context of the word 'sin': 'In this naked word sin, our Lord brought to my mind, generally, all that is not good'. As global citizens we have certainly had our share of 'all that is not good', in varying proportions depending on where we live and our circumstances. We know and accept that this earthly life brings with it many hardships and sorrowful experiences of natural origin, but the past three years in particular have taught us that some agency is hard at work to make our lives much more difficult, and has caused many to lose their lives or to suffer other devastating loss and injury. That people working towards this aim may be controlled and influenced by something of non-human origin, may be discerned in the 'fiend' and his workings, as described by Julian. An extract from her writing (at the conclusion of this essay) could just as aptly apply to the times we are living

---

[2] 'Julian of Norwich: Revelations of Divine Love (Selections)', *Pressbooks* [website], <https://pressbooks.pub/earlybritishlit/chapter/julian-of-norwich-revelations-of-divine-love-selections>, accessed 4 May 2023.

through.

Saint Margaret Clitherow of York had her own spiritual conviction tested to the utmost during Henry the Eighth's reign. That tyrannical ruler, a monarch whose vindictive decrees foreshadowed those meted out by government over the past three years, discharged his own failings onto the populace. He forced many to abandon their spiritual heritage on pain of severe punishment, should they dare to oppose his 'new normal'. Saint Margaret's sadistic torture and execution was the price she paid for her stand against oppression, which led her to give sanctuary to persecuted priests and to educate children who wished to remain Catholic in their religion.[3]

We now anticipate the coronation of another king, Charles III who has already betrayed a large section of his subjects. In the words of Sir Julian Rose:

'In one of the more shocking hypocrisies of this year so far, Charles III, King of England—considered to be a strong supporter of organic farming and environmental causes—has given his Royal Assent to a biotechnology 'innovation' which will provide an open book for UK firms to alter the genome of animals and plants, so as to create novel engineered species and biotech 'foods'.
In taking this step Charles has committed an open act of betrayal of all bona fide farmers, and particularly of organic farmers.'[4]

It will be up to all of us who care about our children and

---

[3] 'Great Britain's Martyrs—Part II—Margaret Clitherow', 25 February 2023, *The White Rose* [website], <https://thewhiterose.uk/great-britains-martyrs-part-ii-margaret-clitherow>, accessed 4 May 2023.

[4] News Wire, 'Disbelief as "Green King" Charles Gives Royal Assent to New Gene Breeding Technology', 30 March 2023, *21st Century Wire* [website], <https://21stcenturywire.com/2023/03/30/disbelief-as-green-king-charles-gives-royal-assent-to-new-gene-breeding-technology>, accessed 4 May 2023.

grandchildren's future, to stand against Charles's betrayal of our farmers. We must ensure that his ascension to the throne is nullified should he seek to erode any more of what is our rightful heritage through his obeisance to the World Economic Forum. It is good to see that several experts in Common Law have come forward, to remind him that his remit is to serve his people, not Klaus Schwab and his like.

Dr David Bellamy staked his entire career as a much-admired naturalist and TV personality on the fact that anthropogenic climate change was a fabrication, which he dismissed as 'poppycock'. A 'Daily Express' article from November 5th 2008 quoted him as saying:

> 'Global warming is part of a natural cycle and there's nothing we can do to stop these cycles. The world is now facing spending a vast amount of money on tax to try to solve a problem that doesn't actually exist'.[5]

His refusal to back down in the face of the manufactured media and establishment storm which followed, cost him nearly everything but his life and the love of those who knew he was right.

As noted by Kieran Sutherland in his 'Belfast Telegraph' obituary,[6] Dr Bellamy's banishment by 'cancel culture' is in contrast to the national near-beatification of Sir David Attenborough. The latter can hardly contain his contempt for the rest of us—we are an affront to his Eugenicist world view,

---

5 Anna Pukas, 'David Bellamy: "Global warming is nonsense"', 29 November 2008, *Express* [website], <https://express.co.uk/expressyourself/73486/David-Bellamy-Global-warming-is-nonsense>, accessed 4 May 2023.
6 Keiran Southern, 'David Bellamy, the broadcast giant with unfashionable views on climate change', 11 December 2019, *Belfast Telegraph* [website], <https://belfasttelegraph.co.uk/news/uk/david-bellamy-the-broadcast-giant-with-unfashionable-views-on-climate-change/38776344.html>, accessed 4 May 2023.

which feels no shame or remorse for endorsing fake images of polar bears stranded on shrinking ice floes.

Dr Kevin Corbett has a long and distinguished career in standing up for truth and the right to life of his fellow citizens. His first test came during the 'AIDS' scare in the eighties, as a nurse employed in the first dedicated 'AIDS' ward in London. It became clear to him that diagnosis was being based on an assumption of lifestyle, with those outside the socially approved norm being fed toxic medication or euthanised. Dr Corbett put his own career on the line by challenging a Consultant, who ordered him to administer a lethal dose to a gravely ill patient. Using his own medical knowledge, Dr Corbett saved the young man's life and was a true 'ministering angel'. He has since written and spoken extensively about the 'AIDS' and 'COVID' scams[7], both being manipulated in a strikingly similar way—not least, because neither suspected 'virus' has ever been isolated.

In 2001, Dr Judy Wood was a professor of Mechanical Engineering at Clemson University in South Carolina. She was alienated from her teaching colleagues when she refused to accept first the official story of 9/11, and then the similarly unlikely alternative versions of what happened. Watching with them in the staff room as the terrible events unfolded on live television, she witnessed a monumental contradiction to the laws of physics[8]. Thus started her epic struggle through a miasma of falsehood, in which thousands of people had been sacrificed in the pursuit of a fabricated 'War on Terror'. In a later interview (to paraphrase) Dr Wood said simply 'if you see something is wrong, you have to do something about it'.

What it was that others, blinded by the official cover story of terrorist 'airplane crashes', could not see was that a previ-

---

7 *Dr Kevin P. Corbett* [website], <https://kevinpcorbett.com/coronahysteria>, accessed 4 May 2023.
8 *Dr Judy Wood* [website], <https://drjudywood.com/wp/>, accessed 4 May 2023.

ously unknown technology of potentially limitless power had been deployed to destroy the WTC buildings. Controlled demolition of military high-grade explosives, the theory first espoused by those who believed that a government 'inside job' was responsible, would have breached the WTC 'bathtub' with massive amounts of rubble and a resultant flood engulfing the area. During her research into the dust cloud seen from space satellite imagery, Dr Wood also discovered that a scarcely mentioned category three hurricane ('Erin') was at its closest to New York at eight a.m. that morning, before making an abrupt 135 degree turn and heading up the coast the next day. Dr Wood's book *Where Did the Towers Go* is her forensic study of the 9/11 phenomenal events, resulting in her conclusion that this act of incalculable evil was in fact an inversion of free energy technology, which had fallen into the hands of those who hate humanity.

Andrew Johnson is another truth seeker, whose many books stand up against a constant stream of fake science from our Establishment and MSM (and indeed a fair proportion of alternative media). His work *Climate Change and Global Warming Exposed*[9] covers some of the details in 'WDTTG', which point to weather manipulation technology as a weapon of warfare against our populations. Equally reprehensible is the co-opting of scientific discoveries which could be used to help humanity, but which are kept hidden away in an anti-human tool kit. Andrew notes that

> 'In (Dr Wood's) book, the development of "super cell" storms is examined and a comparison of their structure to that of a Tesla coil (used to create high voltage electrical discharges) is considered. The possibility is suggested that the electrical

---

9 *Barnes and Noble* [website], <https://www.barnesandnoble.com/w/climate-change-and-global-warming-exposed-andrew-johnson/1127121541>, accessed 4 May 2023.

properties of large storm systems may have some similarities to those of Tesla coils and that there is a possibility that technology exists to utilise or manipulate the energy in these storm systems for "secondary" purposes.'

Information contained in WDTTG now resides in Bath Literary and Scientific Library, where a donated copy will hopefully serve to enlighten members of the library (if not the general public). Dr Wood's book was refused a local library place a few years ago. Last year, however, another council-run library was pleased to accept the 'White Rose' volume 'Hope in a Tsunami of Evil'.[10] (It is, perhaps, a sign of progress that those given charge of disseminating information to the public, are actually capable of putting their fears of an authoritarian backlash to one side) Cutting through various plausible-sounding alibis for genocide, the 'Tsunami' book also speaks to us through the stories and poetry of ordinary decent human beings. As noted by author Veronica Finch:

'...it especially hurts because when they begin to target the smallest in society, the most vulnerable and the most precious gifts—the babies, humans at the beginning of life. Doesn't evil expose itself most effectively by attacking those precious little ones? How many pregnant women have lost their baby due to the shot, and how many newborn have died due to their mother's injection?'

---

10 *Check the Evidence* [website], <https://checktheevidence.com/wordpress>; 'Book: Climate Change and Global Warming—Exposed: Hidden Evidence, Disguised Plans', 24 September 2017,
<https://checktheevidence.com/wordpress/2017/09/24/book-climate-change-and-global-warming-exposed-hidden-evidence-disguised-plans>, both accessed 4 May 2023;
The White Rose [website], <https://thewhiterose.uk/white-rose-products/Hope-Amidst-a-Tsunami-of-Evil-p482143116>, chapter 20: 'A very strange vaccine'.

How Things Will Turn Out Good In the End

The back cover starkly illustrates what we are all facing, and what with the help of God and our fellow ordinary decent citizens, we must overcome:

> 'It will become clear that nothing can be labelled easily or dismissively as a conspiracy theory. Humanity is now experiencing conspiracies that have been in the planning for decades—or even longer. It is our duty to do everything we can to stop these plans, or else we will all be dragged into a dark abyss.'

Lady Julian gave her long life over to sharing the gift of her vision, Drs Judy Wood, Kevin Corbett and David Bellamy paid with the loss of their careers, Saint Margaret paid with the sacrifice of her young life, and endured not only the intolerable pain of a savage execution, but the heartache of separation from her children. Countless others are now standing up for humanity, from refusal to comply with stupid and harmful rules to simply sharing truth and knowledge which empowers others. Returning to Julian of Norwich for the definitive answer as to why things will turn out good in the end, we can see (as she did) that our Maker will never allow our destruction, though we must use all the skills we each were given to raise ourselves up from it. When the level of resistance reaches critical mass, we can laugh with Julian at our crestfallen enemy:

> 'Our good Lord shewed the enmity of the Fiend: in which Shewing I understood that all that is contrary to love and peace is of the Fiend and of his part. And we have, of our feebleness and our folly, to fall; and we have, of mercy and grace of the Holy Ghost, to rise to more joy. And if our enemy aught winneth of us by our falling, (for it is his pleasure,) he loseth manifold more in our rising by charity

and meekness. And this glorious rising, it is to him so great sorrow and pain for the hate that he hath to our soul, that he burneth continually in envy. And all this sorrow that he would make us to have, it shall turn to himself. And for this it was that our Lord scorned him, and [it was] this [that] made me mightily to laugh.'

7

The Brigadoon Inn

By Andy Thomas

In the English Lake District, two young men of the post-lockdown era stumble on something that should not exist.

'The Cloud is down,' said Leo to his designated *social buddy*, Jaxon.

'I've lost signal as well,' replied Jaxon, speaking through the perspex safety screen which separated them.

The self-driving EV in which they were travelling rolled to a standstill high on a remote mountain pass somewhere in the English Lake District. The road was just beginning to plateau as they were almost at the very the top.

'And we've stopped,' said Leo in surprise.

Why the vehicle had selected this route was anyone's guess, for the road they were on carried almost no traffic these days. Perhaps the route-finding algorithm had gone wrong or it had found an unusual short-cut. Whatever the reason, the car had somehow got lost and then died on them.

These two young men had never driven (for) by? themselves, nor had they ever had the need to navigate or, for that matter, even to know where they were. They placed unthinking trust in the vehicle's Cloud based navigation system, as everyone did these days. Both had been immersed, cocooned inside VR and social media throughout the entire journey. They had never even looked out of the window—until now.

Jaxon tried speaking to the car. 'Teri,' he said to the dashboard.

There was no reply.

'Teri,' he repeated.

'Teri!'

There was still no reply.

'Perhaps she's lost connection as well,' he said finally, now with a hint of concern.

Just then, a smiley face flashed up on the car's display and Teri announced in her synthetically buoyant tone: 'Oops! I seem to be having a problem. Sorry about that.'

'Yes. Teri's down as well,' said Leo. 'She'll be back up soon,' he added reassuringly.

They waited.

Every minute or so, each of them would reach for their handset—only to put it down again when they remembered that there was no 6G signal. This instinctive pattern of behaviour was to be repeated uselessly by both of them many times over the next few hours, but always to no avail. Periodically, Teri would remind them that she was having a problem too, but that's all she would say. They were on their own.

Leo looked out the window. 'I think we are high in the mountains,' he thought out loud, 'But we can't be.'

'No, we can't be. We would never have come this way,' his buddy agreed.

Leo, however, was beginning to realise why the last part of their journey had felt like they were going up a hill. They had been!

It was getting cold inside the vehicle. The Cloud was ubiquitous and everything was connected to it—even the car's heating. Without it, nothing worked.

Jaxon became anxious, but Leo continued gazing out of

the window and began to wonder on their surroundings. The road snaked upward a short distance and vanished over the top of the pass. On both sides of them lay steep rolling hills of various shades of green and brown and, on some of the peaks, there was snow. Rocky outcrops littered the landscape here and there. And dark foreboding clouds traversed the pale blue sky above, casting fast-moving shadows against the hills.

Beside the car, only a few feet away, a stone wall stretched upward alongside the road. Leo noticed that the stones were of various shapes and sizes, but all locked together perfectly nevertheless. It would be hard to make all those stones fit together like that, he thought to himself, as he wondered who had built it. Then, looking back over his shoulder, he realised that there were miles and miles of such walls stretching across the hills in all directions.

The hours passed and the sun began to dip behind the mountains. It became dark and very cold. Neither had any clothes other than those they were wearing.

Jaxon tried many times to get Teri to switch on the heater and interior light, but she remained stubbornly quiet. Both had started to shiver and the wind picked up, occasionally buffeting the car.

'Why doesn't someone come?' complained Jaxon, 'I'm freezing.'

Leo didn't answer. In the distance, further up the road and at the very top of the pass, he thought he could see a light. It appeared a little unusual to his eyes because, in his world, all lighting was made by LEDs and all gave out the same blue-white colour. This one had a yellow hue.

How strange, he thought as he watched. It was rather dim, but occasionally it would brighten a little for a second or two.

Finally he said, 'I can see a light.'

'About time,' replied Jaxon, listlessly.

'I don't think it's moving though.'

Jaxon looked, but said nothing.

Until that moment, it had never occurred to either of them to try to get out of the car. There was no internal door handle in any case. The doors in modern vehicles were like those of washing machines; they remained locked for unknown safety reasons until a timer had expired—even after the power was cut.

Leo, for the first time, tried pushing at the door.

'The door's open,' he said in a hushed voice. There was a long moment of silence between them.

'We can't get out!' Jaxon exclaimed, having contemplated the implication. 'We have to stay safe.'

'There may be someone over there. They may be able to get help for us.'

Leo pulled down his full-face visor over the mask he was already wearing. All vehicles were legally required to carry a supply of disposable gloves and he put on a new pair from the dispenser.

'You can't leave me here!' cried Jaxon, becoming agitated.

'We shall go together. It will be OK,' Leo replied, doing his best to sound reassuring.

Jaxon, realising he would be left alone, reluctantly agreed. He applied sterilizer from the in-car dispenser and donned his extra protective equipment. When he had finished, they slowly pushed open the car doors and the pair stepped hesitantly into the night wind.

The dark shadows that were the mountains surrounded them all around and above, while the lightweight clothes they were wearing did nothing to stop the wind. In the moments when it died down a little, the sound of a running stream could just be heard somewhere nearby.

They were explorers in an alien landscape.

Leo led the way, and they began to walk toward the light

while holding on to their face visors. The incline soon became mild as the road flattened off.

Within a few hundred yards or so, the source of mystery had revealed itself to be an old building with light coming from its windows. There was smoke coming from the chimney which the wind blew sideways.

Suddenly, a heavy-set woman emerged from its entrance. Leo was close enough to see that she wore old-fashioned dress, but Jaxon was a little behind him. She did not notice them in the dark, but collected a pair of logs from a stack at the side of building and quickly returned inside.

Shivering, the two of them went up to a window and peered in together. And what they saw was a scene from another time.

The interior was lit by oil lamps, and a real fire burned in the hearth. The woman who they had just seen outside was now doing something behind the bar, and a man in a black jacket stood leaning against it with his back to them.

'I can't believe this. It looks just like a pub!' Leo exclaimed in surprise, turning to Jaxon.

'It can't be. How is this even being allowed?'

There were a dozen or so people inside, and a couple were sitting together at a table not far from the window through which Leo and Jaxon were looking. He was wearing a black waistcoat and a flat cap, while she wore a plain-coloured simple dress. They caught the sound of muffled conversation.

Leo's eyes, however, were drawn to a girl who was sitting on her own by fire. She was about his age, he guessed, and had thick black hair that fell to her shoulders.

She's beautiful, he thought, feeling ashamed for thinking so.

'They're not wearing any protection and that guy over there is actually smoking,' said Jaxon under his breath.

'I know. It looks like a simulation of the past. But it looks so real. What is it doing out here?'

Leo kept watching, but Jaxon stepped back from the window and hugged himself to try to keep warm. While he did so, he checked his smartphone again, hoping for a connection. His device, however, was useless—he couldn't even take a video of the scene through the window as all modern devices saved their data *direct to Cloud*.

In this place, here and now, there was no Cloud.

Leo was also extremely cold, and found himself contemplating guilty thoughts of being inside in the warmth, with the girl and the fire, regardless of the consequences. Eventually, he could bear it no longer.

'I think we need to go in. We're freezing out here.'

Jaxon's reaction was one of horror: 'What do you mean? In there with them? We need to get back to car!'

'We'll freeze if we go back. We've no heating.'

'But they're not even socially distanced!'

'I'm going to go in. You stay here.'

'You can't leave me!' Jaxon whined.

Leo took a step toward the heavy wooden door that was the entrance. It did not open automatically, but he could see that it had a handle that needed to be turned.

He took a breath, gripped the handle and pushed. It opened inward and he was met with the warm air of the interior, the smell of pipe smoke, and the sound of conversation. There was nothing for it now. He stepped fully inside. His social buddy clung to him just behind.

'Oh my God!' the landlady cried out.

All conversation ceased as a wave of a silence washed across the room and echoed off the walls. All eyes were on them.

The moment of silence endured, but was eventually broken by a sudden shout from a huddle of young men in the corner...

'Spacemen!' some spark called out, and the denizens of this long-lost place all burst into laughter.

Leo stood hapless, not knowing what to do or say. Jaxon remained in the doorway, holding the door wide open so that he could draw breath from the safe air outside.

'Where have you two come from, Mars?' the landlady asked, trying to keep a straight face.

'No, Stockport,' Leo replied earnestly. There was more laughter.

'Well you better come in, then. Hadn't you?'

Leo looked at Jaxon. Behind his face visor, his eyes were wide.

'Are you coming in or not?' she demanded, but this time sternly. 'And shut that bloody door! You're causing a draft.'

Jaxon, now momentarily more afraid of the landlady than of the atmosphere, reluctantly let the door swing shut. But he remained stood with his back to it, with one hand holding the handle just in case. The laugher was beginning to die down now.

'And what are you two doing in these parts?'

The question came from the man standing at the bar. As he turned toward them, they could see he was wearing a police uniform of yesteryear, but one which they recognised from images they had seen on the web.

'We have permission,' Jaxon said quickly, as he let go of the door handle to reach for his smartphone. 'Look!'

He was going to show their *travel authorisation QR code*, but the screen displayed only the manufacturer's corporate tag-line, 'Making life better', and a yellow smiley.

There's no connectivity, he remembered again.

'Please,' said Leo, 'Our EV is not working. And we are cold.'

'No WiFi either,' said Jaxon, still shivering, while looking forlornly at the thing in his hand.

'I don't know what tha's talking about, lad. Speak sense!'

'Awwh, leave them alone Bob. They look lost,' said the woman at the table they had seen from the window.

'Are you lost?' she asked Leo.

'Yes,' he said simply.

'Give them both a drink, Barbara,' she called to the landlady, 'Something hot maybe. They look half frozen to death.'

'What do you two want then?' Barbara asked Leo, but this time a little more kindly or, at least, less sternly.

'A latte,' he replied, not knowing what else to say.

'Well, not sure we have one of those, but I can do a hot toddy. You look like you both could do with one.'

Leo wasn't sure what that was, but nodded anyway.

'They can come and sit with us,' said the woman at the table to the man who was her husband.

'Suppose,' he said back.

'Come and sit with us you two,' she called to them.

Leo glanced again at Jaxon who looked positively stricken.

'We just need to...', but Leo trailed off. He was about to say, 'submit an emergency request,' but had caught himself. 'We've just broken down,' he finished instead.

'We'll run you down to the village on our way home,' said the woman looking to her husband who nodded. 'There's a call box there.'

Leo looked around at the surreality of where they were. There was a thick oak beam which spanned the low ceiling and bare stone flags made the floor. The stone walls had been painted white and were decorated with small paintings and various gold-coloured tranklements which looked like they had something to do with horses. Oil lamps were strategically positioned here and there.

The girl with the black hair, whom he had seen from the window, was sitting beside the fireplace. She had been watching them, but now turned back to fire. A new log was just beginning to burn fiercely. He could almost feel its warmth from where he stood.

If this is not VR, he thought, then it is a dream. But it was a dream he dearly wanted to remember. The pressing reality of just a few moments ago was receding, and he made a curious decision.

'I'm Rosey,' the woman said as he reached the table where the couple were sitting, 'and this is Tom, my husband.'

'I'm Leo,' he replied, not knowing whether to add anything.

'Well sit down lad, and tell us all about yourself,' said Tom. 'And what's that thing on your face for?'

Leo hesitated one final time, and then pulled up a chair.

As he sat down, he caught Jaxon glaring at him with fierce eyes from his position at the door. He knew that his buddy wasn't going to join him, but it didn't seem to matter anymore.

'It's to do with my job,' Leo replied eventually. Something had told him not to talk about viruses.

'Do you work for the Government Leo?' Rosy asked.

'Well...' he started. He thought for a moment. What did his job actually mean here? 'I work in the media,' he said finally.

'You mean like newspapers?'

'Kind of. But more like radio,' he answered.

'Oh, we don't have a wireless, do we Tom? There's no electricity in these parts.'

'Don't need no electrickery if you ask me,' Tom muttered as he picked up his pint pot and took a swig.

Leo's mind filled with questions but before he could ask any of them, the landlady placed a glass of hot whisky on the table for him.

'I'm not sure how I'm going to pay?' he said, remembering that his phone wasn't working and that they probably did not accept *UK-Coin* payments anyway.

The questions had faded.

'Don't worry about it this time. It looks like you need it,' she said to him over her shoulder as she headed back toward the bar.

Leo glanced again at the girl beside the fire. He noticed her scruffy brown cardigan which was far too big for her. Her dress was tattered and on her feet were heavy black boots. He decided, however, that he liked how she looked. She brushed the long black hair over her shoulder and caught him looking as she did so.

She smiled at him. Leo looked away.

'Oh that's Harriet,' said Rosy noticing, 'She keeps herself to herself that one. But she's a good little worker.'

'Why? What does she do here?' he asked.

'We both work at the mill. She often catches a lift up here with us,' Rosy answered.

Leo became aware of Jaxon once more. He hadn't moved, but seemed so very far away now.

'You like her, don't you? Harriet I mean,' asked Rosy softly.

'Yes,' he replied, because it was the truth.

Tom pulled out a pipe and began knocking it on the table. 'If you're staying, hadn't you better take that thing off your face then?' he asked.

Leo looked at him for a moment. 'Yes,' he replied again.

Jaxon, having watched powerless from afar, had snapped. He left his safety spot by the door and rushed over to the table where Leo was now sitting.

'Leo! We have to go right now!' he demanded in terror.

'I'm not leaving,' Leo answered quietly.

'But it's not safe!' Jaxon shouted, his voice becoming shrill.

'I don't *ever* want to leave here.'

At this, Jaxon turned on his heels and fled. Leo saw the

door swing shut as he ran out of the pub.

Outside in the wind, Jaxon tried his phone in desperation, but still it wasn't working. He started to push through the gale back along the road to the EV, his mind reeling in despair. He clung to his full-face visor with both hands to keep it from blowing away.

Leo had never experienced a real fireplace in *actual reality*. Unlike the ones in VR, it was mesmerising.

'I could watch the flames forever,' Harriet said as they sat together beside the fire.

'So could I,' he replied to her.

She reached over to him and lifted his visor.

'There,' she said, 'I can see a bit more of you now.'

Leo looked into her eyes—they were blue. He took his face visor and dropped it to floor beside his chair. Then he removed his mask and watched it burn on the fire.

'You have a nice smile,' she said.

Back at the car, the door opened for Jaxon. The interior light came on and there was a comforting chime from the dashboard as he climbed in.

'Hi there!' spoke Teri in her faux-friendly synthetic female voice. Oh thank you, Jaxon thought as the door closed, locking him in.

He looked out through the car's windscreen and back up along the road to where he had just run from. The light that had shone for them had gone.

8

Built on Rock

By Eileen Coyne

It was New Year's Eve, 2022 and, as she did every year, Margaret made sure she gave herself some space for quiet reflection: reflection on the year passing and some speculation on the year ahead. She summed up her feelings for the 'COVID' years 2020 to 2022 as being the years of loss of faith. Not in God, but in human institutions and, in some instances, loss of faith in the wisdom of others.

It seemed that all that was familiar in the world around her was falling away, that the foundations of human society were being washed away systematically by incoming tides of malice.

Margaret had done her own internet research on mRNA vaccines right at the start. Had seen that they had not undergone the rigorous ten- to twelve-year clinical trial studies, where nine out of ten drugs failed during that process. The only testing that had been done was on animals where there had been organ failure and death. She had tried to communicate this. It had largely fallen on deaf ears. She had made a decision, back in September 2020, never to have the jab. Her stance had cost her friendships. Pressure had been applied by her employers to make her take the jab but had been resisted.

Public opinion was against her but Margaret made a firm decision to rely on her own judgement.

But public opinion had been against Margaret before. She had come from a dysfunctional family, had never fit into their mould and had painfully walked away from much of what was familiar to her during her late twenties. It had been a necessary step for her own sanity and she had, for a time, lived without the social support network that most people take for granted. What she had retained was her faith in God, her belief in living a truthful life and a sense of her own worth that she would not allow anyone to take from her. She felt that her previous life experience had been of real assistance when meeting challenges faced over recent years.

There had been a loss of faith in Government, in the health service, in the integrity of media, a seemingly complete failure of common sense but there had been silver linings amongst the storm clouds. Margaret lived in Belfast, in what had sadly been a divided society. Still, decades after the ceasefire, an undercurrent in all human interaction was to define from which side of the fence people were on: Catholic or Protestant, when meeting someone for the first time. However, when Margaret took the decision to protest outside of Belfast City Hall at what was going on, a fundamental shift had occurred. The old, blinkered, social judgements had flown out the window. Everyone embraced everyone. The recognition that an existential threat had emerged had eradicated old fears and prejudices. This was a powerful good.

The pressure had eased somewhat in 2022, Margaret noted. Many news stories had erupted during the year not least of which was the Russian invasion of Ukraine. Margaret didn't remember much fuss being made during the Russian annexation of Crimea in 2014 and saw it for what it was, a distraction. Behind the scenes, major changes were being brought forward by unelected groupings. Talk of Central Bank Digital

Currencies, restrictions on farmers and food sources, crippling energy price rises while the energy companies still raked in Billions in profit. The fact that the same measures were being experienced, planned and rolled out to different timings in different countries told Margaret that what was going on was far from normal. Some dark power seemed to be intent on breaking ordinary people. So she recognised that, soon, she would no longer be able to trust financial institutions and would no longer have any guarantees on food safety or the ability to heat her home.

2022 had been a stockpiling year. A pantry full of long-life food stocks, candles, seeds, a comprehensive first aid kit and a small pot of silver coins which could be used as bartering tools in the event of a financial crisis. Everything within her limited means had been organised to help her weather the next tempests that she felt, in her bones, were coming.

'Well, so much for the review' thought Margaret: 'Now for the year ahead. What do I need to take with me for 2023?' Margaret made herself another cup of warm coffee and, curling up on the sofa with a warm cuddle-blanket, she tried to still her mind; to meditate; to pray. After a time, a phrase came to her: 'Resist, but Rest in Me'. 'Resist, but Rest in Me' she pondered for a while.

'Resist' was a wide-ranging topic. Margaret had already made up her mind to resist any future mask mandates or vaccination calls, to use cash wherever possible to try and stave off digital currencies. She had also undertaken to offer her secretarial services as a volunteer to one of the many resistance groupings which had sprung up; she could afford to give a couple of hours a week of her time to help. She also recognised it as a call to resist despair. To keep on reaching out to people, despite past hurts; to continue to believe in the fundamental goodness of most human beings. To share, to hug, to console, to empower others, whenever possible. To show the younger generations that this was not normal, that this litany of fear, condemnation and restriction was not how life should be lived.

'Rest in Me' brought a smile to Margaret's face. She had long ago realised that some of the greatest challenges and times of disruption in her life had also been times of greatest growth. That blockages and challenges had necessitated that she take a different path from the one she had mapped out for herself and that whilst, for a time, she had felt frightened and overwhelmed, new pathways and relationships had opened up to fulfil her. A constant throughout her life's journey was faith in God. God was her cornerstone. Her determination to be true to her own principles and true to herself and her own nature and let no-one take away her natural autonomy was the essence of her being. She felt safe in God's hands.

Finally, Margaret picked up her family Bible. Every year, she allowed the pages to fall open randomly and read the first verses that caught her eye. She remembered mentioning this to one of her friends, a Priest, who had said that many people did this but that he called it: 'Bible Bingo'. They had laughed over it at the time but kindly, recognising that everyone had some superstition, some need for the tangible. Sometimes the message was clear, sometimes obscure, but every year without fail Margaret wrote it into the first page of her diary for the coming year and would return to read it as the year progressed.

Margaret's Bible opened at Matthew:

'Therefore, everyone who listens to these words of mine and acts on them will be like a sensible man who built his house on rock. Rain came down, floods rose, gales blew and hurled themselves against that house, and it did not fall: it was founded on rock.' (Matthew 7: 24-25)

The quote mirrored her thinking perfectly.

9
Controlled by Technology

By Alyssa R. Mills

What is apathy? The Oxford dictionary states that: 'Apathy (noun) means an absence or suppression of passion or emotion; a lack of interest or concern'. To be apathetic is to be indifferent. To be apathetic shows a puzzling inertness and impassivity when it comes to a moral issue at hand. We, as a society, are undeniably apathetic and we have become so desensitised to the dangers which have infiltrated our lives. We have allowed people in positions of power to take advantage of us and we are now beginning to suffer the consequences.

Back in 2019, a 21-day trial was conducted in China on 10,000 schoolchildren between the ages of 10 and 18. Focus Headbands, a thin U-shaped device which sits across the forehead, allows teachers and parents to assess and monitor the average level of concentration in students throughout the day. Developed by BrainCo (a US-based Technology company) and its local Chinese partner, Zhejiang BrainCo Technology Co. Ltd, these headbands purportedly use three sensors—one located behind each ear and another on the forehead—to detect electrical signals sent by neurons by the brain. From here, this neural data is then sent in real time to the teacher's computer so that they can quickly detect the level of attention in each student. Afterwards, a general report is generated, giving details for each pupil at 10 minute intervals.

Teachers have reported that these headbands have forced their students to concentrate—and this is not all. Some Chinese schools[11] offer a glimpse into what a high-tech economy would look like: robots in classrooms that interact and analyse the student's health and their engagement level; facial recognition, with the aid of cameras positioned at different points in the classroom, to determine how many times a pupil looks distracted, raises their hands, yawns, checks their phone, or looks angry or frustrated; and uniforms with chips embedded in them to monitor the location and movement of students. Despite the concern of some parents, it was not difficult for the schools to gain parental consent. For the majority, these, the world's largest experiments in AI technology, were for the betterment of their country and its future.

In this guise, the Chinese government has implemented a campaign of social credit, surveillance, and digital currency. The idea of a social credit system began back in 2007, with official plans for the future of technological China being released in 2014. The credit system aims to become country wide, poisoning every aspect of life, judging people's behaviour and trustworthiness; using this, government authorities have the power to withhold basic rights from citizens if they are caught 'behaving badly'—if a person wishes to claw back social credit points, he must first complete a government approved task. Those who openly oppose or refuse to follow government rules will find themselves blacklisted. Taking out a loan, or travelling out of the country will become im-

---

[11] Hangzhou Number 11 High School in Eastern China is noted to have trialled the 'surveillance system'. The head teacher stated that it was like having another teacher assistant in each classroom.

possible. Imposed mass programs of intrusive surveillance across China (the most invasive of these located in Xinjiang) allow domestic police agencies to collect valuable personal data, making it easy to detect so-called troublemakers; resources such as mobile apps, biometric collection, big data, and artificial intelligence make this tyranny possible. In conjunction with this, the central bank has adopted a digital currency, allowing Beijing to control and monitor citizen's financial transactions and movements. The CCP believes that these coercive and totalitarian measures will force people into 'positive behaviour' and will induce an even greater form of compliance, one that will meet the material needs of the populace and engineer mindless obedience.

Whilst China controls its citizens with these overt displays of tyranny, it may seem that we have not yet reached these extreme levels. But yet, are we really that far behind? Are we any less controlled? Technology surrounds us and there is seemingly very little that can be done to escape its forces in everyday life. Each form of technology has been carefully crafted to make life easy and convenient, with millions of dollars being spent to increase the addictive nature of these devices and social media. All of this, without a doubt, aided those in power in manipulating us and further exploiting the mental instability of the population during the 'pandemic'.

I am reminded of the saying, 'The devil finds work for idle hands', and this was clearly illustrated when the world's governments forced its people into isolation, many with only technology to keep them company. TikTok, the international version of the Chinese platform Douyin, owned by Beijing-based tech company ByteDance, was launched back in 2017. (Incidentally, the content on Douyin is focused on self-improvement, travel, art, and the like.) After procuring Musical.ly (a similar platform) in 2018, its popularity grew with amazing speed and has now accumulated over 850 million downloads, the majority of which occurred during the pandemic. For those who were looking to alleviate the boredom of being locked at home, or those dealing with a loss of income, apps like this offered a seemingly benign but truly sinister solution.

Alongside this, OnlyFans boomed during the pandemic. In August 2019, the site had 7 million users; in May 2020 it had 30 million; in October 2020 it had 75 million. Now, it boasts over 170 million registered users whilst having 1.5 million content creators. Each day (as of 2023), 500,000 new users join the site.[12] In conjunction with these appalling statistics, Pornhub, at the beginning of March 2020, offered free access to its premium service to people who lived in Italy. Data shows that, during 2020, worldwide, the site had 42 billion visits with 115 million daily visitors. Simultaneously, through the aid of the media, influencers such as Andrew Tate have continued to advocate for the use and consumption of the aforementioned content, helping to feed the impressionable minds of young adolescents. Whilst I hesitate to write about such a tawdry topic, these are statistics which we must be informed about. People controlled by technology in this way are easy marks for the technocrats—it is no wonder that our opinions and ideas have become so depraved and perverted.

We believe that young people, like myself, are more susceptible to the dangers of the digital age and, although we are certainly at considerable risk, we are not the only ones. The older generation have also allowed their lives to become governed by their phones, social media, and Google Pay. All of our lives are taken over by it and it is therefore no surprise that our mental growth, critical thinking skills, and cognitive

---

12 According to Tim Stokely, CEO of OnlyFans.

Controlled by Technology

ability has become severely limited. This brings us back to the point of apathy. I believe that our apathy is due very much to this digital age. We have become desensitised, very deliberately and carefully, over the years as we have been fed a steady diet of material designed to move us closer to a moral morass.

> *'Yes, it is shocking that old people are being euthanized in our hospitals, or that someone was arrested for praying outside an abortion clinic, but I'll just watch another YouTube short before I attempt to think or do anything about it.'*
> *'Ye shall know them by their fruits. Do men gather grapes of thorns, or figs of thistles? Even so, every good tree bringeth forth good fruit; but a corrupt tree bringeth forth evil fruit. A good tree cannot bring forth evil fruit, neither can a corrupt tree bring forth good fruit.' (Matthew 7:16-17).*

Throughout the course of history, there have been countless empires: the Roman, the Ottoman, the Macedonian and the British Empire are regarded as some of the greatest to have existed. Each one changed the course of history. Each one wrought great good as well as great evil. We, too, are currently living in an empire—a technocratic empire. We are being governed by fanatical ideologues who are determined to erase all forms of beauty and morality, and it is through the power of technology that they plan to ultimately gain full control. How can we expect to reap goodness from their diabolical creations?

Each empire has fallen, and this empire will too. It can only be done by rejecting all they have to offer and trusting in God and all the beauty that He has created. Read a book—take spiritual and mental advice from C. S. Lewis and Dickens, not Tate. Watch an old film. Listen to beautiful music. Walk outside and appreciate nature. Remember the art of conversation—actual face-to-face conversation. But, above all, pray.

10

Don't Succumb to Fear

By Stephen McMurray

The recent, fake pandemic was not one of a deadly virus rampaging through the world, decimating the population. It was one of fear, created by government and the global elite that own them, being disseminated through the media and decimating truth. It wasn't a case of vast swathes of humanity succumbing to a respiratory virus but a story of huge segments of the population succumbing to lies and propaganda. It was a horror story and, like all good horror stories, it had to hold the audience captive by using fear and it did that by imprisoning us in our own homes with 24-hour coverage, by a captured media, spewing out apocalyptic tales of death and destruction.

If we, as freedom-loving human beings, are not to be forever locked away in a digital surveillance prison, by the psychotic, anti-human tyrants that think they control the world, then we must not give in to fear. However, it wasn't just the fear of a deadly virus that allowed those in power to cower us into submission it was something even more dangerous, it was the fear of what others thought about us if we digressed from the officially-approved narrative.

Throughout the 'pandemic' censorship was rife. The press,

the mainstream media and the social media platforms all vehemently suppressed any and all dissenting voices. So vicious was the verbal assault on anyone that managed to break through the censorship to question the pandemic orthodoxy that people started to censor themselves. This was the biggest betrayal—the betrayal of ourselves. By curtailing our own free speech, we ensured that all our other freedoms could be ruthlessly purged.

Some of us, however, did not capitulate to the fear. When the 'pandemic' started I refused to believe in the apocalyptic hyperbole. The fact that the whole thing was merely a scam to eradicate our freedoms was apparent from the outset when, just days before the first lockdown in March 2020, the UK government removed covid from the list of High Consequences Infectious Diseases because it didn't have a high enough fatality rate. That, combined with the ludicrous images in the media of Chinese citizens just dropping dead in the street from a respiratory disease made it obvious that the government and their minions in the media were perpetrating a Psyop on us all.

Rather than give in to the fear, I challenged it. The first thing I did was complain to the Daily Mail, who were one of the worst offenders, for spreading fear and outright lies. They had a graph that purported to show the number of covid cases rising steeply. However, despite the title of the piece, on the actual axis of the graph, it said it was the number of people tested—not the number of people with covid. They were clearly trying to terrorise everyone with deliberate misinformation. I accused them of this and said the heading above the graph was misleading. In their response they stuck to the story that we were at the beginning of deadly pandemic but admitted that the heading on the graph was wrong and they subsequently changed it. It was a minor victory but it showed how insidious the media were and that their narrative had to be challenged.

After that I decided to focus on the politicians. I live in Northern Ireland and there are about 90 members in the assembly so, in the early summer, when the idea of compulsory mask-wearing was being mooted, I wrote to them all explaining why masks won't work, providing them with all the scientific evidence and how they would have a huge detrimental effect on people's mental health. Of course, I was totally ignored but it didn't deter me. From then on, I sent emails to every MLA every few weeks, until the end of all the covid restrictions, detailing all the latest scientific studies about the ineffectiveness and dangers of masks and lockdowns, the figures highlighting that covid wasn't anywhere near as dangerous as they were claiming, the false positives being created by the PCR tests and how the cycle threshold they were using was too high to be of any use.

As the vaccines were being rolled-out I sent them information about the numerous side effects that the FDA in America were expecting from the vaccine and those that became apparent during the vaccine trials. I challenged their fear-mongering statements by quoting actual statistics form the Northern Ireland Statistical Research Agency (our version of the ONS) which totally contradicted their propaganda. I challenged them when they brought in vaccine mandates. I challenged them on a regular basis about every single aspect of the whole scam.

What was the result of my persistence? Well, on the surface it may not have appeared to have achieved much as 99% of the MLAS even refused to answer any questions. However, we do have one MLA who has been posting on social media for many months now about how lockdowns were totally unnecessary, how our Health Minister has misused his power and questioning why nobody is addressing the ongoing excess deaths. I would like to think that, perhaps, my constant emails, showing the real science, may have had a small part in his sceptical stance. However, whether any MLA listened or not, when the tsunami of truth eventually breaks through the dam of lies and the politicians all claim they weren't aware of any of the evidence that contradicted their narrative, I have the e-mails proving that they were informed of it all. Pleading ignorance is not going to be a defence.

    In my place of work, they made masks compulsory. I refused to wear one. I was never challenged. From early in the 'pandemic' I would try to enlighten my work colleagues by telling them on a regular basis about all the evidence that was contradictory to the mainstream narrative. However, I didn't do it in a condescending or argumentative manner. I realised that people believed what they were being told by the government because of the constant fear-mongering. If anything covid-related came up in the conversation, I would simply point out that certain doctors and virologists disagreed with the government line or tell them the latest official statistics didn't actually back up what the government were claiming. By the time the 'pandemic' was coming to an end a number of my colleagues, who had mocked me or ignored me from the beginning, had taken the red pill and admitted that I had been right. They were now doing their own 'conspiracy' research without any prompting from me.

    When the vaccine passports were being introduced, I attended a number of freedom rallies in the city centre. I met like-minded people. Everyone there realised they were not alone. Other people had seen through the scam. We exchanged information. We exchanged ideas. We gave each other hope.

    I started writing articles on the subject of the covid scam, dangers of vaccinations and net zero and how the government was using these to crush our freedoms and implement the tyranny that is becoming more obvious every day. Even-

Don't Succumb to Fear

tually I got some of these published and am now an author for The Conservative Woman website, a well-established political website that was brave enough to challenge the narrative. This, of course, reaches more people and presents the evidence to a broader selection of the population.

Even if nobody listened to me I would, at least, be able to look myself in the mirror knowing that I had done all that I could to challenge the lies, fear and propaganda. When the truth comes out, what will all those people that played along with the scam and kept quiet tell their sons and daughters when they ask them what they did to stop the tyranny? Will they be able to look them in the eye or will they hold their head in shame?

To avoid ever having our freedoms stolen again and being perpetually imprisoned in a twenty-four-hour surveillance, digital ID nightmare I would suggest the following:

Never believe what the authorities or experts tell you, always do your own research.

Completely ignore the mainstream media and seek out alternative news sources.

Use cash whenever you can. If a shop doesn't accept it, go elsewhere. A cashless society and digital currency is one of the tyrant's ultimate goals as they then have total control over your life.

Whenever and wherever you can, do not comply with their Draconian rules. As with all abusive relationships, the more you comply, the more they abuse you.

However, the best advice of all I can give is to never be afraid of what people think of you. That's how they imprison you. They start off by threatening and harassing you themselves but eventually by their use of behavioural science, they get us to threaten, harass and belittle each other until, eventually, we censor ourselves. We become our own prison guards, imposing the tyranny on ourselves. Never be afraid to go against the narrative. Be true to yourself. If you lose friends along the way, they were never true friends in the first place. Never be afraid to say what you believe. Never be afraid to speak what you know to be the truth.

As George Orwell said, 'In a time of universal deceit, telling the truth is a revolutionary act.'

That is all it takes to start the revolution to take back our freedoms and our world—the truth.

Remember, even if you speak the truth to 100 people and only one person listens, it is one more person that is awake and, when you are awake, you never go back to sleep and so our numbers always grow. We are many and they are few. We are the ones that ultimately hold the power. We just need to believe in ourselves.

11

My Week In Southern Turkey

By Fiona Cullen-Skowronski

In November 2021, my son and his family enticed me to join them in southern Turkey by telling me they were basking in the warmth of an Indian summer there, with ripe pomegranates and oranges falling off the trees.

I had only three days to get the coNvid documents ready. I squeezed the chemical in a lateral flow test into the thing where you see the line or lines and sent it off in order to get a document to show I didn't have covid. It arrived just before I was due to go and catch a train to the airport.

I spent the flight with a small carton of juice in front of me in order to be allowed not to wear a mask.

It was so good to land at Antalya Airport and join the crowds of people packed together and not wearing masks. I was met by the brother of the man who owned the bungalows where I was to join my family. The brother's wife was holding up a board with my name on. Though we had never met, she hugged me.

Oh, the relief after all the months of old friends stepping backwards off the pavement in order to avoid being near me. After all the months of old friends at church having changed into Gestapo members, checking names and contact details before letting anyone in (while the devil laughed). I was the only one who held a switched-off phone up to the black-and-white square on the church door or who didn't write my name, address etc on a slip of paper to hand to the Gestapo. If one of the particularly observant Gestapo members were on duty, I would go in through the loos where no-one was on guard duty. Once in, I'd wait for a moment when no-one was watching so that I could slip into the main part of the church without using the hand sanitizer that replaced the holy water. (Lady Macbeth would have been no match for the people religiously sanitizing hands and benches in church.)

The week in the Turkish village was idyllic. No sign at all of coNvid rules. Chickens wandering around just being chickens. No-one saying 'Stay safe'. (When anyone says that to me, I say 'God bless'.)

When the day before departure came, a young man came to the village and tested me for coNvid so that I could board the plane. He hardly touched the inside of my mouth (probably because he wanted the test to be negative for my sake), but I suppose that thanks to that one cotton bud the centralized digital controllers now have a sample of my DNA.

Checking-in was an unexpected nightmare. The ground stewardess said something to me through her mask. When I said I couldn't hear her, she pointed to her mask and then at my face. I remembered that there was a mask in my rucksack. I'd packed it in case of such eventualities. It took me ages to find it, and I imagine the people in the long queue behind me wished they'd joined a different queue. People in the other queues were showing their mobile phones to the staff and being sent through quite quickly.

I got out my folder of documents that I'd had printed at the shop round the corner from where I live before leaving England. (The new digital home printers are purposely made to be temperamental. Goodness, if they worked easily, we might start printing untraceable underground newspapers.) The ground stewardess flicked through the documents and took out one that had UNVACCINATED printed in huge bold letters above some other information. She called her manager. He came quickly. They both looked aghast. (It dawned on me that they were worried about sending an unjabbed passenger to the UK as the UK had a reputation for being extremely strict re coNvid.)

Meanwhile the people in all the other queues continued to shuffle through to the departure area. I was clearly the only person among the many hundreds there who had not accepted the injections. All those people queuing were probably too decent to believe that anyone was evil enough to want us all dead or enslaved.

Phone calls were made and finally I was let through. I got the feeling that when the manager finally let me through he thought I had dementia, as he was speaking to me kindly. The only explanation he could think of as to why I hadn't been hypnotized by the 'vaccination' propaganda was that I was a dotty old person.

Once back in England, it was quarantine time. That's the price one paid for a holiday in the winter of 2021. I spent the quarantine period catching up on chores and paperwork and looking down through an open window at God's creation. Tiny goldcrests flitting around in the tree behind the building while huge woodpigeons clumsily landed on the branches. Badgers coming out at night and doing their funny fast walk along the pavement.

Once out of quarantine, it was good to go shopping again, buying fruit and veg from market stalls for cash, and starting conversations with everyone I met about the importance of not paying by card. I ordered meat for Christmas from a local traditional farm. I thought back to the previous Christmas and also to my mum's funeral Mass and lunch the week before that Christmas of 2020. I'm still in contact with her old friends, but the conversation isn't the same. They didn't come to her funeral because they were frightened of coNvid. I had thought the government rule that only up to 18 people could go to the meal after the funeral was very restrictive. But fewer than 18 came.

No, the conversation isn't the same. Old friends enjoy their Orwellian Five Minutes' Hate of Putin. They talk of a cock-up rather than a predatory globalist plan. They affectionately or impatiently call me a conspiracy theorist. They really think that they have come up with these terms and opinions themselves. And they tell me to stop wittering on when I answer their virtuous words about how they are doing their bit re their 'carbon footprint' with a reminder of what we all learned about photosynthesis at school: that carbon dioxide is vital to life.

The conversation isn't the same. Young parents close their ears when I suggest they ask for information about each injection on the ever-lengthening list of childhood vaccinations before allowing the needle-wielders near their babies and children.

The conversation isn't the same with some of my young students of English as a Foreign Language either. Some are keen to study hard, but others think they can rely on Google Translate. And the other day, one of them watched his bus journey on an app on his phone instead of looking through the window to see where we were. We were on the bus to his GP surgery in the town centre. Once we had arrived at the town centre, we walked around looking for the surgery and then realized that it was a swish-looking place called Digital First. The staff were kind and warm and professional and gave the student excellent treatment. But it is chilling for a GP surgery to have such a name.

After the visit to Digital First, we went to the Post Office.

My student asked why I was paying cash for my stamps. I showed him the black and white oblong down the side of each stamp. Put that oblong together with my bank details and you'll know of every letter or parcel I ever send.

It's a battle. But we know the end of the story. Christ wins. He has won already. Let's claim Christ's victory in prayer and by constant non-compliance.

12

The Scrabble Group

By Maronica

Part 1

That's how it came in to being, the name of 'The People First Together', at the end of another Saturday night's hotly contested Scrabble. Who knew it could get so noisy and nail biting! Looking back, for pinpoint accuracy Jamie thought, it was really set in train one mundane Monday morning queueing for vegetables in the local supermarket.

Meat and dairy were haphazard in their appearances in the chilled department over the last several months, and now it was the turn of certain vegetables … onions, potatoes, carrots … with no explanations other than 'supply issues' (aftermath of Brexit, allegedly), or, more 'exceptionally bad weather' in the various growing regions. People had lost track of how the food production and supply problems had arisen on such a great scale, with no signs of their end.

There were daily bulletins, morning and evening, to advise the public what was in short supply in which particular area, particular district … yes, the Local Transport and Health Districts (LTHDs) were firmly put in place at the end of 2023. The whole of that year had seen a mass installation of cameras on practically every road junction; many of Jamie's family could no longer visit at will, or whenever, her gran was well enough to get in to the car. Many a time Betty had sat in it, had been driven a few miles, but demanded to be taken back as she felt sick. Having crossed the LTHD boundary marker and been the recipient of a camera flash, Jamie's dad had lost another of his 'permitted journeys'. Occasionally he had got annoyed with her and muttered a couple of choice 'swears', but, Adrian always quickly reproached himself. It wasn't his mum's fault, not one bit, it was the 'system', unrelentingly rolled out across towns and cities in the name of cleaner air, safer highways and byways, and, always, 'health'.

There was the bitter recognition felt by Adrian and many (millions of) others that 'health' was a misnomer. It was simply a tool for universal control, tied in to the Digital Identity Platform (DIP). How was it healthy to deprive families of their normal social contacts, Nanas like Jamie's who sometimes felt like going on a visit in the car and sometimes didn't. 'Mental health', touted as vital by 'famous people', (paid-for puppets, in Adrian's opinion), was undermined daily, not supported; a shoddy pantomime, to reassure the masses that their government was listening and hearing their concerns.

His understanding from the past three years was that the 'health of the nation' was acting like a conveyor belt to transport billions of pounds to the pharma and tech cartels. The 'health of the nation' was now a national concern, which only the government, by obeying the WHO's shiny new 'Pan-National Pandemic Preparedness Legal Instrument' (what a mouthful thought Adrian, when it was announced during a tea-time news bulletin after the latest list of food shortages), could solve by mandatory medical interventions.

Like a juggernaut the mRNA vaccines rolled off the production lines, no shortages of those ever included in the bulletins.

The DIP was still in the process of assimilating doses with individual digital identity, and there had been numerous technological problems over the past three months or so. 'Little gremlins in the system', chortled the new PM, at the last bi-weekly Prime Minister's Questions (PMQs). 'Like unsatisfactory employees they will soon be toeing the line!', which elicited an audible murmur of disquiet in one or two sections of the Chamber, but were quickly covered with coughing and odd sneezes ... it didn't do to draw attention to expressions of disquietude. If Members of Parliament weren't ardent supporters of the Prime Minister's policy agenda, then they were no supporters at all.

People seemed to have forgotten about looking after their own health because they had been told every day that the government was responsible for the 'health of the nation', and would legislate to ensure that 'everyone was healthy from the cradle to the grave'—vaccinations would be the means to achieve this 'all-encompassing and most praiseworthy of goals'. That had sent several shivers down Adrian's spine although his mother had commented on the new government's 'kindness and caring' ... 'really looking after us all after all those deaths in the pandemic', she wheezed.

Part 2

As Jamie stood in the queue for potatoes, deciding it was a bit shorter than the onion queue, a large round potato suddenly came rolling towards her feet. A bit of excitement for a Monday morning, runaway potato! She bent down to pick it up to see who had dropped it, or if it had just rolled off the shelf, and as she lifted it up to her face she met the face of her old partner at the tennis club, Luke—they had played Mixed Doubles in the Second Team for a couple of seasons before the club was closed owing to straitened financial circumstances. The Treasurer's Report at the last AGM went down like a lead balloon ... no money for the electricity bill, no money for repairs, and decreasing membership down to the LTHDs. 'Hardly the way to support the 'health of the nation', depriving people of sporting outlets, was Jamie's pithy response at the Report's conclusion.'

Luke claimed the rogue runaway vegetable with a quick grin and a whispered message to meet outside, 'away from the cameras'. The queue seemed to move even more snail-like after that, and the designated serving employee was grumpy and officious. 'No, you have two kilos and that potato you have picked up will take you over the limit ... think of others', he admonished the elderly man. The latter mumbled an apology and quickly left, red-faced, to pay at the special outlet for those without the required Store App.

Going to the supermarket and having to worry about limits on potatoes and onions, and be told off for going over the limit, made Jamie fume inwardly on the old man's behalf. She seemed to be doing a lot of fuming these days, it was like a fire stoking up inside her, igniting a resolve to 'do something', to throw off the shackles of this enormous prison that was enveloping society. What was that term she had heard at college? Oh yes, it was the Panopticon... Jeremy Bentam's imagined prison of supervision, so arranged that an inspector can see each of the prisoners at all times without being seen by them ... and the here and now is mankind's digital Panopticon, on which very unhappy thought she exited the store.

Part 3

'Why did you need to whisper, to meet outside, Luke? Something top secret?' He nodded and moved further away from the store towards the car park.

'Not really "top secret", I just want to share with trusted friends'.

That response warmed Jamie's heart—it was a compliment

to be thought of as a 'trusted friend'.

Luke opened the door of a white hatch back car and said he knew of a cafe which was quiet, off the beaten track, and not one of the major corporates.

Seated, with steaming mugs in their hands, Luke told her about the Scrabble 'league' he was setting up, and would Jamie like to join it?

'Do you have any other players signed up?', queried Jamie who liked the sound of a new format of competition.

'Six already, you'd be the seventh, and I'd make it eight, so two teams straight away.'

'Is there a venue for this?', asked Jamie, becoming keener by the minute, rather more keen than on the date muffin Luke had split between them. Like sticky cardboard, she decided. 'I'll drive us over when we've finished here, and you'll be surprised when we get there', answered Luke with a grin on his face.

Yes, Jamie was indeed surprised to find out the place for the Scrabble games was around the corner from where she lived. It was a large old building converted in to six residential units, and Luke knew all the occupants by name. He'd only moved in three months ago, but that was Luke, he had always been the friendliest and most sociable at the tennis club.

'My flat is at the top in the eaves so there are good views over the parks, and, the sunsets in the west are cool ... if I was a painter I'm sure I could make a living, or, maybe not.'

'Perhaps an Art GCSE didn't promise that much,' he conceded.

Part 4

The following Saturday Jamie was enjoying the views from Luke's eaves flat, and meeting the other players, David and Ellie, making up their four, and Brian, Mark Steve and Annie,

The Scrabble Group

as the other four. There would be an individual winner and a team winner by adding up all the scores.

Over Bring Your Own drinks following the first game, Jamie learned that all the players lived in the same building as Luke, who pointed out that it was ideal as no one had to travel, no crossing of districts so no camera recordings. There was no getting around that surveillance devices had become ubiquitous over the past eighteen months. Did people know that the street surveillance units affixed to lamp posts could also pick up voices quite clearly? Steve, the ex-officer for the Department for Home Security, didn't think many knew, or maybe they did, because he'd noticed people meet, say, 'hi', and then carry on as if they had somewhere else to be, most likely a meeting place clear of cameras.

Jamie discovered that amongst the eight of them there was David and Ellie, both paramedics, Brian, a retired Police Sergeant, Mark, an IT genius, (Luke's description of his friend from Sheffield University), and Annie, who had the larger flat on the ground floor and the use of the garden. Her brother had built two raised beds for growing vegetables when she had first moved in, and her flatmates had enjoyed donations of beans, peas, potatoes, carrots, swede, and various herbs.

They didn't always play their games in Luke's flat, far from it, as after the first few weeks she saw the inside of David and Ellie's, then Brian's—he'd done a very hot chilli for them all—and Annie's most recently. She had regaled them all with tales of the goings on at the allotment, the strange habits of one particular gardener—he had erected a 2 metre bamboo fence around his patch, always shouted, 'is there anyone in there?', as soon as he arrived, and then put on a battered straw hat with a toy bird attached to the top before he got to work. No one liked to ask why he shouted, or why he had a plastic bird bobbing around on his hat top.

As the weeks had gone on, with Jamie sensing her companions' cautiously unbending reserve towards her, their post-match conversations had veered (or rather steered, by Luke) on to the increasingly dystopian developments in the UK and beyond.

Brian had been a card carrying member of the Conservatives for most of the time he had been in the Police force but had cut it up soon after the 'three weeks to flatten the curve' had been extended, and fellow citizens were being tracked by drones as they took solitary walks across hills, and chastised and moved on for partaking of a socially distanced coffee with a friend on an isolated park bench.

Steve had been an ardent member of the Green Party but couldn't agree with its newest policies, parroting unfounded claims about the 'climate emergency', for example, that the climate was already changing 'at unprecedented speed'. Did someone have a stop watch on the climate? Who had decided it was an 'unprecedented speed'? Steve became an ex supporter after statements such as this.

Jamie, like David and Ellie, had no ties to any political party; they were all disillusioned and had looked beyond sound bites and slogans, formed their own views about the state of the UK and beyond.

While playing games, and waiting for others to take a turn, they talked about the iniquity of the traffic restrictions, and how there were fewer places to use cash, and, the repeated appearances of the ex-PM, Blair, extolling the virtues of the digital health pass, because, 'you know, there'll be new vaccines involving multiple shots, which will need, um, to be tracked digitally'.

One Saturday night in late August Luke pounced on one of the words Jamie had played. 'Spearhead' had scored her 26 points on a Double Word score, and he suggested that they needed an actual living 'spearhead', a driving force, to move forward with plans that he knew were bubbling away under the radar.

Part 5

'Let's talk about it over a drink and, something to eat', piped up Annie. 'Come down to my flat, it's a bit bigger with a few more comfortable chairs. I don't think we'll last long on these hard ones Luke has for the Scrabble table.'

Annie's flat was very comfortably equipped, and provided with hot drinks and chocolate flapjack, they began to discuss the idea of a 'spearhead' and a movement to counter the dystopian dragnet of the Local Transport and Health Districts, the forthcoming fully operational Digital Identity Platform and the banishment of cash. The DIP was supposed to be a voluntary attachment, but what credence could be attached to that after four years of lies, half-truths and government U-turns.

Ellie raised what she hoped wasn't an objection early on. 'Luke, we are just eight people here, what movement could we form'? David and Brian nodded their support, adding that they hoped Luke didn't think they were being wet blankets.

'Not at all', Luke responded, and then held them open-mouthed for nearly an hour explaining what was already underway, and what could happen in the next months and years. Theirs wasn't the only games group, they were spread around the country, not just Scrabble but chess, cribbage, poker, Backgammon groups, to name a few. They aroused no attention from the 'authorities', they weren't visible to the myriad of cameras, they had gathered in no public places.

He told them of a national and international Directory of Expertise, not 'experts' because that label no longer had currency. In the Directory were many with high level I.T. qualifications, lawyers, medical professionals, linguists, horticulturalists, farmers, electricians, stone masons, carpenters—the list went on. Plans had been made to 'subvert the system', from the inside as well as outside. Luke explained a little of the work around some of the I.T. 'tinkering' that had led to the 'little gremlins in the system' He didn't reveal his own very significant role in such subversion.

'You can all be added in to the Directory if you want, no pressure from me', said Luke, and, 'nor me', added Annie. She was not only a competent gardener but a multi-lingual officer, retired from GCHQ, a period of employment she didn't advertise, and to which only Luke was privy.

'You mentioned the "spearhead"', Jamie reminded him, 'what will that be?' 'Yes', Steve had been thoughtfully digesting all the information from Luke, and also almost absent-mindedly digesting several slices of chocolate flapjack, 'I've been thinking of a name to encompass what you've been saying about The Directory of Expertise, it's full of people and their jobs and skills, so what about The People First Together?' he continued, after another drink to wash down the last of his flapjack. 'There's nothing political attached to this title. Do you remember that Party called "New Reform UK"? It got going late 2021 but didn't get a lot of support because it was mainly about reforming politics, personally I'd say the current political system is irredeemable, never capable of reform ... anyway, remember it folded within a year.'

Jamie, David, Ellie and Brian in unison gave a 'thumbs up'. They turned to Luke and Annie to see if they liked the name. 'Yep', declared Luke, 'I think you've nailed that Steve, it really has a ring to it and can act as the "spearhead" as our various groups cooperate, coalesce and organise. In fact, I'd say, it's genius really—it is the ordinary person in the street, or at home, (thinking of his mum and dad with their chronic health problems), who keep the world going at the micro level, and, who are in contradiction to what the technocrats and autocrats have planned for societies all over the world.' He went on, '"The People First Together", goes across national boundaries without "offending" other nationalities, it's a broad term but it also draws people in. People like acting together, and looking after each other. History is full of community in action, think of the Berlin Wall coming down in November 1989, that was people in action, people acting together to change a course of events, the shaping of a different future! We don't want people fearful for the future, we want people to be part of making the future.' The group, listening to the passion in his voice, felt quite uplifted, and Steve felt very proud of his small contribution. Just a title, but it's what that title came to mean beyond the room in Annie's flat.

Part 6

The year end was a milestone for The People First Together as group numbers grew in the cities towns and villages of the UK, Europe, North and South America, Africa and Australasia. The variety of games and activities engaged in across cultures never failed to amaze Jamie, who had become a District Coordinator, liaising regularly with Regional Coordinators to share information and expertise.

What she and the other members of their Scrabble group noticed towards the end of 2024 as they went about their daily business was an uplift in the morale of the people they lived and worked among. They could meet in a shop or a railway station and ask if they had 'played any good games recently?' It was a cue to start sharing news and information, interspersed with games scores/wins/losses!

The improved public mood lift had been picked up by local newspapers—the Newport News had a column in its New Year's Eve issue, 'Has this end of year celebration boosted the quota of smiling faces among Newport's inhabitants' 'Has a lottery syndicate claimed the super jackpot?'

The Broadsheets avoided paying too much attention to the new phenomenon of 'positivity'—their large funders were hopeful it would soon die down; they did not understand nor like what they had started to detect among the populace.

Part 7

Before 2025 was too old the balance (of power) had started to shift inexorably to the people. The DIP was beset by many I.T. glitches, not just in the UK, but across the world. The authorities couldn't understand the reason for its frailty, its frequent 'blackouts', and could not implement the individual digital health pass to marry up with the Local Transport and Health Districts.

Large scale, apparently uncoordinated protests, kept springing up everywhere on all the policies governments everywhere had set in motion to achieve a one world approach. People were no longer feeling cowed by oppressive diktats, past and present, exercised their free will, and did not comply as often as was possible. It was much harder to squash morale, governments discovered, once it had recovered and strengthened, and, yet, they could not put a finger on its source.

When some of the big name journalists had long and passionately worded articles published asking whether the pursuit of centralised digital identity was really worth pursuing, and even, asked if putting the people first was not the right way to go to achieve fully functioning and socially cohesive societies, Luke and his small group recognised one battle being won, the ramparts starting to crumble around the global dystopian Panopticon.

There would be other skirmishes between the people, and what David and Ellie termed the 'global oligarchs', over the drive to Net Zero, the permanent place of cash as a means of transaction, making Big Pharma accountable for harms caused and curtailing the reach of the WHO. No one underestimated the future challenges but it was getting out, across all principalities, that People First Together was the spearhead to meet such challenges.

People were connected, still getting connected, meeting across a chess board, playing cards, Scrabble, Sudoku, being involved in newly set up market garden societies and so forth. From the roots of these small groups came the sharing of 'expertise', the rebuilding of communities with the emphasis on locality as opposed to global hegemony.

Jamie confided in her dad, as they dug over Annie's allotment for fresh plantings, that had a potato not rolled towards her one grey Monday morning she might never have experienced real hope about their future, never met so many interesting and kind people, learned new skills, and got much better at Scrabble. Adrian laughed, replying, 'agreed on all counts, and since then I've become a champion digger of vegetable patches.'

13

The Warning

By Nicole Katie Sedlak

My experience of the Warning? Where do I start? 13th April 1984, it was a windy evening and I sat alone in front of a roaring red fire after a long day of work. Everyone had gone to bed, but I had felt a sort of uneasiness stir inside of me. I was also troubled as lately I hated the slow pace of life, especially the days where time slowed down, so that I felt I needed to escape. The days where nothing happened, nothing even worth writing in my diary.

As I conjured up stories of my getaway, I felt myself drift off to sleep. The warmth on my face and the soft howling wind fading into the background.

I awoke to a different sort of howling, the mechanical kind like a tractor would have made on the farm. The grandfather clock ticked twelve and I wondered who was out in the field at this time. Forcing myself to stand, I stumbled into the kitchen and peered through the window. As quick as the wind, I jumped back in surprise and sprinted for the door. Opening it, I staggered out and took in the scene. About a hundred meters from me stood a tall cement building in construction and next to it another. These abnormal looking structures covered what was meant to be my father's field.

The Warning

The field that I had spent all day working on! I glanced up at these newly arrived buildings that stretched as far as the eye could see in all directions. They towered above the clouds, and stretched out all the way to the neighbouring field. Next to some of the unfinished constructions stood tall cranes, better adapted than even the ones in main cities.

People were everywhere, screaming at each other and giving instructions. I turned around in bewilderment and there by the wall of the house stood me. Me, but older me. Once again, I shuffled back in confusion, but then the mysterious figure spoke. She told me that she was from the future, and was here to give a warning about what was to come...

That's when my vision began to blur and I shut my eyes, expecting to black out. However, when I reopened them, I was fully conscious. My surroundings had changed, I was standing in what looked like a classroom, but duller and more depressing, if that was possible. The walls were bare and the windows were covered. Black paper stopped any natural light from entering and a blue light shone from above, hurting my eyes. Children sat in rows; their heads erect, eye lids baggy. They sat strangely straight with no sign of emotion on their skinny faces. In front of them sat small computers, on which they typed away obediently. No sound was made except for the tapping of keys and the occasional cough. A musty smell enveloped the classroom and through the sickly light, I could see dusk particles swimming around the room.

I remembered the cheerful children whenever they came to visit the farm. They had no connection to technology and how happy they were to just be with the animals and nature.

That's when Future me walked into the classroom and glanced at the dead looking children, calmly. I had stared at her in horror, half expecting her to say something like don't worry, it's not real, but instead her gaze darkened and she began to speak in a low voice.

'This is the sad reality of most people's lives. The cycle that had been made so difficult to break out of ... it's practically impossible. Though, looking at this it may seem like the only way of life, I can assure you it isn't. Many people these days, wonder what the meaning of life is, our purpose on Earth. Whatever purpose you go by is what will free you from the never-ending cycle of the system. The system where innocent souls are born into this world. They are indoctrinated from kindergarten to primary, secondary to university, where they are finally released into the world. Completely unprepared and out of touch with themselves. In my world 44% of students don't know what they want to do after graduation. Meaning they have no real knowledge of what awaits them, or what to avoid and how to maintain a healthy, stable life without the need of technology. Technology was created to solve human problems and do things that we can't. For example, save millions of photos in our memory. Technology was successful when it came to solving issues with food, shelter, communication etc. However, in some cases technology has taken over human jobs; self-driving cars, eliminating the driver. Self-checkout, removing the cashier. These may all sound like harmless interactions, but it removes jobs and valuable life skills. People can now start and run businesses online, but this impacts our natural skill attainment abilities. 81% of college graduates wish they were taught more life skills before graduation. This means that they assume that they don't have enough skill to start working. Essentially, young people will be drawn to social media where they believe they will learn life skills which they were never taught. Our Earth has turned into a technology dependant world'.

    I gaped at her unable to speak and unsure, whether I should believe her. How could we have done this to ourselves? My mind raced with possible explanations, but I couldn't find an excuse. I was then led to the hallway where students

The Warning

walked like zombies, their noses buried in their phones and Air Pods blasting in their ears. She told me that the new iPhones were tested for safety on a plastic dummy called SAM. Air Pods were not tested for safety at all before being released. At the time I hadn't fully understood what she was telling me or what this new technology would have meant for us as a species.

A crumpled newspaper lay on the floor next to me, as I bent down to pick it up, I noticed the date read 13th April 2034! Suddenly everything began to make sense. I was in the future! A bad future as I could see, but why was I here? I continued to read the newspaper. It featured an interview with Elon Musk about the new AI technology that has recently been released. He had said: 'It's all probably for the best, you can't beat it, then join it. These people merged with the AI robots are much smarter than the smartest person on Earth. It maximises the freedom of action for humanity. It means that there is more of you in the cloud, than in your body.' Then he continued to quote about how a robot rebellion would be possible and that some people would use this new power in a bad way. Keeping this in mind, he still had said that it would be better to have an AI extension of yourself and he didn't see a problem with any of this and that this was the only future.

I could see many problems and could think of many different possible futures. Including the one I had back home. I remembered how ungrateful I had been that I couldn't live in a big city and couldn't follow my ambitions. I finally knew, that if I went to the city I would become a zombie, stuck in the system with no way out. As I put the paper down, Future Me came and stood beside me. She looked into my eyes and said, 'This is your mission, live a free life, be with your loved ones and cherish the time you have left with them. You will not find yourself in technology, but in nature, live alongside it. Restore your lands and follow the laws of Mother Nature with regenerative agriculture. This is the only way forward. Real experiences cannot replace this simulated life that I live in. Now, everyone on Earth has had the same warning, the same chance, to put things right. It all depends on how far you are willing to go to save humanity'.

With that she began to fade away as well as the school around me and I was left in total darkness. I sat up to find myself wrapped in a soft blanket, the last flames of the fire were dying out and the light of dawn was creeping up from behind the trees. The sound of bird song and the smell of burnt wood wafted in the air. I stood up and walked into the bright kitchen wondering if it had all really just been a dream. Or had it been a terrible warning prophesying the dreadful future that was to come and overtake the human race? Just then my sister ran down the stairs, her blonde hair, elegant as always flowing freely through the air, and gave me the biggest hug. I could feel her warmth and her grip on my back. I asked her what was wrong but all she said was, 'I saw it, the end of humanity and the age of the robots'.

That's when everything became clear for once and for all. It had really happened; it was The Warning that had come to everyone. It was one last hope for humanity...

From that day, everyone on Earth received similar warnings about our devastation. By the end of the week, it was on the news and we were all on edge. However, as time passed, we began to understand and stopped ourselves from slipping into the same cycle of self-destruction. We began using regenerative agriculture and the school system was changed worldwide, to begin teaching our children how to live a fulfilling life without being technology dependant. We let them know that their real life was out there, and they could find peace in connection with Mother Nature and mainly each other. That is why our society is what it is today...

14

Technology Detox

By Daniel Greene

It started like every other morning, from the warm slumber of dream-world and fantasy rudely and abruptly interrupted by the alarm siren from a nuclear submarine. It was my own fault. I had selected it as the alarm ringtone on my phone to wake me up, so concerned was I that anything less abrasive would wake me up from my nice warm conformable bed. On autopilot, I got out of bed, as Frankie stirred next to me. 'I thought I told you to change that noise!' She moaned into the pillow before turning away to sleep in just those precious ten minutes more.

I took up my phone from the bedside table and unplugged it from its nightly nesting point and took it into the bathroom with me. Time was more precious now than it had ever been and I had been seeking as many multitasking opportunities as possible. This now included reading the latest political, constitutional, climate emergency or pandemic or crisis—all of which were interchangeable on any given day depending on the voltage that was left in the hype machine while taking the morning constitutional.

I leaned forward and twisted the taps on the bath, which filled while I read the latest shocking miserable headline without a glimmer of light. If all worked according to plan I would be finished at the same time as the bath filling just enough so as not to use the overflow and skim read all the important news, not of course forgetting to read who was just eaten in the jungle or thrown on some ice somewhere and told to skate. I often wondered who, let alone, why these celebrities insisted on going onto these programmes telling everyone that they could not dance or sing or whatever the show was supposed to be about. Not another plug for their third autobiography due to come out this Christmas. But this is the one where they find happiness which has so alluded us all.

Right, reading is done and now to enjoy the next 15 minutes of bath time. This was the last fort of peace and solitude. The warm water penetrating the worn muscle tissue and does its special magic for the day ahead. I had started a new comedy series on Netflix which I would play during this time. Not that I was really paying attention but I could listen and follow along while I washed.

Out of the bath and towelled down I pause the video to finish up with tomorrow's session. I went downstairs and threw two slices of bread into the toaster, laid out two cups, put the kettle on and used the next three minutes to scan the emails that I had received between last night and this morning.

Junk, junk, con, spam, opportunity, newsletter, LinkedIn spam, '*someone has looked at your profile,*' good for them, your Amazon delivery is coming today. 'What amazon delivery?' I questioned myself not remembering any recent orders.

I heard the click from the kettle to indicate that it is done but I ignored it, just a few more seconds and I will have gone through all of them, sifting through to find that one new job offer, that one new opportunity, that one competition that will win us that dream house next to the sea. I finished with a

Technology Detox

mild sense of satisfaction and poured out what was now cold water into the cups. The butter sat in lumps on the toast rather than sweating in the orifices of the bread giving it a lovely flavoursome release with each bite.

I looked at the clock on the wall, 7:34 already—I was late and I still needed to brush my teeth, pick up my lunch out of the fridge and jump in the car.

Frankie was just coming down the stairs slowly. She had her glasses on, one hand on the handrail and the other on her phone and she was still in her pyjamas. Her preference is to have breakfast and then get dressed which works in wonderful harmony with our morning schedules.

'Morning Goose, sleep well?'

'Hmm, until someone's annoying alarm woke me up!' She tilted her head forward and looked over the top of her black-rimmed glasses.

I smiled back, 'Okay, I'll change it later to something more peaceful.' Full well knowing that was a lie. 'Oh, did you order something on Amazon by the way? Something is coming today?'

'Ahh yes, I meant to tell you about that. Alexa the echo device was listening to me while I was on the phone with Kerry and I mentioned that Ninja air fryer you keep going on about and Alexa ordered it while you were logged into it. I could not stop it but anyway, I know it's something that you wanted anyway.'

'Huh well that is true but I think I found a better deal in John Lewis but if it's coming today it doesn't matter. Less hassle, I guess. See you later.' I kissed her on the cheek and dashed upstairs to brush my teeth before leaving the house.

Within a flash, I was in the car and I was listening to the podcast from Martin Lewis on my phone. I had noticed how Siri on my phone had gotten smarter and was now suggesting podcasts to me rather than me going looking for them. Of course, I also now must contend with adverts popping up every five minutes but it was funny because I could have sworn that I was only talking to Simon at work earlier this week about lawn mowers and now suddenly I had heard three adverts from Screwfix, B&Q and Argos all for their deals on lawn mowers. I was slightly suspicious as it is November and not the time of year that you typically associate with garden tools.

The upbeat tones of Martin were suddenly interrupted by an officious digital female voice, '*Incoming call, incoming call—Frankie*' I pressed the green receiver button on the steering wheel—a repeater button of the one just a bit lower on the central console screen. It did annoy me a bit that there were so many buttons doing the exact same thing just in slightly different positions on the car. It seemed very wasteful and not well designed in my mind. I was one of those that liked Nordic design—simple and pure without unnecessary frills.

'You've left your lunch in the fridge again you wally!' Frankie said.

'Dam it. Ok it's not a problem I've got my phone, I'll pick up a meal deal in Tesco on the way.'

'Ok but make sure you eat—you can't keep skipping meals.'

I pulled into the car park and dashed out. Picked up some crisps, salt and vinegar my favourite, an orange juice, and a BLT sandwich. Easy eating. I went over to the cash desks and none were open, only the self-service ones which I hated. In the time that I had used these never once had any transaction ever just gone through without needing assistance from someone, which took twice as long as just using a normal till, but this was the *'new normal.'* This was the modern 'go-to' phrase to put a positive spin on anything that would otherwise be described as crap.

I played the game, no-bags, scanned the items, and placed

them in the bagging area, item was not recognised (it had to be the crisps didn't it—the BLT or the orange juice I could live without). Smiley deely bopper person comes over to help. Only they are not deely boppers it is a headset with microphone and earpiece. I notice that I'm also being filmed on a body cam. 'Wow', I thought to myself, *'Tesco Metro has gotten rough!'* They have not really come to help but to patronise me on how to use a till. I obviously missed the training day when I worked here on tills, wait a minute I never worked here and why should I be expected to ring up my own bill? I am sure the next innovation in restaurants is you will be expected to cook the food and wash-up yourself before being asked to pay for the experience. That is after all what it is all supposed to be about isn't it—the experience?

The assistant scanned a piece of paper on the till and magically it stopped flashing its big red beacon. Order was once again restored and I could pay for all three items. Not by cash though. Unsurprisingly none of the tills take cash anymore. If you are degenerate enough to still carry disease-ridden cash, you must plead with the store manager to accept it as legal tender. I held my phone up to the touchpad—filthy I might add, and a few seconds later I was being asked if I wanted a receipt or wanted to leave the store looking shifty walking past the security guard, who could not care less, on minimum wage waving a piece of white paper at them to ensure they knew and everyone else that I hadn't just shoplifted these top-quality crisps.

Thirty minutes later I was at my desk in the office tapping away on my computer responding to an email which I knew they had no hope of understanding but we were not allowed to simply pick up the telephone and talk to the customer. Everything had to be done by email to keep a written account of every conversation to make sure that when the claim came everything was fully documented. Another thing to thank

American culture for.

Maybe that is the issue right there. America has lots of bars but no proper pubs. That's how we resolve disputes here, build relationships, create that rapport that cements relationships, mend broken hearts and feel at home from home. 'There's not much that a pint and a packet of crisps can't solve,' I thought to myself. *'Crikey, I can't even remember the last time I went to the pub with Frankie, what with the pandemic, ordering food on apps in restaurants, closures and the cost of living increasing.'* We will go at the weekend for a proper Sunday roast dinner, I told myself. Something to look forward to.

It got to lunchtime and I broke out my lunch from the office fridge. There wasn't much space so I went back to my desk and had a picnic there. I checked some personal emails and there was a friend request on Facebook. I so loth the whole thing but I was persuaded to join it fifteen years ago when it started, by my friends at the time whom I've ironically lost touch with but I have gained at least 250 'friends' some of whom I *actually* know.

Before I knew it five minutes had turned into forty. I had gotten distracted by adverts and other people's posts. I knew the FB trap but I would fall for it every time. 'Steve, you coming on Saturday?'

I looked up from my desk to see big Alan hovering over my cubicle wall left since the containerisation of our open plan office, since the pandemic, which had made little to no difference as we had still all managed to catch colds, flus and other nasties that is the human condition. Thankfully no STI's just yet but I did always spray some Dettol over my desk every so often as I know sometimes people would use my desk when I wasn't in the office. I knew this for sure when I found biscuit crumbs on my keyboard and a half-finished cola can on my desk. Wonderful.

'What's on this Saturday?' I retorted. It was bad enough to

Technology Detox

be here from 8:30 in the morning to 17:30 five days a week let alone leaking into the weekends as well.

'We're going paint-balling and then a curry afterwards. Adam is coming, Jonny, Nick, Dave, Laura and Nikki.'

'Nick? I thought he was still on crutches with the fractured ankle?'

'It's at the VR place—you use a headset and run around in the game shooting each other.'

'You mean I don't actually get to shoot Adam in the knee-caps?'

'No, you wear a vibrating pack that lets you know that you've been hit but there's no pain'

'*Hardly seems like worth giving up a Saturday for,*' I thought to myself.

'C'mon it'll be fun'

'Is this that place that has just opened in the town, erm, "The Reality Store"'

'Yes, that's it, went there for the eldests' birthday last week with a few of his friends. Did virtual bowling.'

'As opposed to actual physical bowling?'

'Yeah, that's right, you have a headset and hand controllers, sit down and strap yourself in because it seems so real. You can do all sorts of experiences like travel to places abroad, visit Roman cities, fly a jumbo jet, be in the old wild west, drive an F1 car... If you can think it, they have a simulation of it and it is so real.'

'Doesn't that scare you a bit though? It all sounds a bit like the Matrix to me, you're plugging yourself in and becoming a digital slave?'

'Of course not, it's all about the experience. You're turning into one of those conspiracy theorists!'

'Whoa, Whoa, calm down, don't get so excited you're not strapped in.'

'I don't get it?'

'Don't worry. I just think that it's better to have real experiences rather than simulated ones otherwise where does it stop?'

'You've always been a bit weird haven't you Steve.'

'Probably, yeah. Listen I'd love to come on Saturday but Frankie and I have already committed to visiting her family in Wiltshire so I won't be able to make it.'

'If you both had a Meta Portal you wouldn't need to go and you could do all your visits using an online conferencing app.'

'Yeah, we could but we like to go there in person and actually see them and go for a meal, maybe a nice pub up there.'

'Good luck, most of them are closed now.'

'Indeed. Have fun shooting virtual paint at the team Alan. I'm sure that'll help the morale deficit in the office'.

The afternoon was no different to the morning and I was still corresponding with the same client from this morning although I could tell from the tone of the emails that were coming back that they were getting frustrated by our apparent non-committal to resolve their case and of course, they were quite right. Not only were we deliberately holding out making any offers of resolution until the third email in the chain, this could have been resolved much earlier this morning with a fifteen-minute telephone conversation. No one wants to talk to anyone anymore. We have lost the human touch, compassion and relatability behind our keyboard kingdom. We can tie up litigation for months or seconds with a stroke and tap from those ebony keys.

I was back home and Frankie was still working on something on her laptop. She had been working from home since early 2020 but slowly the hours have been creeping up and up. She says that she is more efficient at home, which I believe, but I cannot help but wish that she was working the normal hours that we both used to work. We used to go to the pub on some nights or a nice restaurant. Now it had become this episodic existence which is only really interrupted by the odd team-building exercise or a mis-delivery from Hello Fresh who deliver all our food now. I got bored of their set menu a while ago now. The novelty wore off when they started commenting on what we should eat and sending us 'special' meals.

I checked my watch, well it is not just a watch—it was a present from Frankie. It monitors pretty much everything. It even tells me about my sleeping patterns, just in case I did not know. I sat there chewing through the cold couscous. *'I've tasted better stamps'* I thought to myself.

Is all this technology helping us and is it saving time and if so, why am I not actually seeing any benefits?

Then it hit me, I had ineptly become a digital slave. And not just me, no others too had the same. I had heard of some 'weird' people that had come away from Facebook and suddenly had much more fulfilling lives but I had not seen it—well how could I? They were not posting pictures of their dinner on social media.

'It starts tonight', I thought to myself, 'I'm starting a digital revolution of my own—a resistance if you will'. 'If the technology does not actually make something easier or quicker I am simply not going to use it.'

I started by removing the watch—as I took it off to hide it in the bedside table it flashed up amber on its little screen to alert me that I had not yet achieved ten-thousand steps that day. It was liberating to not be judged by a wristwatch. Why did it matter so much anyway? I was not overweight nor was I appearing in the latest Marvel film.

Going to bed I did one better for Frankie. I turned off the mobile phone completely and left it to charge up. I found my old alarm clock and set it for six.

I fell asleep quickly which was unusual. The next morning, I woke up to a softer alarm and I felt more refreshed. I went into the bathroom and thought I would try a shower rather than a bath. I felt nice having the hot water rain down on me like a hydrotherapy treatment. I got dry and made my way downstairs. I glanced at the clock on the wall and I was fifteen minutes ahead of where I would usually be at the time. I had a nice piece of toast and Frankie came down just in time to enjoy her tea while it was still hot. We had a chat about the coming weekend and she liked my idea of having a pub lunch. It had been a while and we felt we deserved a treat after all the overtime.

I was on a mission this morning and even remembered to take my lunch out of the fridge. I got in the car and put on the radio and began singing along to ACDC's Back in Black. Then I realised I did not have my phone with me. How would I cope? *'Well, the same as you did before you had a mobile phone —the world still turned'*. I can only describe it as bliss. I did not go onto Facebook, I didn't search through mindless emails, and I didn't watch the adverts for the new series of Megan and Harry on Netflix. At lunchtime, I went out for a walk along the high street. A place I had long forgotten but what a place of energy and sparkle it was. People were sitting outside cafes talking to each other, musicians were playing in the street, and market traders were calling out pound for a pound of fresh fruit. I giggled my pocket and found some loose change and made a pound. Paid the grocer and walked along carrying my fruit in a sustainable brown paper bag rather than a plastic bag for life.

As I walked it felt good, the sun was out and things just seemed a bit more alive. I looked in the estate agent's window and understood that if Frankie and I wanted to live by the sea the only thing that was stopping it from happening was ourselves.

After this, my digital revolution started to spread. Frankie was the first to buy into the idea of a technology detox. Too much of our life was online so we came completely away from social media. When we were at home the laptops and phones went away. When we were out, we experienced where we were with our own eyes, smells and sounds rather than through a video screen. Soon the revolution reached our friends who were curious why we weren't posting our existence on Facebook.

'We're simply too busy actually taking part and enjoying life.' We would simply say.

15

I Never Thought About It Like That

By Stephen James Gray

I remember reading a story once about the future, and of how the robots would one day take over. The technology to create them was introduced by our own billionaire elite, who assured the population that their creations were harmless. The story's main protagonist hated the machines because they were taking the jobs of the citizens, and he argued with his boss about how his position in the factory was under threat by the new mechanical workforce that was slowly replacing its human equivalent. The manager, however, did not listen and simply explained how the robots were more efficient and cost effective. Needless to say, the eventual cost for the rest of humanity was far greater than the money the company saved by firing the old workforce and bringing in the new, artificial one.

Some years later, upon leaving school, I found myself working in a factory too, and after I'd been there a while, I heard a rumour that one of the smaller units was to be closed for refurbishment. When it reopened, the small group of packers who were employed there had been replaced with two machines that could do the jobs of ten people, only quicker and more efficiently. The two mechanical arms that pulled items from the conveyor belt were hardly as sophisticated as the robots I'd read about as a boy and often broke down on a regular basis, but they did indeed work fast and with human mechanics and technicians to watch over them, were able to keep up with the pace of the employees they'd replaced ... just about.

'Tut, tut,' said the manager, an intelligent older man who clearly didn't like the company's newest acquisitions and could see where the introduction of such things was going to lead.

'What is it?' I asked, following his gaze towards the machines.

'All this,' he said, indicating the two arms, one of which had stalled and come to a standstill as it waited for the maintenance team to come and fix it again. Its red light flashed on and off whilst it beeped out a cry for help, like some wounded artificial animal calling to the people whose jobs its more advanced cousins might one day take. No longer able to continue with the one and only function it had been created to carry out, the mechanical arm looked forlorn and bowed its head in shame whilst piles of unpacked things built up on the conveyor. 'These are already responsible for the packing team having to move on,' the manager continued, 'imagine what could happen in the future. Those people are lucky we have other positions available for them, but there may come a time when none of our jobs are safe.'

'But what about the maintenance team?' I asked. 'Human beings will always be needed to repair the machines when they break down, won't they?'

'Don't be so sure,' said the manager. 'Years ago, we would not have imagined robots would be able to do the jobs of human beings, but now they are becoming increasingly common. I wouldn't be surprised if one day there aren't machines that can actually fix *other* machines, or that factories will be built where human beings are not required at all.'

Surely not, I thought. *Human beings would not be silly enough to hand over the means of production to machines, would they?* That was the realm of science fiction and nothing more. *But then*, I thought, *how long before science fiction becomes science fact?* Thinking back to the story I'd read as a boy, I naively asked whether it might not be a good thing that some jobs may one day be done by machines, leaving us to take up other, more creative pursuits.

'Never happen,' said the manager.

'Why not?' I asked.

'Because people will always need jobs,' he replied, 'and not everyone can become writers or artists. There would be anger at the loss of employment, and even the possibility that people may be pushed to express that anger through the use of violence against those who'd seen fit to replace them.'

I nodded my understanding. 'I never thought about it like that,' I said, just as the bleeping red light flashed to green and the machine that had failed began to move again, carrying on where it had left off. While we had been talking, the maintenance team had fixed the problem and put the mechanical arm back to work, and now it happily went on with its task.

The manager laughed. 'Best get back to the grind ourselves, Steve,' he said, 'or they'll be replacing us as well.'

'Yes,' I agreed, as I watched him walk away.

Once he'd gone, I stared for a moment at the robotic arms busily working away, and as I stood there looking up at them, I felt a little shiver run down my spine. It was as if the machines somehow knew that I was there and were waiting for the day that their mechanical cousins would come and take my job too.

I Never Thought About It Like That

* * *

It is not that I fear change, you understand, it is just the *kind* of changes that are being implemented that I am wary of. That and how fast they seem to be coming. Whenever I watch people go by, I realise that the future may not have turned out the way I feared it might, but sometimes, as they walk past with their heads in their phones, I wonder. It is not the robots of boyhood stories that march through our streets now, but an altogether different and more sinister type of machine that could be used to imprison and impoverish us if we are not careful. The most frightening thing of all is just how many of us carry this machine about with us every day, without realising how much we have come to rely upon it. As the towns and cities grow increasingly empty and shops sit boarded up and miserable, the people that once flocked to them in droves now turn to online shopping for their retail therapy, and social media sites to meet their friends. Although the disappearance of the high street has been a growing fear for some time, it was accelerated by the lockdowns of recent years and, of course, it was the smaller businesses that were most affected. As I walked through a rundown area of town recently, I realised that if the high street were to disappear completely then there would be little use for physical money any longer and the digital age would be upon us sooner rather than later. In that moment, I couldn't help but wonder whether this hadn't been the plan all along, implemented by shadowy people sitting in dark rooms, many years before.

It's possible isn't it?

And, if so, it is important that we counteract this plan by choosing to spend our money in the shops that still remain as much as we can, to support local businesses lest they cease to exist and are pushed into the online sphere, where only digital money can be used and the machine is allowed to grow.

In the supermarkets, I often find myself being directed to the self-service tills whether I wish to use them or not, and I marvel at how many of them there now seems to be. The machines have begun to replace the checkout staff that once sat at the tills, and many of them, I notice, do not appear to like the taste of cash at all, and so I refuse to use them. This doesn't stop me from wondering how long it will be before human beings are no longer required in these buildings at all, however, and an entirely self-service system is put into place where the machines will eagerly feast on payments made by debit card or phone app. How much of the future will become automated, I wonder? Will we be left with no choice but to make the switch to electric cars, or will self-driving vehicles become the norm? And, if so, will they refuse to take us beyond the boundaries of the cities that may one day become our cold and isolated prisons, if those in charge decide we have not earned the right to travel past their borders? 'You've used too much petrol, Sir,' they might say, 'we can allow you no more. We know you've bought it because you paid for it via *our* app on *your* phone. Oh, and as a consequence, your credit score has been affected.' Without physical money, there is little to stop this from becoming a reality, and so we must be cautious.

It's been a while, but recently I heard talk of the long-dreaded ID cards again, and though I thought this particular beast had been put to rest and forgotten, I did not consider the possibility that it may never have gone away at all, not really. It had simply been hidden away in the darkest recesses of the minds of those who come up with these things, waiting for the chance to raise its ugly head again. I do not like the idea of ID cards, and digital ones even less. To think that Government bodies, or anyone else for that matter, might be able to harvest and process my data before sharing it with others, makes me feel very uncomfortable. It is open to all kinds of abuse, and is a threat to the very freedoms we have come to take for granted. Instead, the digital system must be opposed and we must resist it with all the strength that we possess. For the first time, I considered how much personal information I already put online, and the basis of a plan to change this pattern of behaviour began to form.

From a bus stop on the outskirts of town, I notice that a new 5G tower has been erected. Another blot on an already decaying landscape. 'Can't wait for it to come,' says a young lad to his group of friends. 'It's bound to be better than 4G.'

'What about the dangers?' says an older man. 'We don't know what'll happen when they switch those things on.'

'Nah, it'll be safe,' say the lads. 'Course it will.'

'How do you know?' asks the man.

'Because they say it will.'

'Who're *they*?'

The lads think for a moment. 'The people in charge of everything,' they say eventually.

'Oh *them*,' says the man. '*They* say a lot of things, though, don't they?'

The boys look over towards the tower again as if seeing it with fresh eyes, and new questions seem to be forming in their young minds.

'I heard something about them, too,' says one. 'That they're some kind of weapon or something.'

The others laugh.

'Nah, I'm serious,' he continues. 'My neighbour told me ages ago. He only uses those old 'brick' phones now, there's something about the new ones he doesn't like.'

And this conversation continues onto the bus, and, who knows, perhaps all the way to their destination. New thoughts have been introduced and ideas different from those of the mainstream are being considered for the first time...

* * *

Recently, I found myself working for another company after a period of unemployment. During this time, I wondered how long it would be before the people at the job centre would no longer be needed either—their workload being moved online while a Universal Basic Income is sent out automatically to jobseekers who no longer need to speak to human beings face-to-face. By this time, I was not surprised by how automated the system had become and how much the business I now worked for relied upon the intricate workings of machines. Scanners and sensors ruled the aisles whilst hundreds of security cameras watched our every move, just like they seem to do in every other area of modern life. To get to work I had to catch the company's own bus which, whilst convenient and able to drop the workers off outside the building, was also entirely cashless and required employees to download an app to pay the fare. I didn't like this and once again I worried about the loss of physical money which I believe to be a problem that will have far reaching consequences. I have no wish to exchange my freedoms and privacy for the convenience of being able to use a phone app. I do not find it so difficult to go into a real bank where I am able to retrieve real money, or to fish around in my pocket for change. If we don't, how long will either of these things remain? If we don't use them, we will lose them, as the old saying goes. This method of using real money in order to make our purchases has served us well for generations and comes with the added bonus of protecting us against the prying eyes of those who may wish to do us harm in the realm of cyberspace.

Once we arrived at the site, we had to press our badges against a scanner in the gate in order to gain entry into the building; scan our badge a second time in order to clock in and then use a handheld scanner to read our badges before we could start work. My job consisted of using this scanner to read the barcode labels attached to parcels before stacking them onto pallets, much like the job I'd had many years before upon leaving school, though somehow colder and less human in a way that I cannot quite explain. The machines had not yet advanced to the stage where they could replace the human workforce, but whilst at this company I heard stories of those who'd spent time at another site which they described as being 'fully automated,' and I knew that one day they would. The stories I heard about how the workers were treated by those in authority during the time of the recent pandemic, made me wonder whether the robots weren't already there, but made of flesh and blood instead of steel and oil.

During a lull in work one day, when the sensors on the conveyors broke down and the maintenance team were called, I got talking to a younger man and somehow the conversation turned to the digital system and how it might affect our lives in the future.

'I like all that stuff, though,' he said. 'It's much easier to do my banking online and most of my shopping is done online too these days.'

'But what about the possibility of the Government being able to track where you spend your money?' I asked. 'Let alone what you're actually spending it on. Doesn't that bother you?'

'Not really,' he replied. 'I don't mind that the Government might want to spy on me. If they want to, then let them. If we're not guilty of anything then we have nothing to hide and nothing to fear either.'

'The thing is,' I said, 'all the stuff we take for granted requires us to have absolute trust in those in charge. Unfortunately, I no longer have much faith in them. It's not just that they can track you either. If everything becomes digital and we lose physical money, what is to stop Governments from creating laws that will take *more* of our freedoms away?'

'How so?' he asked.

'Well, what is to stop them from passing laws that put restrictions on the things you buy? What if you have eaten too much of a certain food—one that they have decided on a whim is bad for you? Or from saying you have had too much alcohol or spent too much on chocolate this week? They would know because the digital system would allow them to see what you have purchased. If you don't use cash and pay for everything via debit card or a phone app, they can already do this. So far, we've not handed all our freedoms over and so they're not able to control our lives in this way, but that doesn't mean they never will. What if you wanted to travel outside your local area, and jumped into your car hoping to go for a nice drive one day, and suddenly you found that the Government had decided you'd used too much petrol that week? 'Driving is bad for the environment,' they could say, 'and *you* are not helping.' What is to stop them preventing you from buying petrol? In fact, what is to stop them preventing you from accessing your bank account at all? Without physical money our freedoms are severely limited and many people are unaware of this, just as I was up until quite recently.'

'But what about crime?' he said. 'If there's no longer any physical money, crime is bound to fall too.'

'Maybe some will,' I replied, 'but getting rid of cash won't stop criminals who operate online. Besides, this is how the Government will sell you on the idea. They'll say that if we get rid of coins and notes then it'll end crimes such as drug dealing and robbery, but once their digital currency is in place, what is to stop *them* from doing as they wish?'

'I never thought about it like that,' he said. 'I suppose it all got worse during the pandemic. You know, when people were locked in their houses and were restricted to buying mostly online.'

'Yes, I suppose so,' I replied, and I thought again about how many of the events of the past few years had come together seamlessly, and all in a way that appeared to be leading us in one single direction—a digital future under the dominion of those who would tell us that our safety was worth trading in our freedoms for, and so leaving us deserving of neither.

We both turned and stared at the conveyor belts which sprung back to life and began to drop their parcels down towards us again. The maintenance team walked away and the machine rolled onwards, still waiting for the day when it would no longer require human beings to fix it. After a while, my friend turned to me and spoke.

'So, what can we do about it, then?'

'About what?' I asked.

'The future, how do we make it so that it doesn't turn out like the way you said?'

I thought for a moment before answering. 'Little things,' I replied, 'we have to remember the little things and maybe then the larger things will take care of themselves. We can start by remembering to use physical money wherever possible, and don't rely too much on the alternatives. Online banking may be convenient, but we must use the physical ones too, otherwise we'll lose them. If there are shops that refuse to accept cash, we must insist they do or take our business elsewhere. It is an unfortunate but necessary step. If, whilst at the supermarkets, we are directed to the self-service tills, we must refuse or insist that we only use those which accept real money. More and more of them only take card payments and this cannot be acceptable if we want to preserve cash, and through that our freedoms and privacy.'

'Anything else,' he asked with a smile.

'Yes,' I replied, 'tell your family and friends. Tell everyone you know and spread the message. Print leaflets and put them through your neighbours' doors. If you find an interesting website, send the links to people you speak to online. The more of us there are who are aware of the threats of the digital system, the more of us there will be to resist it.'

'Good idea,' he replied, as we both returned to our jobs. As we worked, I became lost in thought and my mind wondered again as it often does. I looked over at my friend and he looked back and nodded and we both began to smile. The machine marched on, but it was not in charge yet, not as long as there were people who were willing to stand against its progress.

For the rest of that day I was lost in thought, until finally I realised that it is not by force or by coercion, but by gentle, subtle reasoning that an idea can be shared and an understanding reached. When this happens, a single fragile light that seems to flicker alone in the darkness can become a dozen and then a hundred lights, growing stronger with each new flame that is ignited. Before long, a small group becomes much larger and a million lights will burn bright enough to ensure the safety of the next generation that will continue the struggle in our absence, never to fade, and never once growing dim...

16

Always Make a Fuss

By Radical Nan

It was during the first part of lockdown when I noticed a control creeping in from the bank I used. The recorded message when I rang had taken on a sort of 'end of the world 'quality telling me how they were all working very hard but services were under pressure.

The bank is already a digital world, one I had tried to avoid but digital nonetheless.

My son was looking at mobile homes to buy. He had a site all lined up and had found a van and put a deposit on it and then lockdown arrived.

He was unable to collect it. The money I had agreed to loan him remained in my sole account and when he needed it, I was going to transfer it to a joint savings account for him to access. As this meant my going to the branch, I did not bother straightaway as the bank was closed most of the time anyway.

When the lockdown was lifted, he needed the money asap. I rang the bank to arrange a transfer of my own money between my own accounts and was told that due to lockdown this could not be done.

I asked why and the call handler could not tell me. I asked

to speak to someone higher up and the customer services manager told me that if 'I asked again she would have 'legal action taken against me'. She sent me this in writing too.

I rang the head office to complain and after a lot of being passed around found someone vaguely sensible who arranged for a colleague to ring me to arrange the transfer.

A charming young man rang and told me he was prepared to do this as a 'one off never to be repeated transfer'. When I asked him to explain he said that they 'have a list of approved transactions and mobile home purchase is not on the approved purchases list. I asked to see the list. He could not produce it.

We played a game. He told me that 'I could have money for food but not for a sofa'. I asked to see the list 'where is it on your website.'

He said it's not on there.

'Ok', I said 'what is on the list, can I have a new hat or a goldfish, slippers or knickers or tyres for the car? He said 'only essentials were being permitted'. All this nonsense had taken far longer than a transfer of money from one of my accounts to the other would have done.

There was no list.

The head office listened to the recordings of the call. I was not rude, swearing, threatening but very insistent. Megan the customer service manager had no idea that she had overstepped the mark at all. She was completely unaware of her own shortcomings. She told her manager in rather insolent terms I believe.

The woman from head office sent me a bouquet of flowers.

She gave me her direct line and email just in case I had another problem. I did of course exactly the same thing. I tried to email and ring her. She had disappeared from head office.

The Ombudsman told me I should receive £75 compensation and that if it happened again, I was to tell the bank about his ruling.

It happened again and I told the bank. They did not listen.

Moral of this tale is, your money is their money when it is in your account.

They can block you from using your own funds, entering the branch and threaten you with legal action just for asking.

I believe that early lockdown was a trial run to see how much control they can exert over the public and get away with it.

Always make a fuss. Never let it go. They are testing to see what we will put up with.

Once this type of control becomes acceptable and that is almost upon us, we will never be free of it.

Controls build confidence among control freaks and corporations are all control freaks.

When I ring anywhere now bank, insurance company utility the hold message is the same;

'We are working very hard to help you. We treat everyone the same and will tolerate no abuse of our staff ... etc, etc

Translated this means: 'You will shut up and put up with whatever shoddy services we offer, we are superior beings and if you complain you are an abuser, racist, homophobic/transphobic bigot.'

We are constantly being groomed and we need to resist.

17

August 2025

By Moira M. Malcolm

I don't have a mobile phone.'
'More and more people don't. What's your landline then?'
Celia reels off her landline number holding an old-fashioned cord phone next to her ear. Celia, now 45, had to learn the hard way that radiation from mobile phones causes all sorts of health problems. It's why she's deaf in one ear.

The polite, cheery-sounding receptionist in the Health Centre, who hasn't experienced verbal abuse since covid protocols were dropped and face-to-face appointments reinstated, confirms: 'That's you booked in for the Digital Detox Seminar on Wednesday 3rd September.' She adds, 'You'll be amazed at how much more time you'll have when you learn to limit your screen time.'

'Sounds good. Can't wait.'

'Thanks for phoning Celia. See you in September.'

'Okay. Thanks.' She places the phone back in it's cradle and paused to reflect how her life will improve when she rids herself of her technology addiction which is, she admits herself, ruining her life.

Celia turns to gaze out the window which, during hot weather in August, she likes to keep open. She feels grateful to hear, with her good ear, the high-pitched sounds of birds chirping away in the garden. To her delight she sees a Blue Tit balancing on the rod of the metal bird-feeder. She watches as his small, blue-capped head bobs in and out extracting the sunflower seeds. A Robin flies in to join the party which Celia decides to view through binoculars, an item she received recently from her local Swap Shop when she handed in a Thermos flask.

Suddenly feeling lethargic, Celia climbs the stairs to her bedroom for a lie down. She has never felt right since taking those covid injections, now known by all, apart from those who ended up in prison over it, as 'Rat Poison'.

The view from her bedroom window is of tiled roof tops and terracotta chimney pots. She sees smoke rising into the sky from some of them. The sun makes an appearance from behind a natural, not man-made, cloud and rays of sunlight transform the chimney pots into a reddish brown colour. In the distance Celia catches a glimpse of the final 5G tower in her town being torn down.

In a few weeks' time the tree planting team will begin to replace the avenues of trees which were mowed down to make way for the 5G weaponry. Celia hopes she is able to get involved with that. All the children in her town are excited. NOT going to school has given them a real zest for learning and some of them have become a real joy to be around.

Children of all ages have been involved in planting vegetable seeds in the receptacles the council had bought to block roads in town and to stop people parking. The receptacles were moved to the new allotment area where Celia, and anyone else on a low income, can pick up vegetables free at the point of need. The new NHS (National Horticultural Service) is going from strength to strength.

Since telecommunication companies had been forced to correct the wrongs they had done (by removing harmful cell towers they had sneakily constructed during the unlawful lockdowns), various little birds had returned to her garden, and bees had returned to pollinate the enormous sunflowers she grew each year against the high back wall.

The yellow colour of the sunflowers was a reminder of the hope she felt inside that the world was finally heading in the right direction. As her eyelids close, Celia slips down underneath the bed clothes and within minutes is fast asleep. Beyond the bird song, petrol and diesel cars roar on the main road not far from her home in the background.

People are again free to travel anywhere they please and councillors who had introduced measures to restrict movement are long gone. The most senior ones are already in the clink, along with pharmaceutical salesmen and women, including doctors, nurses and midwives, who coerced patients to participate in the biggest clinical drug trial of all time.

Celia abruptly awakens and, for a split second, feels frightened. Her rigid body relaxes when she reminds herself, as she does every morning, that it's all over now. The terror regime which began in March 2020 is no more. She can live on her own terms as a free woman in an energised community which is free from government interference and surveillance.

Celia fires up her laptop, because old habits die hard and also because she has yet to buy a paper diary from her local newsagent. It's the shop where she buys *The Light* newspaper every month. The majority of print newspapers have gone under since all the lies were exposed but for some reason that paper's readership continues to grow.

After reading an article on a website about the benefits of detoxing, fasting and drinking rosemary tea, Celia focuses on dates in her diary. She smiles when she remembers her nephew is taking her, on Saturday, to a matinee at the Uncensored Theatre, to see *Death of a Vaccine Salesman*.

18

The Overbearing Octopus

By E Mc M

When I think of the global control system (of which the push towards digital ID is just the latest part) I picture an octopus sitting on humanity, wrapping its tentacles around us and squeezing tightly. What the octopus needs to survive is our resources (money, energy, time) and the more we withhold the weaker its grasp becomes. What are these tentacles and how can we loosen their grip?

Big corporations/Big food

Reduce money spent with online giants or large international supermarket chains. Switch to corner shops, independent retailers, local craftsmen and markets.

I now buy a weekly local veg box, shop at the market, buy handmade gifts from local traders, frequent charity shops and only purchase online when there is no other option.

Big food is largely about profit. My grandmothers, raising families in the 1940s, would have cooked every day using mostly fresh, fairly local ingredients. Convenience or processed foods were not common, eating out and takeaway fish & chips a rare treat. How much has changed in a short time.

I have started to cook from scratch and avoid processed

and convenience foods as much as possible. (In the time it takes to unpack and heat a supermarket pizza it is possible to whip up a tomato omelette with new potatoes and a green salad.) I noticed that my tastes soon changed, I no longer want to eat the processed food I used to and I have lost some weight too.

Big pharma

How much money do you think big pharma makes from you through over-the-counter drugs or prescription medicines every year? The industry depends on repeat customers. Side effects of some medications will present as new illnesses often requiring further treatment, more drugs.

Lifestyle changes can greatly improve health and reduce reliance on pharmaceuticals.

Better diet, regular exercise, rest and relaxation, fasting and detoxing, vitamins and supplements, alternative therapies ... the list goes on.

I found it quite liberating to accept more responsibility for my own health and now I view a trip to the GP or pharmacist as a last resort. Two things that really opened my eyes to the impact of lifestyle (particularly diet) on health were listening to a talk by Patrick Holford (author of 'The Optimum Nutrition Bible') and watching Jason Vale's documentary 'Super Juice Me!' (available on YouTube.)

Big tech and 'smart' gadgets

Aside from the monetary cost big tech, especially social media, is a distraction, draining time and energy. Smart gadgets in your home are perhaps doing far more than you realise. Reducing dependency or removing both can be a good idea.

I have never owned a smart phone, my basic model is fine for texting and calls. I use a laptop when necessary but don't go online every day. Whenever there is a choice between online or offline (eg: completing tax returns) I take the paper option. We still have a bank branch in my town so I visit in person rather than using online banking.

Banking/Digital currency

Resist any push towards digital currency, even when this becomes inconvenient. If you are lucky enough to have savings, don't keep them all in one place (perhaps look into tangible investments such as gold, silver or jewellery). Reduce the use of credit and debit cards and switch to cash.

Since joining the globalwalkout.com last year I have used cards only a handful of times, paying instead with cash at every opportunity and avoiding shops that are cashless. Using cash also makes it easier to keep track of my spending.

Education

If you are a parent of children in the education system, are you happy with what they are being taught? Aside from home schooling, which is not an option for everyone, perhaps you make time for discussions at home so that your children at least have another viewpoint. You might think that they are not listening, but you will have planted a seed that may cause them to question what they hear.

As an adult, what knowledge or skills could you acquire to make you more independent?

The situation that we find ourselves in is odd. Everything that we need to survive (food, water, space to live) has been freely provided but, at some point, it has been taken away and sold back to us in order to keep us reliant. Becoming more self-sufficient, less dependent, is another part of the process. Whilst weakening the grasp of the octopus we can simultaneously build up our own self-reliance.

An interesting exercise is to run through your typical day and note when, and for what, you rely on outside sources, then consider what you could do to become less dependent. For me, the three obvious ones were food, water and power.

Food

Start to grow what you can. If you live in a city flat you can grow tomatoes on the balcony and have pots of 'cut and come again' salad leaves or microgreens on your windowsill. Stock up on supplies of dried and tinned goods. Frequent farm shops and farmers markets in your area. Personally, I have enjoyed learning to forage—once you know what to look for, the nearest common or riverbank can supply a variety of edible leaves.

Water

Since I am not in a position to make major changes to my home, I spent some time wondering how I could solve this one with minimal cost and fuss and ended up buying a selection of water filters, all of which are designed to make rainwater drinkable. They range in price from around £10 to around £300 and I have passed one onto each of my extended family.

When it comes to bathing I set myself the challenge of wild swimming throughout last winter, so I now know that even on a drizzly, windy day in February I can go for a swim and get clean.

Power

Aside from candles and matches, I have picked up a few useful solar powered items: a phone/laptop charger, radio, torch and lights. If the power is down I will be cooking outside on my barbecue so I have a supply of wood on hand too.

Of course, everyone's circumstances are different, we just do what we can. Even knowing that you have taken the first small steps to becoming more independent will build confidence and make the future seem less daunting.

This, too, shall pass.

19

The Party Is Over (and It's All Our Fault)

By Dee

The beginning of the industrial era in the early 20th century led to booms in technology, and the machinery required to mass produce items gave birth to what is called 'consumer culture'. Local, community driven jobs and ways to earn and live were replaced with a workforce and ruthless capitalistic corporate entities. We handed over our responsibilities and power in exchange for the chance of 'success' (without knowing what success actually is).

Hypnotic advertising, catchy labels and addictive process of sale was thrust onto people to which they were caught up in. This consumer culture has lasted around 100 years, and I think we are now coming to the end of it. The post-industrial era. In this new horizon, a rapid and traumatic change from analogue to digital 'tools' that form our society and world has taken place without enough time to process and adapt. This not only creates a massive dissociation from 'Boomers' to Gen X/Y/Z in regard to relationships but creates a dissociation in the environment with a hollow space in the work and play-field that was ripe for the taking and is now filled with 'oddities'.

Our industries have become 'stale', this is because the human essence was put through this turbo capitalistic machine at a gargantuan rate. This 'essence' of creativity has been exploited and formed into algorithms to produce wealth for the big owners of the particular industry. Think of a pop singer who signed a deal to make 10 songs for a record label, the way the song is orchestrated, the intentions and emotions, the basic message would not be of organic nature. The singer is not depicting an experience, a feeling, a story, but rather just building their outside image, persona and aesthetic while using AI tools for the sound, then selling this package to susceptible consumers.

The problem here is that there is only a limited amount of songs, movies, art, cuisine, TV, fashion, hairstyles, car shapes, games and even ideas available to conceive before you start cloning them and adding minor nuances (which aren't enough to change the concept). Perhaps the only area we *do* have new concepts in is the technology field (this is really only the category that can 'advance'). Efficiency and convenience through tech which is forced upon us are removing the 'journey' aspect and the process of adventure. For what reason is there such a hurry to get from point A to B if the destination is as hollow and empty as the place from which you began? Eating apple pies made by unknown hands with unknown ingredients and corporate intentions is a bad spiritual practice.

We are now at a stage where a 'deafening silence' is in the air due to the lack of fresh stimuli. These stimuli were thrown out, and factory line assembled at such rates, people could catch and harbour what they liked, formed into their identity, incorporated into their lifestyle, choices etc. Well the machine is 'empty' now and people are stumbling for a hysteria to acquire which replaces these stimuli. Gender identity, sexual orientation, extremist politics, woke, anti-woke, cult and gang culture, new age ideologies, attack and defence of aligned sub culture, new drugs, new perversions, new 'madness' to explore and insanities to form.

People will create and cling to something, anything, in order to not feel what is a 'deafening silence' that is the leftovers of the post-industrial era. The hustle and bustle calming down. We are at a collective crossroads, there are stakes at play and people are unconsciously willing to be swept up all over again as long as they do it together, even if in an unsavoury process.

The remedy is what benefits the people first, a new system, the death of the old and sickly archaic system where we are all exploited, we need time to build and replace our essence that was stolen. With the proper foundations and strengths to truly flourish, a framework that doesn't allow accumulation of power and authoritarian systems. Local, decentralised 'power', a town hall which 'governs' a very tiny surrounding area where you can turn up and perform a speech or voice concerns with your local representative mandatorily attending. Community will be re-established and attempt at helping the social isolation and mental health issues plaguing the modern world. Also, each voice will have weight to it in this form as you are physically present, rather than sending a letter to an anonymous bureaucrat receptionist which takes months for a response and where you are treated as a statistic in a data hub.

20

Seek

By Jeanne G Dust

Heavenly Father, creator of heaven and earth please help me to get through this day. This is my first prayer on awakening and if anyone thinks I am a religious nutter you don't know me so don't judge me please. I think that you would pray too if you had my life. My first thought on that Friday morning was how in the world am I going to get through today. I felt tired and drained and demoralised. At least it's Friday. But I had no inkling of how the day would turn out. I set off as usual walking briskly in the chilly spring breeze down the hill to the bus stop. There is a cemetery adjacent to it and I usually while away the time looking across the overgrown weeds to the gravestones. There is only one name that I can make out from here 'Fez'. I've wondered before and was wondering again on this particular morning who Fez was when I was joined by Jed. He lives in the flat above mine. 'Who do you think Fez was?' I asked indicating the gravestone. 'RIP FEZ is all it says on the tombstone.' 'Good morning Gloria. Fez is a city in Morocco. I've been there'. They must have had to dig a pretty big hole if they buried a city here'. Jed goes on protests. He has been labelled an anti-vaxxer but I've got to know him quite well lately and surprising even myself, I quite like him.

    I gazed out of the window on the bus journey. I was in no mood to talk and Jed respected my need for solitude. The usual route, past the park with the man on the park bench with his 'I need job' sign. He never seems to do anything to get a job. He always seems to be sitting or lying on the same park bench usually with a can of lager by his side. Past the statue of a dictator in the square. His name is Jurine but as the statue is invariably urinated on late at night by revellers who congregate there after the pubs have closed it is known locally as the urine statue. Past the posters on the billboard. There is a new one today with a government minister grinning and holding up a book. His name is Tom C Khan and someone has already defaced it by adding two horns to his head and writing Cat over the letter C. Further along we passed the hideous building Furnace e-link. It's ugly. No one knows quite what goes on in there but there is something sinister about it.

    I walked with dread to my workplace after parting from Jed. For those of you who have always loved your job, who are in your element you wouldn't understand and for those who hate their job as I do you will know only too well this feeling. A colleague I recognised was just ahead of me and I called out a greeting to her. She continued as though she had not heard me. When I finally caught up with her inside the building going up the steps to the office I saw that she was weeping but before I could ask anything she was met by a senior manager and whisked into an office. You could cut the atmosphere with a knife when I walked into the office. No one answered when I wished good morning to all present. And then 'Haven't you heard?' I hadn't heard but I knew by the sombre faces and silence that it was something bad. I knew I should have checked my emails before I came in. I just should have checked. I resent doing work stuff when I'm at home but this moment when they all know something bad and I don't, I wished I'd checked. There were exchanged glances 'Who is going to tell her?' looks but in my paranoid mood I thought it was something that I had done wrong or failed to do with dire consequences so it came as a relief at first when someone said 'It's Tony' pause ... and then with a sob 'he's died'. Oh, why if someone had to die did it have to be Tony? Why couldn't it have been Eckbi? Eckbi is spiteful, mean and critical; she's also lazy and stupid but talks to me as if I am the stupid and lazy one. Everyone loved Tony. Unbelievable! Tony.

Tony was popular. He was the kindest manager and such a sense of humour! And so alive! He was alive and well only yesterday. I know what Jed will say about this: 'Sudden Adult Death'. I don't take much notice of most of what Jed says but there are moments when I think maybe Jed is right. Jed thinks that the government has a plan to turn us all into cyborgs. Gloria. Read the government document 'Dawn of a New Paradigm' and then come back to me and tell me I'm a just a stupid conspiracy theorist. There is a conspiracy to harm us and to turn us into slaves. If you haven't got time to read the whole document then read one sentence. Page 53, the sentence beginning 'People have human rights, machines do not have human rights...' There is no full stop after this sentence. You need to read more. Knowledge is power.

The day dragged. All the days here do but more so today. I didn't see Eckbi all day. Usually I would class a day without seeing Eckbi as a good day but today is going to be remembered by me for the rest of my life as one of the worst days I have lived through so far. Jed thinks that things are going to get a whole lot worse. Jed knows all the latest conspiracy theories and he talks a lot about them. Jed encourages me to read and Amie encourages me to pray. I don't do much of either.

The bus journey home was long, noisy and tedious. A child sitting next to me had a computer game with cartoon characters. Lord Something fighting with Mr Something over a bag of money. So I had to glance across as some of the words sounded inappropriate for a child. Yes, I am sometimes nosy. Words that sounded like 'fock 'ell' were the man's name which was spelt 'Mr Fockereller' and his rival 'Lord Schith.' Then Mr Rainy Blot got on the bus and as usual spewing the words 'Idiots, idiots' the only word that always seems to come out of his mouth which today he was saying with more venom than usual. He was wearing the same jacket that always looks as though he has got wet in the rain hence the nickname Jed and I have given him.

On arriving home I called into my neighbour Amie to ask for her prayers for Tony. Amie is sweet and always kind. She seems to radiate peace. I know her views on sudden death. To her it means that they may have died without repentance. Tony was a good person but a believer? Oh no. Apart from Amie I don't know anyone who is. I certainly know a few churchgoers but Amie is the only person I know who would definitely get to heaven.

I then went to my flat shut the door and switched on the TV. There was only the usual Uncle Ramon and Emma talking on their favourite subject—climate change. I switched channels but it was just more advertisements for medication and so I switched it off. I lay on my bed and cried. I cried for Tony and for me. My life hasn't worked out how I thought it would. I didn't think that this is how my life would be. When I was a child and thought about the future I didn't think it would be like this. Working day after day for an income that is barely enough to survive on in a job that I hate. I'm stuck. I'd love to leave and move away and start again. The thought came to me that I could pray. Amie taught me. She asked me one day if I ever pray and I said that I did once. I prayed for a bike as all my school friends had one and I prayed for one but didn't receive it. 'How old were you?' 'Ten'. She didn't reproach me. She didn't say 'All those years ago and you haven't prayed since?' She explained to me how you just need to be still and believe that there is a God who is there listening to you. I made the sign of the cross, imagined myself sitting in front of the throne of God and I prayed silently. I prayed for everyone. I prayed for God to forgive us, to enlighten us and pour out his blessings on us.

I could hear Jed's music. I couldn't make out the words but I recognised the song—Uprising by the rock band Muse and I know the words 'They will not control us. We will be victorious'. I implored God for victory and my mood lifted as if by a miracle.

21

Slavery

By Mev Berwick

In my younger days, I was employed in the paper-making industry. At one particular paper mill, once through the main gate we had to pass through a big storage yard to enter the mill proper. In this yard there were various containers, packing cases etc. including a large cable drum some six feet in diameter. On this drum was coiled a few hundred feet of soft copper tubing. The drum lay there for months, and it was just one of those things that registered in your mind as you passed on to your place of work.

Then one day the yard was full of police and mill management, the cable drum was cordoned off. Why? Because the copper pipe had disappeared from the drum. The question being: where did that copper pipe go, since it had not been used for it's intended purpose? The only conclusion was that it had been stolen, but how had the thieves managed to steal it all without being noticed?

The thieves, who must have been employees or contractors, were never caught; their plan had worked brilliantly. How? Quite simple really. Over a period of months, a few feet of pipe at a time was cut off, probably every day, just enough to shove in a bag without anyone noticing; until the removal of the last remnants left the drum empty!

So you're probably wondering what this (true) story has to do with slavery? Let me give you an analogy; let's assume that the copper pipe on the cable drum is now your Freedom. Then assume that the thieves are your Government. (The difference here is that we know who the thieves are, and they don't give a toss about you or me). Over the last three years, our government has been stealing your freedom, stealing what little wealth you have, all without you noticing, all under the guise of 'it's for your own good'. Three weeks to flatten the curve has come to this.

Sherlock Holmes: 'When you have removed the impossible, whatever remains, however improbable, must be the truth'. I use this quote to try and impress upon the multitude of trusting souls who would never believe governments could be capable of the crimes against humanity we have witnessed since covid was foisted upon us. A wrecking ball has been taken to our way of life, our economies, our agriculture, our health services, all to 'build back better' and remove 'useless eaters'. Oh, and you will have nothing and be happy! Anyone with half a brain would refuse an experimental treatment that isn't even a 'vaccine', does not confer immunity, and causes more problems than it solves.

Albert Einstein: 'Unthinking belief in authority is the greatest enemy of the truth' and 'question, question, question everything'.

Only when you realise that you live in a corporate world where you are mere assets to be used and abused; that the inhuman psychopaths running the show are the biggest criminals in history; that they own governments, Mainstream Media, big pHARMa, much of the judiciary; that their propaganda is the only news allowed; 1984 and Animal Farm indeed; only when you understand this will you be able to begin to fight back; and when you do understand, when the light finally comes on, you will never change your mind or be taken in again.

The realisation that unelected organisations hold sway over our governments is hard to take. The likes of the UN, WEF, WHO, can be seen as criminal organisations intent on the massive reduction of the human population. Fearmongers, preying on the uninformed, all they want is what's left of the planet's resources to themselves, using the fraudulent climate change as a lever; and what's left of the human population as their slaves.

But what can be done about this? Do we just accept it? Knowing the extent of the problem helps, and with the enemy in full view, we can only hope that more and more people start to see the truth, however slowly that happens. Does evil really always defeat itself? Resist, defy, do not comply, are good starting points. Keep using cash, boycott card only businesses, fight against digital currencies, digital IDs. Subscribe to local businesses, farmers etc. Campaign against the roll-out of 5G via your councillors. Your MP's are, in the main, useless self serving puppets. And don't think a Labour government will fix all of this; they are all part of the same beast, beholden to the City of London. Democracy is dead, Parliament is a joke (maybe Guy Fawkes was right?). It's very clear to me that the whole political system needs to be restructured for the benefit of we, the people.

But where I see the weakest link in their chain— everything these evil cretins rely upon is powered by electricity and electronics. Many people would suffer, but why not take down the power grids for as much time as it takes? Back to the very basics of life would soon expose who the really useless eaters are. In the meantime, lamp posts and ropes should be the order of the day.

Finally: Benjamin Franklin: 'Those who would give up essential liberty for a little temporary safety, deserve neither

and are sure to lose both.'
    Will you live on your knees, or die on your feet?

22

Survival of the Smartest—A Beginner's Guide

By Tony Zhang

According to the Pope we have entered World War III so now seems a good time to offer guidelines for helping newcomers survive the present onslaught on their life and liberty. We have little space for explanations so it's more a pot pourri of signposts for bringing you up to speed with what's happening now, readying you for what's coming down the line, and joining with the resistance.

Don't panic!

In the immortal words of Lance Corporal Jones, 'Don't panic!' We are living in the age of 'nudge' and many have succumbed to a whole raft of extraordinary demands, the end aim being 50% population reduction and full techno control of the masses. In truth there was no COVID-pandemic, though the so-called vaccines were and are dangerous and, as planned, they continue to kill and injure millions around the globe. The Climate Crisis is another hoax but, rather than panic, take time to find out what's really going on. A visit to Telegram is a good place to start. Also check for local activity, for instance by searching 'a stand in the park'.

Masks

Never wear one it's all nonsense. Most of the masks you see and wear are not masks at all, they are splash guards designed to protect medical staff from the bodily fluids of patients. They are not a barrier to viruses and they dull your senses by restricting oxygen and increasing intake of carbon dioxide. They also collect possibly malign bacteria when damp and are even thought to contain carcinogenic material. On the other hand they are apparently making a fortune for the shady characters who supply them.

Geo-engineering

Stay inside and keep out of the rain! For years, those outside who look up have noticed long white trails that seem to hang around for hours and eventually form strange looking clouds. These are made by specially converted aircraft that spray a wide range of noxious chemicals onto the people below. When pushed, the official excuse is they are controlling the weather but when rain is captured and analysed, the data include such toxins as arsenic, lead, barium, mercury, titanium, aluminium and uranium. Why they want to make us ill is another conversation but our advice is to stay inside as much as possible when trails are around (especially when raining) and detox regularly with Zeolite Powder (ultra fine) and other forms of chelation therapy.

Health

A top pharmaceutical executive once responded:'Why would we want to cure anyone ... we'd go out of business in no time?' That greedy and cynical reply sums up the parlous state of the health 'business'. We've been brainwashed into believing only allopathic intervention can make us well but that's patently not the case. The body is a stupendous machine that comes free of charge and, with help from flora and fauna, will look after us better than anything Big Pharma has to offer. It's therefore no surprise that, with the NHS in a state of collapse, natural and holistic treatments are making a dramatic comeback with community-based services appearing across the country. For instance, take a look at The People's Health Alliance at https://the-pha.org/.

Vaccines and pharmaceuticals

Where possible avoid jabs and other pharmaceutical products. The human race has survived for millennia without chemical concoctions and it's a scandal the way 'health' has been taken over by profit-hungry corporations. Parents are coerced into having their offspring vaccinated yet independent research shows that, if anything, jabs have a negative impact on health (though not on the Big Pharma wallet). For instance, over a period of some 50 years, autism alone is said to have increased from around 1 in 30,000 children to 1 in 25 and the finger has been pointed at vaccination. Schools too are being coerced into jabbing kids, sometimes without permission of parents. Where that is a concern, legal letter templates can be found on the internet.

Detoxing

How do I detox the noxious chemicals I've been jabbed with? It's a question we hear all too often from the newly awakened and the full answer is too long and complex to be considered here. However, serious efforts are being made to find detox protocols and these are changing and developing all the time. Up front in the fight is the World Council for Health and its latest advice can be found at https://worldcouncilforhealth.org/resources/spike-protein-detox-guide/. It's wordy but there's a helpful summary at the end.

Supplements

Take supplements as you grow older. Healthy young people who consume fresh, natural and organic food are unlikely to fall ill because the body's needs will already be met. However, once past the age of around 55 you become less efficient at producing some of these extras and help is needed. Vitamins C and D come high on the list. Take for instance one of our authors, who is 77, takes no pharmaceuticals and has been without illness of any kind for over 12 years. It takes ongoing personal research but, for the record, his current list includes Vitamins A, B, C, D, and K2, Glutathione, Magnesium, MSM, NAC, Omega 3, Probiotics, Selenium, Turmeric, Ashwagandha, and Quercetin. That sounds a lot but he still runs a full-time business so it seems to be working!

Mainstream news

Avoid mainstream news, especially from the BBC. They appear to have been 'bought' by key figures from the World Economic Forum and today offer propaganda on a par with anything Russia gave us in the past. They want to control our thinking on many levels. For instance, the Ukraine war reports paint a very different picture to independent reports coming from those on the ground. Thankfully, we still have small news operations that are honest, accurate and truthful. One in particular is called UK Column and you can find it at ukcolumn.org. It's said to be attracting more viewers and listeners than BBC News.

Money

Our day-to-day spending is planned to go fully digital, under the control of a new world bank. This sounds melodramatic but it's already starting to happen. The fight back rule is for everyone to use untraceable cash wherever possible and slow down on, or even stop, using digital cards. Banks too are no longer considered safe and many customers are withdrawing funds and moving them elsewhere. Some are buying gold and others are switching to crypto. As yet there are no perfect answers and the advice is to stay alert.

Power

We can no longer rely on gas and electricity to appear on demand at a price we can afford, so it's time to consider possible alternatives. These include firewood, LPG gas, solar (not cheap!), wind and even a camping gas cooking stove. One very useful gadget is a water distiller, so if the water supply fails you can take it from any stream or river and distil it. The result will be perfectly safe to drink although lacking in minerals. Then there's the question of personal transport. Electric cars are *not* a good idea because energy prices will soar and malign forces are likely to control car usage via the internet. However, some of the older diesel cars run happily on cooking oil.

Food

Where possible eat locally produced fare that's organic. The human body is an amazing thing, but to remain healthy it needs good food. The mass produced products sold by global chains often contain little in the way of nutrition while some is said to include substances intended to damage our health. The ideal diet is one that is organic, low in carbs, high in good quality fats, and contains fresh fruit and vegetables. The keto diet encompasses this. Always check labels … foods that are heavily processed with ingredients that include artificial flavouring/colouring and 'e' numbers should be avoided. One excellent source of (delivered) organic food is Riverford, at https://riverford.co.uk/.

Drink

Avoid both sugary drinks like Colas and water from the tap. Run tap water through a purifier or use the bottled variety. Tap water is said to be anything but pure, with chemicals like fluoride (not the natural variety) now being added in some areas. The adult body is said to need at least two litres of water a day and many low-sugar drinks (e.g. tea, coffee, beer, wine) will count towards that.

Growing food

Food scarcity is already on the way, so why not grow your own? We are seeing a concerted attempt to seize farmland across the world. Fortunately Bill Gates had the great foresight (ha!) to buy up huge areas in the US and no doubt we will be expected to eat his expensive and GMO-based produce with air miles attached. So what to do? Well, if we are living in World War III we need once again to 'dig for victory'. Even the smallest of gardens can make a difference and pages of practical advice are given by the People's Food and Farming Alliance on their website at the-pffa.org. Collect seeds and swap/barter with like-minded people in your neighbourhood. Also try to make sure you always have at least a month's supply of food in hand.

Finally, remember you are not alone. There are millions of us and probably only a handful of 'them' calling the shots. Help set up self-supporting communities. Stay positive and be strong. If you're told to do something you don't want to do, politely refuse. If we are resolute and united, we will win.

23

The Enemy In Your Pocket

By Harry Hopkins

We are well aware of the central role that smartphones play in many people's lives. Haven't we all seen young folk walking along the street gazing at the screen in their hand, oblivious to what is going on around them? How many times have you seen people sitting together in the pub, cafe or restaurant with their eyes fixed on their phones? Groups who come together supposedly for friendship and conversation retreating into the virtual world as if a spell has been cast. Can this be a good thing? Can the random capture of a person's thought processes ever be healthy?

There is no doubt that Silicon Valley engineers have designed, and are constantly upgrading, applications which are as addictive as gambling, alcohol or drugs.

All of this is intentional. If those who would seek to control every one of us, and indeed every aspect of our lives so that we could not function in society without subservience to them, how would they go about it? They would seek to make us totally dependent on their highly developed technology, so that any kind of acceptable and worthwhile life would be impossible without it.

Are these the ravings of a modern-day Luddite? Well, I

love technology. I have a computer and an iPad, but I have an old-fashioned mobile phone, the kind whereby you talk to people and send the occasional text. I use technology as a tool when it suits me. As with alcohol, I know that over-indulgence might lead me down the slippery slope to hell. I firmly believe that 'smart technologies'—I mean not just phones but anything with the word 'smart' in its description—are being pushed not for our benefit but because they are all part of the Big Brother society that we are being herded towards; it is a vision of a totalitarian state that is a danger to us all.

Here is just one example: energy suppliers are very keen for you to have so-called smart meters installed. These provide a continuous display of your use and automatically send details to your supplier. The myriad alleged benefits include being able to monitor your energy consumption and adjust your behaviour accordingly, receiving accurate bills instead of estimates, and no need to open the door to a meter reader.

However critics have warned for years that a smart meter enables the supplier to control your use, even cutting you off, at the push of a button from the control centre. Now this aspect is coming to light. Customers who are behind with their payments are finding their smart meters are being switched remotely into prepayment meters, which have a higher tariff.[13] Although the supplier is supposed to discuss the move with the customer, in some cases the only warning given is a text message.

Meanwhile the closure of bank branches, which has been going on for years, is gathering pace. Older people cannot go into banks because they are not there. They cannot contact their banks because of the computerised systems replacing

---

13 Rebecca Wearn et Colletta Smith, 'Energy firms remotely swap homes to prepay meters', 9 November 2022, *BBC* [website], <bbc.co.uk/news/business-63554879>, accessed 4 May 2023.

human beings. 'You are number 27 in the queue' is enough to dishearten and depress many people who live alone and have minimum support.

Life is becoming increasingly difficult for millions of people who cannot or will not take on board the technological revolution. The push for 'apps' to pay for everything rather than use cash is all around us; supermarkets are champing at the bit to accept card/phone app payments only. Public transport, public car parks and public conveniences are moving to app payments only. Already some shops will not accept cash at all. In short, there are millions of people who are excluded from society because they are not up to speed with technology, and this will only get worse.

Where is this headed? I'm afraid that those who are unworried by the swish of a phone at a checkout or the monitoring of their digitalised money online are in for a huge shock. Rather than a Utopian dream of having life simplified by technology, what in fact is heading down the tracks is the entire opposite. A complete and total loss of freedom. A life where your every waking moment is monitored and controlled by the phone in your pocket. Your phone knows where you are; how fast you are driving (if you are one of the fortunate few who can still afford to drive); how much 'digital money' you have and what you can spend it on; when and where you can access medical care (not in person of course, the digital doctor will see you now); where and when you can holiday; if and when you can work. And much, much more.

And once your 'cash' is just an online number completely outside your control, you will be totally and utterly dependent on the State to allow you to function at all. You will be a non-person and subject to any qualifying conditions which the authorities impose on you in order to live. It's already this way now for millions of people in China.

So what can you do about this? How can you say, 'Enough

is enough, I want a better world for my children and grand-children'? You can make a major start right now. You can ditch 'the enemy in your pocket', because if it is allowed to control our lives, it becomes the self-inflicted instrument of our own incarceration. When that happens, life as we know it will be but a distant memory.

24

The New Resistance

By Ray Wilson

Early in March 2020, I applied to be a first responder. I wanted to help in what initially looked like a potential tsunami of devastation that was about to befall us.

I signed up because I was not prepared to remain at home, essentially doing nothing during the enforced lockdown. Therefore, I might as well do something that would be useful to others and also beneficial to myself. It would give me a chance to at least ride around on my motorcycle. The boss (my missus) said to me, 'Make sure you remember to polish your boots.' I did. I switched my NHS first responder app on, and I was off. Well, not exactly.

It didn't quite work out that way.

I was logged on for a grand total of 56 hours In that time, I was not called out once to perform any essential tasks. I did, however, find out some of the things that were happening. Things that the mainstream media did not cover. I also realised that our government, and indeed all governments worldwide, had no interest in keeping their populations safe. Everything is the opposite of what they say. There is a war on, and it's a spiritual and psychological war. A war waged by governments around the world on their own people. AI is a valuable weapon used in this attack.

The NHS is changing beyond all recognition, and the transformation will be unrecognisable in comparison to what we are used to. Genomic medicine, digital medicine, AI, and robotics will change the roles of our clinical staff over the next few years. The roles of the doctor, nurse, and paramedic are changing, and by 2030, remote hubs and online diagnosis will operate via computer and smart phone. There will be autonomous ambulances driving the most efficient route to an emergency, supported by a crew of cyborg paramedics. Well, probably not, and I will explain why.

Meanwhile, my life as a first responder came to an ignominious end. I did eventually get a request for assistance when I was away in Cornwall. This was a year later, and it was a request to help vaccinate people. This was not something I was prepared to do.

The NHS reported that the number of applicants was three times higher than initially targeted. It went on to say that those who have applied will be helping the NHS by performing simple but vital roles. These include transporting equipment, supplies, and medication between services and sites. Volunteers can also provide telephone support for individuals at risk of loneliness. This is the biggest call for volunteers in England since the Second World War. Chief Nursing Officer for England, Ruth May: 'We have been absolutely bowled over by the staggering response'.[14]

The Royal Free Hospital in London struck an agreement with Deep Mind in 2015 to build a system for alerting clinicians when a patient was at risk of becoming seriously ill. An investigation by the National Data Guardian and Information Commissioner's Office found that the privacy agreement

---

14 Source: 'NHS volunteer responders: 250,000 target smashed with three quarters of a million committing to volunteer', 29 March 2020, *NHS* [website], <https://england.nhs.uk/2020/03/250000-nhs-volunteers>, accessed 4 May 2023.

between the Royal Free and Deep Mind was not robust.

So, what exactly is artificial intelligence, how can we avoid it, and how can we use it to benefit society? For full disclosure, before I continue, I should mention that I was and still am involved in electronics and have had involvement in building the internet of things. I am not comfortable with this fact. I have learned a lot in the last three years, which has literally turned my world on its head. I still believe technology can help us if we use it correctly. Yes, we should clean up our lives, not use 5G networks, and protect ourselves from electromagnetic radiation. After all, if the government truly wanted to keep us safe, they most definitely would not want us carrying smart phones around 24/7.

I believe that the sneaky insertion of software onto smart phones under the auspices of keeping us safe, is, in reality, using AI to spy on us. The UK government says that text alerts will be sent directly to phones in the event of a life-threatening event, such as flooding or a fire. Similar systems exist in other countries, including New Zealand, where they are credited with saving lives. Alerts could be sent for public health emergencies, floods, industrial incidents, and terror attacks. It will be possible to opt-out of some alerts through the phone's settings.

For most people, the chance of receiving an alert will be low, or so we are told.[15]

One of the damaging effects of social technology like the internet and social media chat features is the decline of interpersonal communication. When you communicate online, it is a very limited form of interaction compared to face-to-face communications. Technology can encourage viewers to imitate an action played out on a screen, no matter how hard we may try to resist it as it slips into our minds at a subconscious

---

15 Lucy Webster, 'New emergency text alerts to be trialled', 17 May 2021, *BBC* [website], <https://bbc.co.uk/news/uk-politics-57145675>, accessed 4 May 2023.

level.

Turn off your TV. Limit exposure to mainstream media, especially the BBC. Get the latest news from trusted alternative platforms, such as UK Column or GB News. Ask people at Stand in the Park for their recommendations.

Youngsters are increasingly getting carried away by social media, and it's affecting their social skills and their ability to form meaningful and lasting relationships. The less face-to-face communication you have, the worse your social skills become; the more frequently you use social media, the worse your social skills become. Youngsters are also giving up their privacy by giving private information to the likes of Twitter, Tik Tok, and Facebook. Big Tech 'friends' or government organisations have the power to pry into personal information. AI is hoovering it all up and making it easily available. Profiles, life stories are littered all over the internet. The use of anonymous VPN routers can help, at least to keep some of your searches more private.

> 'Whether you're a human rights activist or you're on forums discussing a medical condition, a degree of anonymity on the internet can help you stay safe. It's important to understand the difference between privacy and anonymity, and to avoid free services that tend to have no real commitment to the user' (Isik Mater, Director of Research at independent internet monitoring organisation).[16]

YouTube changed its algorithm most recently in (2022.) The changes to the algorithm are in a purported response to some of the inappropriate material that people upload to the platform. YouTube recently announced that they have modified the algorithm to ban 'borderline content'. I uploaded footage

---

16 *NetBlocks* [website], <https://netblocks.org>, accessed 4 May 2023.

of an event in central London showing hundreds of thousands of people peacefully protesting. This event was not covered at all by anyone in the mainstream media. It was not reported, so therefore it didn't happen. That's what the powers that be want us to think, at any rate. The NHS100K gathering outside BBC HQ met a similar fate. Again, there are no proper reports except for a bit of footage showing nurses and doctors throwing their uniforms at 10 Downing Street.

The pandemic and accompanying lockdowns have been wildly successful, creating the right environment for total control of society. Huge portions of the population, influenced by fear and mind control, are in complete submission. Use cash. Tyranny comes in the guise of convenience. Avoid using store cards, credit cards, and smart phones. These are tools of the AI beast that gather your personal data, building an individual data set and creating your profile. Use cash. Use barter. Use local, non government currency, like the Lewes pound. Become self reliant. Start doing what we know to be right. Stop relying on all government systems. Disconnect from them. Use alternative health care, even if you have to pay, in the end it will cost less. Grow plants to eat, start guerrilla gardening clubs, move out of cities. Build independent power grids, water supplies, home school. Do what needs to be done.

So this is the good news. We are all sovereign human beings, not artificial intelligence. not part of some transhumanistic agenda. When we are united without fear, we are strong. When we forget our small differences, we are strong. When we are together, we are strong.

Not only can we control the algorithm by feeding it the information we want it to use to generate positive outcomes for humanity, we can disengage from all other areas that are not beneficial to us thereby denying it the ability to grow.

'The danger of AI is weirder than you think' I would recommend listening to this TED Talk by Janelle Shane in which she points out the following outcomes, which are not only extremely amusing but give us a true idea of AI's weakness.[17]

In the movies, when artificial intelligence goes wrong, it is usually because the AI has decided that it doesn't want to obey humans anymore and has its own goals.

In real life, the AI that we actually have is not nearly smart enough for that and has the approximate computing power of an earthworm or maybe at most a single honey bee.

Today's AI can do a task like identify a pedestrian in a picture, but it doesn't have a concept of what the pedestrian is. It doesn't know what a human actually is, or how big a brain it has—it's just a collection of lines and textures and other things.

Artificial intelligence (AI) is a computer programme that can take a collection of robot parts and assemble them into some kind of robot to get quickly from Point A to Point B.

In a traditional computer programme, you would give the programme step-by-step instructions on how to do this.

With AI, you don't tell it how to solve the problem—you just give it the goal, and it has to figure out for itself via trial and error how to reach that goal.

It turns out that AI tends to solve this particular problem by assembling itself into a tower, falling over, and then proceeding to land on its head at Point B, the desired destination.

Technically, this solves the problem. The danger of AI, is not that it's going to rebel against us, the danger is, it will do the task, but it won't do the task, exactly as we expect it to.

How do we set up the problem so that it actually does

---

17 Janelle Shane, 'The danger of AI is weirder than you think', *YouTube* [website], <https://youtu.be/OhCzXoiLnOc>, accessed 4 May 2023.

what we want? We feed it the data that we want it to use to generate the outcome that we want.

The tech giants, big media, big Pharma, and big government are mining our precious data so we now know exactly what we need to do.

25

The Scamdemic

By Ryta C Y N Lyndley

As soon as I was aware of the nonsense trotted out on the TV which we didn't watch just heard from friends, as I had already cancelled our TV licence due to the extraordinary lies perpetuated by the BBC. I had written to the BBC to say the reason we were cancelling was because when Tony and I went to London to a peaceful demonstration against the Iraq war, I asked a policeman on the embankment how many folk had passed by him that day he said about 25,000. When we arrived home, switched on the news the reporter said a few thousand! The BBC wrote back and said sorry you feel like this.

Most people do not realise that paying the licence is mandatory and not a legality, and there are no vans knocking on folks' doors as this is just to encourage the fear factor, the fear of authority. I said to Tony we are not taking any notice of this toffee we shall go out daily and to the coast weekly as we always did, ignoring this so-called lock up. We knew in our hearts this was to brainwash us all, to try to curtail our freedoms, which cannot be done as we are all free spirits. When folk asked me, supposing the police catch you, I'd say there are only three policemen in Norfolk and I'm sure they are all after me!

It was a delight to drive on empty roads and the fresh sea air is so good for the soul. There was always a fish and chip shop open to fulfil our simple needs. Meanwhile I did not buy a mask and wasn't apprehended in any shops, only once on the bus. I went past the driver on boarding saying exempt and went upstairs, being the only person not masked up. He quickly came upstairs, 'you have to wear a mask!' I said I didn't, so he reiterated his request by pointing at a notice on the nearby window. At this point he was looking a little exasperated and realised he needed to be driving his bus. I explained quite calmly that under the Human Rights Act article 10, I had freedom of speech, thought and movement. At this point he left to drive his bus.

Since this incident I have engaged folk in conversation and if they show any interest, I have offered them a copy of 'The Light Paper' or a small flyer saying cash is king and why we should keep cash in circulation. I do ask them to think about the tooth fairy, car boots and craft fairs. I do this daily on buses, at the swimming pool, at yoga and line dancing classes as I am very active and meet lots of people. Also I feel it is my job to try to awaken those who are asleep.

Another contributory reason for my positive attitude is I joined 'Stand in the Park' so spend my time learning and exchanging ideas with like-minded people. They also organise events with speakers who keep us informed of important facts hidden from us relating to health.

One event was given by two doctors who said there are no viruses it is just your body detoxing. As a yoga teacher I would verify this as, aged 76, I do not take any medication, never had a flu jab, and have declined the vaccine. Mostly I swim three times weekly, go to a yoga class weekly, go dancing monthly and have just joined a line dancing class. It is a little difficult trying to get my feet to listen to my brain but hey, I won't give up!

There was another talk by a young man who had a cancer on his leg. His parents advised go to the hospital, he did, and they wanted to operate immediately. He refused, went home, and decided to cure himself by changing his diet and using electrical equipment that cleared and cleaned his blood of toxins. His cancer shrunk, he squeezed out pus, it dried up so he returned to hospital to ask if they would be interested in his self-healing method. They refused, were not interested in his help and cooperation and there have been six more cancer charities started up in this area.

Sadly, it is all about making money for Big Pharma, healthy patients are no good for business. So, similar souls, keep up the good work that all of you do, well done and have faith that goodness will prevail.

26

The Wake-Up Call

By Wayne More

Professor Iva Sour had glimpsed the future, and it had hurt his eyes.

Rows and rows and rows and rows of them, all their robotic little unpeople. They lusted for the taste of death ... it reflected really their inward desire for their own demise and what that brought with it: escape finally from their hell on earth from the Chinese-style world order. And it was the only way anyone could escape.

They ate bugs regularly anyway, and they were dead, but they lusted for the substance of animals who were part of their own family, mammals; beings who suffered like they did.

It was satisfaction that they should suffer, for when there is no relief from your suffering, the only kind of consolation must be that others have also suffered, that you are not alone in this suffering, and so the reward of steak eating was reserved for the best slaves only, the ingestion of the divine moo-cows endowing them with comparative God-like status, as once ones points reached that level, they generated yet further points, and those qualified to eat cow may easily earn points enough to travel by taxi, plane, or train, in first class, even as the master prison wardens did.

Professor Iva Sour leaned back into his black leather swivel chair and grinned. For the first time in an age; after a long, dark age he had glimpsed a light at the end of the tunnel.

It was an idea that actually seemed feasible, an idea that actually could work. While the resistance had long been racking its collective minds trying to think of ways to make people 'allergic' to the smartphones, they had all the while been missing what was in fact staring them in the face: If the foul devices, the phones, didn't work, then the foul system, social credit, couldn't work either. Result: Collapse of the artificial society complete, a great reset of the people, for the people, by the people.

The wall of the professor's conditioning tried to block out the light. And that wall to Iva was the wall of the room he was staring at, daring to think what he was thinking. His eyes scanned across the almost featureless off-white wall ... they fell upon a single postcard, fastened to the wall: it was a picture of an old man in golden robes with a long, scraggly beard. He sat at a desk, on it a large, thick book open, in his hand a feather writing quill.

Professor Sour recognized the man as St Augustine, the old world hero of Catholicism. Somewhere in him a light was switched on as he considered a line this saint had once manifest: 'Love and do what thou wilt'.

And suddenly it all made sense; there were reasons why this way had been so professionally demonized, but there was nothing wrong, and everything right with folk doing their will, doing what they pleased to do.

(There was a reason that this very noble expression, this expression of divinity, of this saintly way was much later perversely corrupted into the perhaps more readily remembered these days *Do what thou wilt be the whole of the law*' by the likes of A.Crowley, who worked for British intelligence; it's very important to those who do intentionally, covertly create our culture that the basic concept of people 'doing what they want to' be, in the public's perception, something terrible and unwanted, as, in most peoples programmed beliefs, it is.)

The screwy fact is, that this way, this doing as we please, so long as we are coming from a place of love, has every as much and more power as does doing what we please when coming from a dark place; the facts we fail to see these days, due to our media-reinforced conditioning are that although it may be true that if someone pleased themselves to plant bombs (and very few have actually ever done that, or anything similar, that is actually planted bombs because they pleased to, they did that as part of a perceived duty, it was the result of following orders, not a product of their free time) it would not do for them to do as they will, every bit of damage they would cause would be equaled at least by the positive power of good people doing as they please.

He saw then, how that eureka moment had led to this point. It was ever since that moment that he had put his scientifically inventive mind into finding the solution. It had come to him in a blinding flash: White hot fire. It had entered and illuminated him with the blinding light of pure love, and it had blinded him so utterly, it had let him see nothing but the solution...

The solution was the destruction of each and every single smartphone that there was; in his vision, in his dream they would all be silent and lifeless. Just empty shells, dead as meaty dodos; pointless, and past existence.

They would never ring again, never again bring with them a foul fruition of the system with its electronic grid of barbed netting, surrounding and capturing and enslaving humanity.

Now the Government could no longer exert its automatic control field, now the New World Order would crumble and die as it should; simple as.

The Wake-Up Call

It had taken some time to develop programme: Wakeupcall. It had taken the very best scientific minds on the planet a long time, working diligently, intently. Iva had gained contacts in all the right places; in the offices of Apple and Google for instance; the finest programmers was what it took, and by the twentieth version the Wakeupcall virus was ready.

It worked like this:

The virus first entered through a mysterious call; the recipient of the call heard nothing, but unknowingly opened a software door for the virus to enter; the owner of the phone unaware that the next time their device connected a call, the virus they didn't know they had would leave, and infect the connected phone.

On the phone it had left though, it had left a 'shadow-version' of itself. That stayed dormant, replicating itself again and again, with each connection the infected device made to the next smartphone, leaving new shadow-selves in each one, which in turn lie dormant, replicating across new connections, and so on, and so on; each virus version a kind of time bomb laying silently in wait of activation, the owner of each phone unaware that when the time reached twenty-thirty, the first of January, twelve o'clock precisely, the device would instantaneously meltdown. Simply, the power would out, never to return, no matter what, leaving an empty shell: Vacant of action, useless, pointless and dead. Nothing more than a relic, a reminder of the bad old days.

The effects of the benign virus were permanent; once it had been activated, the programme caused irreparable damage, ensuring each device could never again work. There was no going back, no going back to their New World Order, as the foul social credit system was pivotal to it. It was over, and humanity could rediscover itself, now the road to hell had abruptly ended in a cul-de sac.

27
Children

By Tim Bragg

The head of the village was 100 years old. Sitting calmly, surrounded by children—he bewitched them with his words. James loved to tell tales and the children were his natural audience. He could entrance them with stories from way, way back; to an age and way of life none of them could ever know.

He was telling one of his favourite stories—about orphaned children living in an old rundown mansion. How the adults who ran the orphanage treated the children harshly. Of course the children listening were especially captivated. The mansion, with its facade peeling and its windows barred and sad looking, was close to the edge of an island. The orphans longed to sit on the small cliffs and look out to sea and imagine that their parents lived just over the horizon. Or they dreamt of sailing away on a lashed-together wooden raft, escaping their fate, finding freedom in an undiscovered land. But as it was they simply lived an austere and regimented existence.

One day a child refused to eat his soup, complaining that he felt ill and that they were trying to poison him! A supervisor was so enraged that she pushed the child's screaming face into the hot bowl. Two adults then dragged the poor boy away and beat him. During the ensuing uproar the other children took the opportunity to escape from the old house, kicking and screaming their way out with raised courage and defiance.

Old James let the story unfold slowly and with much detail of course so that the children looking up at him were completely enthralled. And he told them how there was a bounty placed on every missing child's head of twenty gold pieces. And that the people who lived on the island and the people who were on holiday there were encouraged to hunt the orphans down.

He had a way of telling this story so that there wasn't a dry eye as he explained how each child was rounded up and often betrayed for the golden coins.

James followed this sad story with a funny verse that allowed the children to let out their emotions further and then he played them a magical tune on the celeste. And all this was why the children loved him so much and why he loved them too.

Throughout the week the village would meet every lunch time —to share food and their news. A party had gone out at the beginning of the week and was due back that day. They arrived exuding a sense of excitement and expectancy. Everyone who could, sat round the gnarled, wooden table. Children helped serve the food, everyone taking their turn. Andrew had lead this last venture as he had done on each previous month, through the darkest and coldest winter days.

'We've got some news,' he began in earnest. The adults grew as attentive as the children had listening to James' story. 'But first, a present for you, dear James.' Angela nodded to Andrew and took a basket she had placed by her feet beneath the table. 'Here,' she said offering the gift.

'Another basket?' James said laughing. But he could see all the marvellous produce the party had picked and gathered. 'Nothing touched,' Angela said, 'nowhere near the agri planes and sheltered from winds. We don't want you catching anything,' she winked at him.

'And not just that,' Andrew added. 'Look what we've found these past three days.' Two of the party left the table and dragged in a heavy, coarse bag and let the contents drop and scatter over the stone flagging. Any ideas of eating were abruptly stopped as the children left their duties to gather round. There was a tap, some piping, an old battery and a handcart with wheels among the haul.

'A good day to have a birthday,' said James.

'Especially a hundred years,' Amy's small voice piped up. Everyone laughed.

'But not only that,' said Angela. 'Shall I tell?' she asked.

'Tell!' said James, heartily.

'We went close up, as usual,' she began, 'and we expected *the usual*. But. Nothing! Nothing.'

'Nothing!' Andrew affirmed.

The great hall hushed. 'Go on,' said James.

'We went straight to the gate. Right up to it. We could see the markings, everything…' He paused a moment. 'No explosions, no shots … none of the sensors had been triggered. No drones overhead.'

Eyes focussed on the members of the party. Angela took a mug of honeyed mint she was offered. 'Are you ready?' she continued. James nodded for everyone. 'The gate opened for us!'

'And, did you enter?' James asked.

'They were afraid…' a young man coughed, '*We* were afraid,' he added quickly.

'Let us eat,' said James, 'and tell us more, every detail. We must know everything!'

It was soon decided that James would accompany a party that would leave early the following morning. James himself settled in the leather chair with its stuffing hanging out. Sometimes he felt as worn as that old chair but at other times as lively as ever he'd been. Life was hard but also rewarding and they ate healthily. Simply being surrounded by beautiful untouched countryside lifted both their spirits and well-being. Close by, the children were delighted to have found a toy from the scavenged contents of the sack and played before the flames that leapt upwards in the great fireplace. Though it was Spring and the vegetable plots were newly turned and the seedlings nurtured in the village's vast polytunnels, there were still nights of frost. In the hall and the surrounding houses and outlying hamlets that belonged to the village, the rooms were still cold enough for fires. They were a community and though forged through adversity were also tempered by solidarity and genuine love for one another. Of course it wasn't always easy. Life never was and never would be. That too they enjoyed. They had chosen true life over comfort and ease.

James was up shortly after Andrew. The original group was chosen to return to scavenge and try out the sensors once again. James insisted they take some arms with them. But he also had a sense of contentment. His limbs, though old, felt young again that day.

Andrew was surprised that James wanted them to carry weapons, it had been many, many years since they had last used their firearms, though they had always been maintained meticulously. It had become one of their rituals. Over time the need for weapons had diminished. Any meat they caught was trapped, not shot. They had heard tales from travellers about poisoned animals and a new folklore had arisen about an evil spirit that visited at night, plunging its claws inside bodies, squeezing the life out of beating hearts.

Their lives were lived close to the land and the seasons and their tales were always at hand to help educate and entertain. Following many years of struggle they now thrived as a community. Andrew nodded at James and called the party together. As they left, most of the children ran alongside laughing and singing, until they were eventually called back to the old hall.

It was a long way to the sensors and the gate in the great wall of the city. And they needed to camp on the eve of the first night. They were adept at making fires and gathering extra food. They were hardy folk. The night sky was clear. For many years they had never ventured this far and had taken precautions regarding smoke from their fires and shots from the guns when they had been used. But life had changed slowly and the past was either unknown to them or came in disturbed sleep or nightmares. James was the oldest among them. Good food and plant medicine and sheer willpower had forged the man he now was.

Andrew and James slept close by the fire. They had set trip wire and members of the group took turns keeping watch. The two men talked as they looked up at the near full moon and the sparkling stars. 'It's been a long time,' James said into the fresh night air. Andrew turned to the fire, its flames curling round the wood which spat and crackled. 'We must never forget how we have come to be,' he continued. 'Our faith, our authenticity, our understanding has kept us free. My time's limited. And yet I have never felt so alive. We have grown closer to the land and yet closer to spirit too. Maybe they're connected?'

'Maybe,' said Andrew.

'I've often wondered about the city,' James said softly,

'about life inside those walls. Yes I have seen the machines come out and grow their food. I've seen their drones patrolling the ground and the air. But it has been some time now since I have seen one of *them*. Can you recall the last drone you saw above the village?' Andrew shook his head. 'Maybe they have forgotten us as we have forgotten them. They chose their life. And we chose ours,' James said.

'They chose to exclude us,' Andrew spat. 'They chose to close themselves off into their walled world. They probably thought we'd all die. They probably think we're all dead. How could we survive, after all, living solely with Nature.' He smiled wryly as he said this. 'How could you have lived so long, James!'

James laughed. 'My time has been allotted. That is for God alone to say. When I have fulfilled my reasons for being here then I shall rejoin all those who have died before me. Even those who chose poison and trickery. I don't hate them...'

'They probably hate you,' Andrew said forcefully.

James smiled, 'Maybe,' he said, 'maybe.'

The morning sunrise splashed over the sky. James felt his limbs loosen slowly. He loved his people. Felt contentment. As they walked that day and the sun shone warmly he felt it more difficult to keep up. He was not immortal—and nor should he be.

As they approached the city the land changed and they were careful to choose wooded paths between the great wide open swathes of cultivated land. But as the party had noticed previously, no machines worked the land. At this point, now close to the city, four members of the group advanced, including James. They approached the modern castle walls. As before no sensors were alerted. No drones appeared overhead. No explosive devices were detonated as they reached the great gate. As ever, it seemed, the gate was closed. Would it open again? It was only then that Martha saw a slight movement in the sheen of the wall—something was monitoring them. She motioned towards a hidden screen and covered her mouth—'Say nothing,' she mouthed. The four of them looked to each other and then concentrated on James' weathered face. But before he could offer any thoughts they heard movement and the gate began to slide open. Slowly but surely.

Transfixed. They stood silently. 'Should we run?' Martha said breathlessly.

'I cannot run and nor would I if I could,' James answered. 'But you can leave me here if you wish.' They shook their heads. 'I have been waiting for this moment all of my life,' he said. The others looked up at the great gate as it pulled open. And then they gasped, as one, as they saw inside the great city. They were at the threshold of another world. A world created by their fellow men and women. And AI of course. They could never forget or ignore the new robotics.

They held hands—touching the skin of another giving them courage. Facing them within the walls of the shiny city were humans, almost as themselves. But not.

For some time the two groups stared at each other. This was the first time that the two paths had met again after the great separation. Outside-folk had surely been captured and taken into the city in the early days—girls and young women having been most at risk. Cruelly hunted until villages withdrew deeper into the countryside. Now the two paths of humanity again converged, scrutinising each other.

James moved slightly closer, stepping over the city's threshold. Looking into the eyes of those opposite him he searched into their gaze. Their bodies were a confusion of age and robotics. Some of them seemed almost seamlessly machine-like, while others seemed as if the veneer of progress was badly bolted on or roughly grafted to their body. Though they had the air of super beings they also all appeared paradoxically old and tired. The image of a technological junkyard entered into James' mind. Still no-one said anything. The rest of the party joined him, taking steps inside the city. In a sense this was as if stepping foot into their greatest fear.

One of the city folk took a pace forward. 'Welcome,' she said. 'Welcome,' the others (maybe 20 or so) greeted them, timidly to begin with. The city appeared almost empty. James and his people were struck by the immense size of the buildings. The shiny surfaces and the dark glasswork. But it occurred to James that the city was dead. He had memories of cities from before and they were as if alive with people and cars with flashing neon and noise. Now it seemed as if this city was a ghost.

'Where are all the people?' Angela asked. 'Where are all your robots,' she coughed, 'your AI?' She wasn't exactly sure what a robot or AI would look like but their essence featured in many of the villager's folk tales. The air between the two groups was still tense. Then one of the machine folk moved towards Martha. He went to embrace her. She looked at James, fearing she would be poisoned by his touch. James nodded to her. The New Man and Martha held each other. And they both cried—though the tears of the man were partly trapped behind 'intelligent eyes'. With this initial act all of the assembled citizens embraced the small group. Andrew too let go of his fear—for he was still unsure whether this was a simple trap for them and that they would all be killed or experimented on.

James and his group were invited to drink and eat. James said they would talk but it was not their custom to receive hospitality, only to give it—and here he thought fast. He also instructed Angela to go back to the rest of the party. Before she left he whispered something in her ear. He smiled knowingly to himself as he watched her pass through the open gate and across the rough land and then onward to the trees distant. James apologised for her absence but assured their hosts that it was simply for her to let his own people know that they were safe inside the city's walls and that no harm had befallen them.

Around a shiny grey metal table they sat under dim lights.

'My name is Reza. I am the spokesbeing for this city.' Reza appeared more artificial than human flesh and blood and James could not distinguish Reza's sex. Reza continued: 'We thought you would return. At the beginning all Outsiders were tracked. And there was talk of annihilation. But others wanted to see if you could survive in nature.' Reza looked pensive. 'How easily we forgot and forget. But, yes, we knew all about your forays close to the city. And we conducted studies. We were amused.' Reza eyed the three of them. 'We lived in great comfort and—as you can see—were augmented so that those of us who didn't die following the separation were kept alive for as long as possible. We were promised immortality. Some of us lived beyond 150 years. Scientists created further gene-altering medicine. Unfortunately many of our offspring were stillborn or born with severe...' At this point Reza could be seen shaking slightly. 'Many children had problems. And eventually the only new life in our city of comfort and technological splendour was AI itself! And liquid robotics were flooded into the young who had survived —but they turned them into emotionless machines. They had little inclination to produce offspring. One day I watched the last child being born. It was a little girl. She lasted only minutes...'

'Why didn't you ask us for help?' James asked.

'How could we? Besides that is not the end of the story. For a time we were completely governed and dominated by AI. We became, the experimenters became, the experimented on. Their flesh to mould in their image. But we were saved.

Eventually.'

'How?' Martha asked.

'We began to lose energy power. And as power was lost viruses began infecting the—what you call—robots. An irony I appreciate. Both we and they were poisoned by modern medical technology. Not even AI was exempt. The power we had left and devised systems for keeping and storing was sufficient only for our needs. But we wanted our comforts still and all the technology that provided a safe and healthy life. We had to make choices. We were GODS! We could fix any problem—we were greater even than AI and the serf bots. Hadn't we always been gods?' Reza had stood while explaining these last details but now sat down. Softly, 'We were dying. And there was nothing we could do. That is why we decided to let the pathway to our city open up to you. Passively we placed ourselves in your fate. We are in a limbo state between life and death. How long have we to live? Maybe there are other cities distant, cities that cut themselves off, as we did. Maybe they will find us and restore our power and our true POWER. Maybe they will have found the key to life everlasting. Maybe they have become gods. But here we are now. Even our water purification and artificial food is failing us. We allowed AI to do our thinking! We don't know how to survive. We have lost our way, and ability to live a life. I don't know whether I am a human being or a machine.'

James, Andrew and Martha stayed inside the city walls that night and the night after. They were shown all the technological marvels—now defunct but still, impressive. And yet it was all so sterile and pointless. The city was magnificent in its starkness, with its imposing buildings. But decay was also evident. There was much for them to discuss. For James it felt close to healing. But he knew that would come with the final, and pre-arranged, act.

Excusing himself and feeling wearied by all the talk—for it was as if two worlds had collided inside his mind—he passed through the gate, which had been left open, and headed for the trees. He waited there for some time in deep and inconsolable thought. Until they arrived. As soon as they saw him they rushed to him. The children of the village had been brought there by Angela. A great adventure. Now they were to enter into the city. 'Like the old mansion in the story,' James whispered.

Before they reached the gate a crowd of people began leaving the city—they were people unlike anything the children had seen before but some strange power, some deep spirit moved the village children so they ran towards these folk laughing and crying out as they did, throwing themselves into these strangers' arms.

And for the first time in many decades the people of the city cried real tears. Here in their arms was the future. Fragile and robust simultaneously. Healthy, curious, beautiful children.

Holding the children's hands they left the city and certainty behind. Ready to face the world as it always should be faced. With gratitude and thanks. James didn't leave though. He remained. It was as if life had turned full circle. Silently he watched them depart.

It was his time. His allotted time. His stay on Earth was completed. It was now time for him to move on.

28

The Exhibition

By Tim and Annie Bragg

The cock crowed as it always crowed, each morning. Mist hung low in the distant small valley. A goat bleated close by. The sun was rising and spreading its colours across the horizon. The air was beginning to warm and felt fresh. Caleb sat on his verandah, acorn-coffee in hand. His favourite chicken nestled in his lap and his dog Snowy was lying by his side. As he looked out across the land surrounding his farm, he felt content. It was a Sunday. A special day.

After breakfast he would visit the little chapel near the copse and sit inside on one of the old wooden pews in peace and dusty silence. Sunlight would eventually stream through the stained glass—its colours creating a second sunrise. In this small chapel Caleb felt perfect peace. It was a Sunday after all. Outside a number of gravestones told his history. He couldn't stay there all morning, there was work to be done—animals to feed. Plants to tend. Of all days this was the day he felt most content and at one with his surroundings. Leaving the chapel he looked up at the sky and then down across his land. He checked his watch. The watch, on a fob and previously tucked into his waistcoat, was oldfashioned enough not to be anachronistic. And as he thought this he smiled inwardly. Again he looked up at the sky—but there was not a cloud to be seen.

The family was cramped inside the small apartment on the 11th floor of the high-rise. It was a good height to be and if there was a power cut not that arduous a descent.

'Mak, have you got credit?' Jen asked. He nodded. 'Have you told the children?'

'I was leaving that to you.'

'Like everything,' she said, bustling about in the small room.

'Wake Tammy up last.'

'Jed!' the mother called.

'You'll wake Tammy, we need to surprise her.'

'Have you ordered a corp-uber?'

'I thought we'd take the bus ... would be fun...'

'Fun? Who for?,' Jen bit.

'Tammy.'

'Jed, don't wake your sister. Put that down. I don't want you staring at that all day.'

'Hey dad, have you seen this?' The boy went to his father and showed the screen. Mak laughed. Jen opened the closet door where they had installed a small bed. Tammy was still sleeping. The air-con was humming—thankfully no power had been cut during the night, it could get stifling.

'Happy Birthday darling,' the mother cooed as she gently stirred the child.

The traffic seemed denser and louder than normal. Jen had a headache. It was a Monday and she should have been at a meeting—and it had been difficult to get the day off. It used more credit. Maybe that was why Mak had instructed the bus to stop outside their building. Normally she only endured a 40 minute ride to work through the traffic before she could relax for a few moments in the quiet of her office. That small moment of peace seemed to prepare her for the day. Mak would usually take the children to their schools before he went to work. Everything had become mechanical so that the start of their day was as stressless as possible. Look at camera. Swish a wrist. Tap a QR code. Jen could almost forget these actions as they became reflexive ... routine.

'Have I got any presents, Mummy?' Tammy shouted above the noise.

'Wait and see,' Mak said, reassuring his daughter.

'Look at this,' Jed thrust a screen in Tammy's face. The little girl recoiled.

'Jed!'

'Where are we going? I want to go to school...' the boy shouted.

The mother tutted. To Mak she turned and asked, 'Was the boss okay?' Mak shrugged.

Gazing out of the dirty window Mak watched everyone struggling to get to their jobs. Lights flashing. There was a mix of electric whir and diesel throb from the reconditioned lorries. Above them the newly installed cables sparked as the bus's contact shoes bumped against the cold wires. It was a retro system but thought more durable. Mak laughed inwardly. They were always changing things. Always having big ideas. Mostly their great plans failed or reverted to older technology.

The streets were full of people—like shoals of fish caught in a net. The sky was dark and felt cold. But today was special. They could travel out. Mak had had to do lots of extra work and had stayed overtime at the office to accumulate the required credit. In fact, since Tammy had been born, life had got more difficult. Children cost. Despite the number of still-births and the fall in fertility, children meant more tax. In fact the city should have been quieter but they were corralling everyone from the countryside and forcing them to relocate. The city was insatiable.

Mak's digital sounded—'*Fine!* Non-mask wearing!' His gaze went from the window to his wife and children. 'Jen, Tammy's mask!' The girl's mask had dropped below her nose —or she had pulled it down. There had been an on-going struggle to keep her face masked. Mak thought it sad to cover such a pretty face. But at The Exhibition they would be exempt. Everything was controlled there—every last detail. Again Mak smiled. An ironic smile. Everything was controlled everywhere. At The Exhibition they would have controlled fun. He hoped. They just had to pass through the 'medical entry gate'.

Could he remember a different time? Mak checked himself, it didn't do to be too reflective. That was frowned upon.

The bus hissed to a stop. They had never been to this part of the city. It felt different. Before them was the huge arched gateway flashing neon: Welcome to The Exhibition!

As they approached, each of their AI phones joyfully announced: 'Welcome to The Exhibition—where you can learn while having fun!' Mak and Jen's phone added: 'Check your credit!'

Tammy was excited but Jed buried his face deeper towards his phone's screen.

'It's my birthday!' Tammy suddenly exclaimed with much joy. Mak and Jen exchanged a glance. Their rulers still couldn't read minds. Couldn't interpret a near hidden twinkle of an eye. They held hands—and despite an initial refusal, even Jed held his mother's hand. The building before them was colossal. None of them had any real inkling what lay within and beyond. The Exhibition was advertised as 'life enriching' and 'life enhancing', both ideas unusual within the government's normally austere lexicon.

As they entered the foyer of The Exhibition the noise of the city was drowned out. Mak and Jen helped their children regard the cameras and swish their wrists for entry—though Jed found this tiresome and commonplace. The QR codes were activated and they passed through the medical gateway without a problem. They had permission to remove their masks. Information screamed at them. Their digitals screamed at them. Jed squeezed through people trying to find which area to visit first. Mak lifted Tammy onto his shoulders and for the first time she could see across the sea of heads. There were also many trained guides to help direct folk. Every question was noted on Mak's digital phone and credit deducted. The entrance fee had created quite a hole. But it was a once-in-a-lifetime experience. It was Tammy's birthday. They had been blessed.

Photos flashed and the smell of food concentrated its unique flavour around busy stalls. Coffee, tea, richly sugared drinks were pushed on them. There was a kind of limp, repeating melody blasted through speakers—programmed drums marking time. Often this barrage of sound was broken with enthusiastic news delivered by gasping voices. Go to Exhibit A or B where such and such was happening. And so the family was entertained. Mak bought Tammy a stuffed toy dog at the exit of the Grand Safari. He tried to get her to have a tiger or rhinoceros, especially as they were now extinct. But she wanted that dog—it was her birthday after all.

In the War Zone only Mak and Jed entered. The whole family had been to the Space Station before that but decided to follow different experiences. Mak and Jed could pick which war to observe and even participate in. This was the most controversial exhibit as, despite every attempt at 'health and safety', a number of young men and some girls had been killed in the various fighting. Many others had been injured.

But it was the most popular. The deaths were always indirect—even though one could feel the thud of a bullet or the plunge of a bayonet within the virtual reality. It cost extra too. A lot extra. The rules were explained in a tedious monotone and zone and flak jackets handed out. Mak found all this curious. It was dangerous and young folk *had* died—though he doubted that reality. But there they were. Jed reassured him. 'You have no idea what they can do with virtual reality these days Dad. Times have changed, you don't even wear headsets!'

Jed chose the Vietnam war and within minutes they were flying overhead in a Chinook helicopter. Jed was in his element as they were dropped close by to a jungle—immediately breaking into a sweat with the sub-tropical heat. But when they got fired on—he urinated in fear. After about 30 minutes, Mak pulled Jed aside and they made it to a 'safe point'. These were designated and protected areas and constructed to 'melt' virtual ammunition. They also sold clean clothes. Jed wasn't the first to wet his pants and both man and boy were wringing with sweat. Mak's digital fired: 'Credit Completion!'

Jen and Tammy had gone into Wonderland. It was strikingly real to Jen—it was truly real to Tammy. But the two stayed on the visitors', which was crowded with parents and their children. At one point a giant head of Alice came within minute clicks of the visitors and she bellowed 'Curiouser and curiouser'. Jen was taken aback but Tammy seemed to love the experience. When they left, they entered the great foyer again and the noise remained unabated. Tammy was very tired.

'We need to rest,' Jen said to a guide-helper.

'Let me recommend this,' she said.

'Thank you,' Jen replied. 'We have to wait for Tammy's father and brother.' Digital: 'Credit Completion!'

Jen had been texting Mak too, throughout Wonderland. They decided to meet at the 'petting zoo' for some respite. Jen and Tammy arrived to find rows upon rows of small pens with animals of all description within. Tammy was excited at first but the crowds were constantly jostling, thrusting children up close, desperately trying to pet the creatures. Jen felt Tammy beginning to change mood. 'Come,' she said to the little girl.

'Photo, photo—caress the monkey!'

'No, no thank you,' said Jen. As expected there was a huge shop close by and there she bought Tammy some animal-shaped sweets and more sugar-drink. Tammy clutched her toy dog. 'Do you want me to take that?' Jen asked. But Tammy shook her head.

When Mak and Jed finally arrived, Mak immediately put his finger to his mouth. He had sent her a message previously, briefly explaining what happened. Jed piped up, 'It was amazing! You saw dead bodies, Mum. And people getting shot. Planes in the sky and helicopters getting shot down.'

Jen looked at Mak. He shrugged. 'It was as if we were there,' he said.

'I told you,' Jed shouted.

'Was there no warning?' Jen shouted above the noise as best she could. Mak shrugged again. 'He's 13, that was the lower age limit. They play this kind of stuff every day.'

'It was super-vibe,' said Jed.

'Right,' Jen said abruptly. I'm exhausted. We have one last place to visit, it was recommended. I think they've both nearly had enough for the day.'

'Not me,' said Jed with new-found bravado.

Mak paid extra credit to get into 'Pastoral Land—Travel Back in Time'. Only a certain amount of folk were allowed in, though there were special times advertised too—'See the animals being fed' was one of them. Mak was puzzled. It felt so old-fashioned. After his Vietnam experience and the Space Station before that, his head was spinning and he could feel the possibility of an oncoming migraine. The huge glass panelled entrance slid open. With trepidation they walked out and into the countryside.

Mak and Jen looked at each other. Tammy sprinted over the soft, springy turf. Jed pressed his face closer to the screen as if he was eating his digital. But his face seemed frustrated.

'Jen?' Mak asked. Jen looked around as the other people who had entered with them continued down, what was now, a dusty lane. 'Can you hear?' he asked.

'Hear?'

'Yes, listen?'

'I can hear the people talking in the distance.'

'Forget them! What else?'

'Nothing,' she answered. Then checked herself. 'Nothing except some birds.'

'Tammy, wait,' said Mak, 'let the people go on. Let's stay here for a moment, maybe get something to eat, we need to eat something.' But as they looked around there were no stalls or souvenir shops, or cafes or restaurants. There was no pumping, piped music—no announcements. Even Jed looked up from his digital phone, which he was pressing angrily, and quickly cast his eyes about him.

'This isn't as good as virtual reality,' Jed said suddenly. 'And why doesn't my phone work!'

'It's better!' Tammy called out. She was picking something from a hedge.

'Wait,' Jen said, but as she walked, her high-heels sank into the ground. She struggled with these for a few steps, then said, 'Damn it!' and took them off. Mak laughed. She turned about to face him. He thought she was going to tell him off but she just smiled.

The Exhibition

Caleb had enjoyed the evening sunset. He was happy and free. He knew the morning would bring people but he simply treated them as ghosts from the future. He did what he always did and in his own time and rhythm. When he walked across the fields, Snowy followed him with Clarabelle clucking behind. It was a hard but fulfilling life. In his mind he could hear beautiful music. The only thing that truly disturbed him was when the rain came. He hated its regularity. Checking his fob-watch he moved on. The sun was rising in the sky and the air tasted fresh with Spring flowers. He managed to survive well with his cow and goat and chickens. Mending his own clothes and being handy enough to mend any machinery—he took everything in his stride. The farm was big enough to sustain his needs but also small enough for him to manage. They gave him a horse and plough for the land but the horse was always taken back. Yes, he was content in his beautiful world, with his animals to talk to. As he did his work, he would let his thoughts roam. Sometimes he recalled the past and the stories he was told—but for the most part he simply lived in the moment. There was always something to keep him occupied and if there wasn't, he would sit on the verandah and fill his pipe with the tobacco he had grown and puff on it contentedly. He was seldom ill and the only time they had had to take him 'out', he was so distressed by what he witnessed, that he convinced himself it was a nightmare which he just couldn't quite shake from his memory.

Of course he wasn't stupid and he saw the way the ghosts behaved, how they moved and acted. He heard the rougher boys hurl insults—but as their words came, Caleb could take them in his thoughts and dissolve and reconstitute them into butterflies or small birds. Even the harshest words could perch on his shoulder and tweet peacefully. He noticed how the ghosts would look up at the sky as if they were drowning in air. And how the smaller children would run and run and run. There was a little girl close by him then who wished to stroke his dog. She was tightly clutching a toy dog under her arm. As she approached, she looked up into his eyes with curiosity. Caleb could see her parents not far away. A boy was gingerly wandering across a field towards a stone wall. There were plenty of folk about, but again, Caleb was able to merge them into their backgrounds so that a large group of them became indistinguishable from the duck pond they gathered by. And again he was able to transform their shouts—in this case into duck call or the grating sound of frogs—which didn't grate on him.

The little girl came closer. When she spoke, Caleb was surprised that he could hear her words. This sometimes happened. He had to listen carefully. What was she saying?

'May I stroke your dog?' she asked. 'It's my birthday.'

Caleb smiled down at her. Nodded. She moved towards Snowy with his white fur.

'You'll have to put your toy dog down,' Caleb found himself saying. 'Or you can give it to me to look after.'

The little girl looked at Caleb, then her toy dog and then Snowy. 'Here you are,' she said. Caleb looked at her parents, focussing them in from the fields and sky behind. Carefully he took the toy dog, then he dropped down on his haunches as Tammy approached Snowy. The girl touched the dog's fur. Snowy looked up at Caleb. 'It's all right old fella,' Caleb said. Snowy was wary of the younger ghosts—sometimes they didn't know how to behave with an animal.

'He's beautiful,' the girl said. Then, 'Why is it so quiet here? And so much room?' wrapping her arms around the dog's neck.

'This is how it used to be,' Caleb said softly. 'And how it might be again one day,' he reassured her. Eventually Tammy let go of the dog as her parents approached, calling to her. It was as if they were afraid of Caleb. Caleb watched them disappear. Looked at his fob-watch. Time for a shower he said to himself and counted down from 10. 'Three, two, one...' And he felt the spots of rain.

The workers at Pastoral Land were taking photos and clips of film—sometimes simply for their own amusement. They laughed amongst themselves as they saw and heard the folk leaving.

'Look at that boy there,' one nudged. 'Covered in mud. Bet he's never been as dirty.'

'Might be cow pats,' another chirped.

'Hark at you!'

'Hark?' the other teased. 'Careful or you'll be an exhibit too. No escape from there back into the real world!' The worker bit into a meat-flavoured insect burger.

'Look at the woman trying to put her muddy shoes on, looks as if she's going to cry.'

Laughter. 'They're the ones who'll write in asking if they can replace old Caleb.'

'Yes, like saying the farm needs a family.'

Mak, Jen, Jed and Tammy were quite silent in the tidal wave of noise that washed over them. They needed to sit down and eat.

'Let's go out,' said Jen.

'Really?' Jed whined, his digital now firing away as it usually did.

'Where's your dog?' Mak asked his daughter.

She looked surprised. 'I must have left it Daddy,' the girl said.

'Shall I go back and get it?' Mak asked. 'I'm sure the guides will let me back in if I explain.'

'Oh, no Daddy. There's no need. I left the dog with Snowy. It's Snowy's now. He'll be much happier there.'

Jen bent down to concentrate on the little girl's words. Mak also bent down but again lifted her onto his shoulders. 'Happy Birthday darling,' he said to her as softly as he could in all the noise. Then as quietly as he could, bending his head back to hers, 'Yes, your little dog will be much happier there.' Mak and Jen looked at each other.

As they stepped outside into the darkening light of the city skyscape—with neon lights flashing and the plaza packed with people, Mak made sure they all had their masks on.

'I think it's going to rain,' he said.

'How do you know?' Jen asked.

'It's just a feeling,' Mak replied. 'Just a feeling.'

29

Walkies Fido—Now How About It, Mr Prime Minister?

Experiences of the Common Man
By Tim Haselup

When I was very little, I heard my grandmother say that when the trains rolled by, behind the church, and scrunched and squeezed and clanked across the points in the track it made a dreadful din. Every Sunday, the villagers used to shrink in the pews until the service times were changed and the choirmaster gave the order for everyone to stand up and sing louder[18]. The choirmaster knew about the trains and their notorious cargo, yet he enjoyed living in his fine new apartment that had belonged to Solomon from the synagogue.

When I was a bit older, I read for myself about the Pied Piper of Hamelin long ago, and the mean mayor and his cronies;

But, as for the guilders, what we spoke

---

18 Cf 'Sing a Little Louder—The Subtle Conquest of Indifference', 30 September 2020, *Written Lives* [website] <https://writtenlives.ca/sing-a-little-louder-the-subtle-conquest-of-indifference>, accessed 4 May 2023.

Of them, as you very well know, was in joke.
Beside, our losses have made us thrifty;
A thousand guilders! Come, take fifty![19]

I laughed and giggled at the colours of the piper's coat and the sounds and the smells, as any child would. How short-sighted was the mayor's idolatry of money and the finer things, compared to the treasure of the children's lives. Dear grown-ups, the corona virus chancellor Sunak signed off the £15billion spend which is now written off on wasted PPE[20]. Yet at the time of writing, he has refused to pay the nurses their due. Didn't he and his colleague Johnson applaud and speak about fairness and reward for frontline health care staff? Well now, Mr Prime Minister, how about it?

I read of the Emperor's new clothes, sewn to embarrass, written by Hans Christian Anderson two centuries ago[21]. And I laughed and giggled as any child would at such a silly man. How vain and gullible the emperor in his palace so far from the dirt of earthy life? Was it just a fairy tale? Then I caught the headlines about the man in the designer clothes, who refuses to reward the labourer on the frontline[22]. Well now, Mr Prime Minister, are you away with the fairies in Mr Anderson's tale? If only this simple child could believe you are a

---

19 Robert Browning, 'The Pied Piper of Hamelin', *Poetry Foundation* [website] <https://poetryfoundation.org/poems/45818/the-pied-piper-of-hamelin>, accessed 4 May 2023.

20 Victoria Jones, '£15bn written off on PPE and Covid drugs that can't be used', *The Times* [website], <https://thetimes.co.uk/article/180f92d8-9dc2-11ed-8201-2ed91f44d1e8>, accessed 4 May 2023.

21 The emperor's new clothes by Hans Christian Andersen, *Study.com* [website], <https://study.com/academy/lesson/the-emperors-new-clothes-summary-moral.html>, accessed 4 May 2023.

22 Sophie Barnett, 'Nadine Dorries mocks Rishi Sunak over £3.5k suit as MP slams "embarrassing" Tory race', 25 July 2022, *LBC* [website], <https://lbc.co.uk/news/nadine-dorries-mocks-rishi-sunak-expensive-suit>, accessed 4 May 2023.

man of integrity, not vanity.

I watched as the wall went up in Berlin city and how the fleeing soldier from the east leapt over the barbed-wire barricade[23]. He thought freedom was worth the price. Estimates claim that 5,000 others risking their lives followed across the wall[24]. Then I listened from afar and watched as the western emperors, fatigued by war said, 'enough is enough, we fight no more'. They did it in the east, they did it in the desert and they did it in the tropics. They did not understand that they had sold their birthright, like Esau[25]. The story goes that Esau ate and drank and rose and went his way, despising his birthright. Had they understood what they were giving away? Elsewhere it says, 'Samson … did not know that the Lord (his strength) had left him'[26]. Those western intellectuals of fatigue were to become the self-indulgent politicians, professors and accountants scared of the millennial bug. In meta-morphosis they became green media gurus kow-towing to artificial intelligence rather than the maker of heaven and earth. The contrast is plain to see, the needy footsoldier leaping the barbed wire to escape while the western politicos despise their birthright. Perhaps like my grandmother's choir, ashamed, I just look on. Perhaps I even party and sing louder, stamping my feet to the wokey-cokey.

In my desperate dash to escape the innocence of childhood I went off to university, so becoming a grown-up sav-

---

23 [Photo], <https://nato.int/nato_static_fl2014/assets/pictures/history_photostory-construction_of_the_berlin_wall/20161025_03_Guard_jumping_over_barbed_wire_to_join_the_West..jpg>, accessed 4 May 2023.
24 Charlotte Alfred, '10 Great Escapes Across The Berlin Wall', *Huffpost* [website], <https://huffpost.com/entry/berlin-wall-escape-stories_n_6090602>, accessed 4 May 2023.
25 Genesis 25:29–34, *Bible Gateway* [website], <https://biblegateway.com/passage/?search=genesis%2025:29-34&version=ESV>, accessed 4 May 2023.
26 Judges 16, *Bible Gateway* [website], <https://biblegateway.com/passage/?search=judges+16&version=ESV>, accessed 4 May 2023.

ant. Worse still, I graduated to sitting in an office towering over London, daily pen pushing millions of dollars around the fortress square mile. Like all my colleagues in Kafka's bank[27], I would bow and scrape to any upstart naked emperor and do whatever it took to keep my place. Status was everything. Far below our Babylonian skyscraper, that sordid city wall in Berlin came down.

A student came to me from the Eastern bloc. She left behind her family, her heritage and her language. She was hungry to learn English, because embodied in olde England she saw something of value. During a 2010 grammar lesson full of students practising sentence structure, she came out with it. It was a deadly improvised explosive device. Of the famous poetic Jerusalem builded in Blake's green and pleasant land[28] she said, 'I like it here, because here is freedom.'

Isn't it strange? We can be in a room full of people, where we all see and hear the same things but understand them differently. For most of us, most of the time these occasions are transient wraiths, immediately forgotten. But just occasionally, very occasionally, for one or two of us in the room, those wraiths take on flesh and blood.

So it was with the words that came from Red Sonja's lips. This post-communist juvenile from the Eastern bloc had stopped me in my tracks. 'I like it here, because here is freedom', she said. I pondered. What had I missed? All around us Lehman Brothers and countless other banks and financial houses had failed. Toxic loans were blamed. The numbers were fudged by naked emperors saving allies while drowning others. The private parts of EU member states were exposed and national debt was out of control. The Pied Piper was about to whistle away Europe's children. I was seeing only

---

27 Cf. *The Trial* by Franz Kafka.
28 William Blake, 'Jerusalem', *Song Lyrics* [website],
  <https://songlyrics.com/blake/jerusalem-lyrics>, accessed 10 May 2023.

gloom. Red Sonja was seeing, well just what was she seeing? 'I like it here, because here is freedom?' Had Red Sonja just unearthed a treasure. What was it? How does one take and polish and craft this precious stone into something of immense value. Is there more of this strange treasure to be found? How far did I have to look? How much effort was required to dig for and refine this treasure? What land rights would be required to allow the search? Who else was looking? Most important of all, who was trying to hide the 'freedom' treasure?

'Hi Ho, Hi Ho it's off to work we go.'[29] Except that this is not a pantomime. The actors may all be cross-dressing narcissists, yet the villainy is real and they look like giants not dwarves. I didn't see my dear student again, and it would have been construed as gross misconduct in the modern safeguarded era for me to socialise with her. As an aside, isn't it strange that 'Safeguarding' means separation and segregation and isolation. To lose digital bank accounts and social media accounts is to isolate and punish. The imposition of solitary confinement is the very opposite of embracing empathy and inclusion. The psychologists call solitary confinement by a different name. To them it is the war crime of torture[30]. There is no shoulder to cry on these days, no scope to take the cuts and bruises and kiss them better. It's bizarre. How about it, Mr Prime Minister?

As I looked and listened, there was no moral compass available to the common man. The bishops were throwing away the purity of the gospel for selfish pride. The ayatollahs were banning education for half the population, the mandar-

---

[29] 'Snow White and the Seven Dwarfs', *IMDb* [website], <https://imdb.com/title/tt0029583>, accessed 4 May 2023.
[30] Robert T. Muller, 'Solitary Confinement Is Torture—Research reveals numerous adverse effects of solitary confinement on inmates', *Psychology Today* [website], <https://psychologytoday.com/us/blog/talking-about-trauma/201805/solitary-confinement-is-torture>, accessed 4 May 2023.

ins and the cossacks were making a land-grab in territories abandoned by the west. So where could I begin searching? I pondered these things. At the very beginning, the Bible says, 'empty darkness was over the surface of the deep, and the Spirit of God was hovering over the waters'. I didn't understand. There was certainly empty darkness overhead but thank goodness the Holy Spirit was hovering. In the end from out of nowhere, insight came from the unlikeliest of sources.

Every evening, right on schedule, the propagandist megaphone in every home was singing its lullaby—'Follow the science'[31]. One night I finally understood. Now I had a place to start. What was the science saying? Was it saying like Red Sonja 'here is freedom'? Or was it saying 'don't be fooled by digital propaganda, the emperor has no clothes'?

What I found startled me. Firstly, I discovered the sinister symbiosis of population control, eugenics and evolutionary theory. The theories of Malthus, Darwin and Galton are horribly intertwined. It seems impossible to disentangle the Darwinian evolutionary environmentalists from the Malthusian population controllers and Galton's racial discrimination. It is embedded in the science and the history. Why are the conversations between the founders of today's wealthy abortion clinics and the builders of the gas chambers so carefully hidden away[32]? Why is it so? The industry is huge. The tiniest fraction of legalised terminations concerns the frightful brutalisation of women by strangers. The industrial scale reality, however, is that most procedures are not so and that 95% of these parental choice terminations are influenced by available

---

31 Freddie Hayward, 'Why Boris Johnson can't claim to have "followed the science" on Covid-19', *The New Statesman* [website] <https://newstatesman.com/politics/uk-politics/2021/02/why-boris-johnson-can-t-claim-have-followed-science-covid-19>, accessed 4 May 2023.

32 Marie Stopes letters to Hitler, *BBC* [website], <https://bbc.com/news/science-environment-11040319>, and <https://bbc.co.uk/news/uk-54970977>, accessed 4 May 2023.

funds sucked out of the NHS budget[33]. Taxpayers' money intended to provide healthcare for the sick and needy is being siphoned away into the pockets of the clinics' owners. Think about it. This generation is screaming and really screaming loudly. 'Me first'. It is just like Esau's refrain, my pleasure before your well-being. The word of God says it is an abomination when you sacrifice your child to Moloch. This was the old superstitious mechanism to seek your own prosperity at next year's harvest by killing the firstborn[34]. Beneath our sophisticated nail varnish and hairspray, the behaviour has not significantly changed. Those same sacrifices are happening today. Official statistics prove it[35]. The lobbyists on both sides of the debate will argue about different individual 'freedoms', for the parents or for the defenceless unborn child. That argument may need to happen, but more broadly the scale and the severity of modern superstition seems to have been totally misunderstood.

It is not just about the individual. In practical terms, the nation now has teachers, teaching your children, who have chosen to execute their own offspring for material gain. Your daughter has a best friend at school, whose parents chose to kill her sibling. Do you want that? Do you want your child to be taught not altruism but to worship mammon, 'me first' self-indulgence? Do you want your son and daughter to dis-

---

[33] *MSI Reproductive Choices UK* [website], <https://www.msichoices.org.uk/abortion-services/nhs-funded-and-private-abortions>, accessed 4 May 2023: 'Can I get an abortion on the NHS? 98% of the clients we see in our clinics have their treatment funded by the NHS. This means that there will be no cost to you for your abortion'.

[34] See Leviticus 20, *Bible Gateway* [website], <https://biblegateway.com/passage/?search=leviticus+20&version=ESV>, accessed 4 May 2023.

[35] Department of Health & Social Care, 'Abortion Statistics, England and Wales: 2018', 13 June 2019, *gov.uk* [website], <https://assets.publishing.service.gov.uk/government/uploads/system/uploads/attachment_data/file/808556/Abortion_Statistics__England_and_Wales_2018__1_.pdf>, accessed 4 May 2023.

cover their friends' families would rather kill their own than offer shelter to the needy. Is this Red Sonja's treasured freedom? Or is it the tyranny from which the Berlin soldier fled? How about it, Mr Prime Minister?

Did the covid propagandists realise what the science would actually say?

Well, here I am entering the foothills on the search to finding freedom, the treasure Red Sonja described. Why do acquaintances male, female and non-binary from far left to far right condemn me for daring to ask the question? Is this freedom or tyranny? Their condemnation is a spur to go further. On the slope I come across a field of scree, which is a collection of broken rock fragments accumulated through periodic rockfall. The scree is a deadly, slippery slope of broken rock, truths and half-truths resting over ball-bearing lies.

Here I see Health Secretary Matt Hancock gaily announcing in the middle of his own infidelity 'COVID vaccinations are to become compulsory for staff at care homes in England' [36]. Simultaneously it can be read on the government website that the MHRA have only granted temporary licences for each of the vaccines[37]. The 'temporary' status means that their use has not yet stood the test of time and that their safety is unproven. Some people might consider the 'temporary' licence as a signal that these drugs remain 'experimental'. This makes coercive action by Hancock or any other enforcer il-

---

36 Mary O'Connor et Marie Jackson, 'Covid vaccine to be compulsory for England care home staff', 16 June 2021, *BBC* [website], <https://bbc.co.uk/news/uk-57492264>, accessed 4 May 2023.

37 See UK Government website, […This temporary Authorisation under Regulation 174…] [file], <https://assets.publishing.service.gov.uk/government/uploads/system/uploads/attachment_data/file/963841/AZ_Conditions_for_Authorisation_final_23.02.21.pdf>, and *gov.uk* [website], <https://gov.uk/government/publications/regulatory-approval-of-pfizer-biontech-vaccine-for-covid-19/conditions-of-authorisation-for-pfizerbiontech-covid-19-vaccine>,both accessed 4 May 2023.

legal in international law. Nevertheless, Hancock's replacement, Nadim Zahawi, quickly endorsed the move. Zahawi's political reward was promotion to the position of Chairman of the Conservative Party. Some might argue Zahawi faced a later ethical reward when sacked for breaching the ministerial code[38]. That scree of broken rock on ball-bearing lies is truly a treacherous place to be. Is that tyranny or freedom?

Red Sonja had started me on a journey. On this climb I was unearthing serious misgivings, and I had barely scratched the surface. It made me think of the martyred theologian, put to death just before the end of WWII. Dietrich Bonhoeffer had written, 'We are not simply to bandage the wounds of victims beneath the wheels of injustice, we are to drive a spoke into the wheel itself.'[39]

Red Sonja in that grammar lesson had said something profound. For all her youth, she had travelled thousands of miles and traversed national borders and political barriers just to say those precious words, 'Here is freedom'. I was so glad she had made the journey. But what about my own ponderings? I was discovering the profit sitting in the abortion clinics. I was seeing the official records showing that, contrary to the slippery message of the unfaithful propagandist minister and evidenced in concrete terms, the COVID vaccines did not work. I was seeing that the frontline carers were promised and then denied reward, because the man in the designer clothes was diverting the monies elsewhere. The propaganda says it is within the law but is it an acceptable freedom? The self-indulgence is quite shocking. How about it, Mr Prime Minister?

---

38 James Robinson, 'Nadhim Zahawi sacked: The seven major findings from ethics investigation', *Sky News* [website], <https://news.sky.com/story/nadhim-zahawi-sacked-what-sir-laurie-magnus-found-in-his-tax-row-probe-12798225>, accessed 4 May 2023.

39 *Goodreads* [website], <https://goodreads.com/quotes/22884-we-are-not-to-simply-bandage-the-wounds-of-victims>, accessed 4 May 2023.

Then I saw the brutality of the regime behind the financials. A cohort of ministerial colleagues wilfully breaking international conventions aimed at preventing harm to the people from coercive medical experiments. We are now seeing the actual damage done to healthy athletes by those experiments[40]. And for the average citizen it is reported in official statistics that the overwhelming majority of those now being hospitalised with COVID are those who have received multiple jabs[41]. In other words, the vaccine and associated boosters are not offering protection. They do not work. There is evidence they do harm. Will there be an apology? How about it, Mr Prime Minister?

The oxygen gets thinner as I climb. Way back in 2008, Sir James Crosby, in his report to Chancellor Gordon Brown on the proposed UK ID card, coined the phrase 'Identity is the new money'[42]. The report was critical of government strategy and immediately dropped from sight.

But the secret was out. 'Identity' was the new money. And the only scaleable way to store the new money was going to be digital. Another phrase became fashionable as well for describing the cool phenomenon of the information superhighway and its feeder roads, namely *disruptive technology*. At

---

40 Kieran Lynch, 'Christian Eriksen and Sergio Aguero's on-field heart problems "have fuelled suspicion of Covid vaccines in Premier League players—with encouragement from Matt Le Tissier and Trevor Sinclair", say club medics, with around 100 stars still refusing the jab', *Mail Online* [website], <https://dailymail.co.uk/sport/sportsnews/article-10339755/Premier-League-field-heart-issues-fuelled-suspicion-Covid-vaccines-players.html>, accessed 4 May 2023.

41 For example: 'COVID-19 vaccine surveillance report, Week 42' [file from *gov.uk*], <https://assets.publishing.service.gov.uk/government/uploads/system/uploads/attachment_data/file/1027511/Vaccine-surveillance-report-week-42.pdf>, accessed 4 May 2023.

42 'Sir James Crosby report recommends free government-independent ID cards', *Science Direct* [website], <https://sciencedirect.com/science/article/abs/pii/S0965259008700811>, accessed 4 May 2023.

each step I was seeing the free spirit individual obliterated, to be replaced by the digital slave. Our identities as individuals were commoditised, monitised and put up for sale. In this erosion of individuality, the emperors consider digital 'disruption' a highly desirable estate. Measured steps and the maturing process will not achieve the explosive change desired to establish their dystopian world view.

The paper money in our wallets and purses for generations once gave us an assurance. The governor of the Bank of England states: 'I promise to pay the bearer on demand...' The absolute gold standard may long since have gone, but there remain two precious attributes that come with the paper. There is the promise of intrinsic value, and there is the promise of accountability. In the disruptive digital world, both attributes are deliberately being removed by the politicians we described earlier and their kindred spirits.

In January 2023, HM Treasury started advertising to recruit a Head of CBDC[43]. You don't need to have worked at Bletchley Park[44] to crack the code. 'Central Bank Digital Currency' is a way of saying that a nation will move away from the paper notions of intrinsic value and accountability regarding the purchasing power of our wallets. Digital currency, also known as 'Crypto' currency, has no intrinsic value and no guarantor. For the last few years its attractiveness has resided in an absence of traceability for the money launderer, with various high profile criminal investigations underway and speculations that one day the bubble will burst[45].

We have not yet traversed the scree of broken rock on ball-bearing lies. There is more to come in this treacherous

---

43 Tim Fries, 'HM Treasury Seeking Head of CBDC as UK Moves Closer to the Digital Pound', *The Tokenist* [website], <https://tokenist.com/hm-treasury-seeking-head-of-cbdc-as-uk-moves-closer-to-the-digital-pound>, accessed 4 May 2023.

44 *Bletchley Park* [website], <https://bletchleypark.org.uk/about-us>, accessed 4 May 2023.

place.

The 16th president of the United States is perhaps the one who has the greatest emotional connection with his land and his people. Within 50 years of Stephenson's Merseyside experiment with the steam train 'Rocket',[46] here was the great president who signed the papers which would bring modern transportation to the Americas with the Union Pacific railroad[47]. He was a great supporter of new technology and innovation. Yet technology innovation by no means establishes his popularity. The reason why Abraham Lincoln continues to have the ear of the people can be attributed to a short two minute speech. It is known as the Gettysburg Address. It was a requiem speech for scandalous numbers of soldiers who died in pursuit of freedom, but it was more than that. Lincoln stated:

'It is for us the living ... to be dedicated here to the unfinished work ... that this nation, under God, shall have a new birth of freedom, and that government of the people, by the people, for the people, shall not perish from the earth'[48].

In the essence of his character Lincoln expressed faithfulness and a duty to serve others. His dog was called Fido, which in Latin means 'I trust' or 'I have faith'.

---

45 Diksha Madhok, 'Risk takers', *CNN Business* [website], <https://edition.cnn.com/2022/11/14/business/ftx-crypto-collapse-updates-hnk-intl/index.html>, accessed 4 May 2023.

46 'Stephenson's Rocket', *Science Industry Museum* [website], <https://scienceandindustrymuseum.org.uk/what-was-on/stephensons-rocket>, accessed 4 May 2023.

47 'Abraham Lincoln and Union Pacific', *Building America* [website], <https://www.up.com/heritage/history/lincoln/index.htm>, accessed 4 May 2023.

48 'Gettysburg Address', *National Geographic* [website], <https://education.nationalgeographic.org/resource/gettysburg-address>, accessed 4 May 2023.

Walkies Fido—Now How About It, Mr Prime Minister?

Fast forward to the modern era and there is an alliance of superpowers from the digital industry, beholden and accountable to no national state, not under God, not governed 'of the people, by the people or for the people' who have established for themselves a goal[49]. Ironically they have called their alliance FIDO (F̲ast I̲dentity O̲nline). The masters of the modern FIDO have a completely different agenda.

The core message of the FIDO alliance is that in the digital field of the modern era the greatest threat to life exists in the freedom of the individual (to create one's own password). The FIDO objective is that 'password-only logins be replaced with secure and fast login experiences'[50]. In other words, the FIDO alliance's purpose is to abolish the free-willed, free-minded individual capable of making individual choices and able at will to change identity passwords. The aim is to abolish the capacity of the individual to move freely at one's own pace across geographies and media channels. Instead, a person will be given a centrally allocated, centrally controlled number as their monitised identity and their travel restrictions. The right to roam is to be abolished under the FIDO agenda. In an earlier generation less than 100 years ago, the FIDO digital agenda was executed by tattooing the flesh of millions destined for gas chambers. Now the FIDO tattoo is digital.

'Here is freedom'. This common man salutes Red Sonja for her siren call. Unlike the Lorelei whose voice drew sailors along the Rhine to their death, Red Sonja spoke of freedom and life.

The science and the history reveal the actual severe threat posed by the digital emperors. It rapidly becomes apparent that if freedom of any kind is to be preserved, then there is an

---

49 Cf. Tower of Babel, Genesis 11.
50 *FIDO Alliance* [website], <https://fidoalliance.org/what-is-fido>, accessed 4 May 2023.

urgent, pressing and compelling need to speak out in resistance to the bullies and their henchmen. Red Sonja said: 'I like it here, because here is freedom'. With a treasure like that, why sell your birthright?

How about it, Mr Prime Minister?

It is time to tell the modern day FIDO and its masters to go for a very long walk and not return.

30

I Don't Have a So-Called Smart Phone ... Imagine That!

By Willie Fi Fife

Since 2019 I've been without a mobile phone, having previously carried one around for five years. In October of that year my 'provider' told me that I needed an upgrade. I politely declined but asked, why? They gave the usual 'technospiel' about getting the latest 'smart' phone with the latest apps that go with it. Why would I need the latest app? I only used my phone to text occasionally and receive calls now and then. But that fell on deaf ears and a cut-off date was given: 'After this time your present phone connection will be terminated.'

So, for over three years now with no 'smart' phone at hand, life has been moving along quite nicely (apart from the so-called pandemic debacle). Imagine that: no real problems, no major hassles due to people not being able to get in touch. The need for a lifesaving, in the moment response facilitated by a phone, has never happened. Not that I'm discounting any such possibility, but it's not something that happens too often: a mobile phone coming to the rescue and saving the day. No—life just goes on as it always has. No drama, no satellites required.

Having said all that, I do have a land-line phone at home with an answering machine which, 'does what it says on the tin'.

Have you noticed the creeping sense of dependency to always have a phone on your person? It just doesn't feel right to me and I'm no luddite. I have a working background as a QA Inspector which involves working hi-tech equipment at a local engineering firm. Advanced technology does have its place in modern society. There is no argument against the technology used in life or death surgery. But other advances in AI, robotics and emerging nanobots should not restrict, overly intrude, dictate or otherwise dominate our lives. Developing technology must surely contribute to freeing us, adding to our ease and well-being. Liberating us rather than becoming some form of covert super-surveillance and money-making, life defining contrivance. You can see how many of the CCTV and so-called smart systems being deployed are being used as Big Brother revenue streams. Ever found yourself in a bus-lane in an unfamiliar city at a particular time of the day or in the evening, even with no other traffic around? The penalty fine will arrive promptly by post (or even sooner on your 'smart' phone!). Now consider the 15-minute cities and 20-minute neighbourhoods that are, 'coming to a town near you soon' and are just an extension of such big-brother scrutiny combined with daylight robbery.

Getting back to the so called 'smart-phones' with their insidious, subtle and creeping impact upon how we live our lives, we can all see how this is becoming more and more apparent.

Many times, when out for a walk—down by the sea or wandering through the local woodland, I pass some guy so caught up in his phone that he's blind to where he is and everything he's missing. Surrounded by nature's beauty, he walks on totally inured to the sights and sounds that are all around him. Gazing hypnotically, trance-like into the screen of the phone, his face bathed in that strange ethereal light with ears blue-toothed and plugged from the call of nature. Even at the seashore I've passed ladies busy chattering away, their attention focussed solely upon the phone. 'Awaken...! Look around. Open your eyes and ears', my heart and mind calls out to them ... but no, trance-like they wander on, oblivious in more ways than one.

Noticing this sad decline, I resolved a while ago to take a multi-pronged approach to what's going on in the world and the direction we were being steered in. I imagined a combination of inner and outer effort to '...create the change we wish to see in the world' to paraphrase an erudite spiritual-dude from the continent of India.

A practical 'outer' approach combined with a complementing 'inner' heart-based effort. Let's call it: Mind-Based Open-Hearted Activisms.

So, I'm off to a good start with the no mobile-phone lifestyle ... but what else can improve my lot? Here are just a few practical examples which combine head and heart:

➢ Viewing and Listening (AAA)
➢ Interacting with local banks on a *Trust* basis
➢ Broadcasting the necessity for *Keeping the Cash*
➢ *Knowing* what's really going on
➢ The inner silent practice of *Daily Meditation and Prayer*
➢ Unlimited Possibilities...

Discerning viewing and listening without undue influences!

AAA is the art of Active Advertisement Avoidance. Such a simple thing to do:

Imagine you're sitting with your loved ones watching some very erudite (I hope) and enlightening film or documentary and the inevitable relentless adverts come on. A golden opportunity has presented itself. Hit the mute button on the remote (ah, thank you modern technology.) Turn to your loved ones, smile and say 'hi', ask if they want a cup of tea. Or better still have a short chat, *see* how they are doing, giving them your best attention while you wait on the kettle boiling. You have skilfully avoided the relentless devious effects of adverts, adverts, adverts. Over the length of your average film, you will have reconnected with your immediate surroundings, your own body and the other human beings sitting next to you, four or five times, instead of gazing mindlessly at some fat opera guy or a bunch of meerkats telling you what you need to be buying, or some opinion that's allegedly in your best interest. None of which is done to confuse-you.com—honest!

I trust my bank!—No ID required

For 30 years plus I've held an account in a local branch of a big high street bank. The original premises have now been shut-down and I've to travel further afield to do my banking, but in the early days I knew all the bank-tellers by their first names. One lady was at primary school with me. Weekly visits to withdraw 'my' money being held by the bank never required strict ID. You had a passbook and everything was on friendly, I know you and you know me, terms. Since moving house my present-day bank is dealt with in the same spirit. I go there a couple of times a month and still take no ID, no piece of plastic card to withdraw reasonably sized amounts of *my* cash from *my* account. There's been the occasional hiccup, but overall, the tellers have come to know me (!) and any time where they ask 'do you have your card?' followed by '...we need to verify who you are...', I inform them that as a customer of many years, I'm not here to steal cash or launder money. I recount the facts that it's the big banks who are the rogues and are rife with corruption. The Lloyds, the HSBC, the Deutsche Bank, etc., have all been fined millions, sometimes billions for corrupt financial practices which have included money laundering. Hard-working members of the public are not the crooks. We don't need any of this contrived hassle which is obviously designed to make cash interactions vexatious to further reduce resistance to the coercion from cash to digital currencies. After such a conversation, and there's been a few, my face became quite familiar, so next time I'm in they know who I am and there's *no need for ID*. Problem solved! Recently they redesigned the furniture at the entrance of the bank, effectively blocking any route direct to the tellers on the left. All customers are steered to the right so have to pass by, the internal ATM before getting to the teller counter. For goodness sake! When I ask about this strategy and suggest that all of this will ultimately lead to less staff and more technology, they just smile but the smile never quite reaches their eyes.

'*Always cash*' is an approach that I utilize in supermarkets. Especially in Aldi and Lidl, whose employees always feel the need to ask—'cash or card?' at the checkout. Once more a perfect opportunity has presented itself, especially if there's a queue of customers behind me, to very politely and ever so, slightly loudly, reply—'*Always cash* as I don't want to live in a Chinese style dystopian cashless society.' Occasionally I get a knowing smile.

Even at work I take that approach when I see guys using their phones to buy a bar of chocolate from the vending machine. Another chance to talk about *keeping cash by using cash*. A quick chat highlighting that Choice is Freedom and the choices we have a right to are: access to cash, the use of chequebooks, credit-cards and on occasion—electronic transfer. All these forms of financial transaction methods equate to—CHOICE and Choice contributes to Freedom.

As the UK government amongst many others around the world, quietly work to nudge us towards Central Bank Digital Currencies (CBDCs), we need to assert our rights and maintain access to cash, 'cash with integrity' as a friend often puts it.

As Joe Public doesn't know the pitfalls of a CBDC the skilful approach to communicating the truth about this dystopian digital future needs to be concise, clear and informative. The culmination of a Chinese Social Credit system which combines a digital currency and health status monitoring, controlled at source by central banks via an individual's smart phone must be exposed. The essence of this ruse is how a third party can know what you spend your currency on (invasion of privacy) and can control (dictate) what you spend such digital money on.

The upside of highlighting already trialled CBDC systems in other countries is that we can clearly see what the game is and where the control mechanisms will be. Again, China inhibits you from saving by putting time limitations on your digital credits. If your health status does not correspond to government mandates, then the right to travel is seriously curbed. So, let's expose the obvious, self-evident tyranny, and show that none of this is conspiracy theory but an actual dystopian possibility.

Right now, I earn my wage, paid to me every month and I choose what I spend it on. Yes, I have responsibilities, bills to pay and other financial commitments arising from choices I made. I also have the inalienable right to choose exactly how I spend the cash I've earned through my labour, sweat and toil. If a person decides to give money to a homeless charity, munch away on some bad-for-your teeth candy-bar or set up a monthly subscription to a trusted independent internet based news source (see UK Column) that is their right—the right to choose. The CBDCs are designed so that an external third party can, with the greatest of ease, press delete to your digital wallet thereby fundamentally affecting how you live your life and any choices you make. Just think of the Canadian Truckers and Pay-Pal's involvement in freezing the bank accounts of anyone supporting them. The truck drivers had legitimate grievances and were peacefully congregating and exercising their civil liberties, which is their right.

What about the digital grid that's being quietly developed all around us? The goal appears to evolve the 'Internet of Things' and 'The Internet of Bodies' via 5G and 6G telecommunication systems. The relentless repetition of smart this and smart that, has been on-going for years. We now know about smart homes, cars, dishwashers, fridge-freezers ... smart everything! A world where the interconnectivity of everything to everything is in place. Yikes! Your house will know when you're coming home. The car will start up as you approach it, no key necessary. All goods and services silently monitored from the background. It all sounds a bit spooky and disconcerting to me. For example (in Scottish parlance...): 'If a ever found maself in the position where ma fridge in the hoose telt me via ma phone that a wiz runnin' oot o' bog roll (toilet roll) ... *it would be time to seriously rethink my life!*'

Approaching from the heart for unlimited possibilities

At this point, with all the 'outer' attempts to think, act and live in a better world, expressing common sense and clear communication to others is very important, if not *the* most important part of all this. The heart-based dynamic. That inner desire for change. And I believe this is the more powerful part compared to the 'outer' approaches described so far. Working from the inside out so to speak. Activating the Spirit within. I wouldn't say I'm a religious person by nature, but I'm very keen on Truth and a big part of Truth for me is— who am I? What's life all about? Is there purpose and meaning to it all? As a mentally active guy, I've found that sitting still for a period of time each day, to quietly reflect or to allow the thinking mind to become less busy and more settled, has been of great benefit over the years. I also find that spending time in nature to be of great comfort and solace. I'd describe the combination of these two things as healing and meditative, especially when there is apparent chaos and agitation all around. Some may interpret this as prayer and meditation—and I wouldn't disagree. An individual faith has arisen from such personal experiences, deepening my need for this daily time of quiet stillness and peaceful reflective contemplation.

Over the years I've read about many people of good character who consistently spent time alone in silence, only to return to the world refreshed, invigorated with their sense of purpose reaffirmed, and a deep calmness and clarity which aids decision making and sets intention. A healthy daily dose of peace and quiet can nourish the nerves, calm the mind and settle the brain.

Compared with all the other words in this paper, this reference to such inner work, seems small and less important, but the opposite is true. The heart-based intention, prayer and positive imaginings are the foundation to everything that takes place at the 'outer' practical level. I believe therein lies a big part of the secret to success. Yes, let's uncover the truth about what's really going on in this world of deception, determine the best response to such truth and take action. But any action has to come from within peaceful, heart-based action, arising from an imagined world where Love, Peace, Wisdom and Compassion are the motivations.

Having mentioned wisdom, let's compare for a moment the two words 'smart' and 'wise'

SMART: Sneaky Mind-Altering Authoritative Ruthless Tyranny

WISE: Worldly Insightful Sound Evaluation

'Smart' pertains to the intellect and implies goodness and intelligence, but without any heart for guidance, it becomes debased and corrupted, drifting into a word that can be deceptive, a negative, e.g. SmartAlec, smarty-pants and dare I say ... smart arse! It can also relate to sharpness, a stinging pain, and also, brisk. Smart is all about mind disconnected from the heart.

Whereas wise or wisdom points to understanding, knowledge from experience, good judgment, sage-like, insight. In addition these can easily be associated with virtues such as ethics and benevolence. Between the two acronyms and their range of meanings, I know what holds greater depth and value to me.

As an after-thought... Have you ever heard of a *wisdom*-based weapons system?

It's becoming more self-evident that the world and most of humanity are in big trouble. So, to conclude let's imagine a better place in which to live—a world where natural wonders and real miracles can be explored and cultivated.

As the great satirist and hilariously rude comedian Bill Hicks often said:

'...The world is like a ride at an amusement park, and when you choose to go on it, you think it's real, cause *that's how powerful our minds are. And the ride goes up and down* and round and round; it has thrills and chills and it's very brightly coloured and it's very loud and it's fun ... for a while. Some people have been on the ride for a long time, and they begin to question: 'Is this real, or is this just a ride?' And other people have remembered, and they come back to us, and they say, 'Hey—don't worry, don't be afraid—EVER—because ... this is just a ride.' And we always kill those good guys who try and tell us that, and we let the demons run amok. But it doesn't matter because ... it's just a ride. *And we can change it anytime we want.* It's only a choice. No effort, no work, no job, no savings of money. *A choice, right now, between fear and love.* The eyes of fear want you to put bigger locks on your door, buy guns, close yourself off. The eyes of love, instead, see all of us as One. Here's what we can do to change the world, right now, to a better ride: *Take all that money that we spend on weapons and defence, each year, and instead, spend it feeding clothing and educating the poor of the world, which it would many times over—not one human being excluded—and we could explore space, together, both inner and outer, forever, in Peace.*

Wouldn't such an approach to all the oppressive 'smartness' be wonderful! Redirecting all the world's so called 'Defence Budget' into paradigms for peace.

In 2022, the US annual defence spending hit an eye watering $858 Billion. Eye watering in the sense that such ill-advised spending should make you cry!

Original imaginings for a better world

Investigations by Dr Masaru Emoto, would appear to suggest that our thoughts and words have a discernible effect upon water. His experiments involved exposing vials of water to various words, pictures or music, then freezing the water and examining the frozen crystals under a microscope to discover that words of hate or love, pictures of beauty and ugliness, classical music as opposed to the sounds of Gangster Rap or

Heavy Metal, showed apposing effects on the water crystals. The positive words, pictures and sounds creating a far more symmetrical and aesthetically pleasing pattern. Does this imply our thoughts and words can affect the world around us (and we are made of up to 60% water)? The implications surely merit further investigation.

Matthew Manning is a medical healer who has a remarkable track record of working at the interface between body mind and soul—a record which spans over 40 years. He has shown, under scientific scrutiny, that he has a capacity to channel 'healing energy' which has been quantified and the results have been beneficial to plants, animals and humans. His ability has successfully influenced a range of biological targets including blood cells, mould samples, enzymes, seeds and cancer cells. Professors and consultants continue to comment upon his astounding work and against all the odds, his healing energy has shown positive results for both cancer patients and those suffering from other life threatening illnesses.

It would appear that even in the heady world of Quantum Science, by the act of observation and intention, we bring wave form into existence as a particle. Can it be true that we have much more influence on the substance of reality (subatomic matter, molecules ... water! etc.,) than we realise? Could it be that the never-ending daily distraction of war, disease, fear and uncertainty are redirecting our attention so that we inadvertently *perpetuate* negative 'possibilities'? Do we need to just acknowledge their existence, then *imagine* a world without such hazards? Is it all down to how we *imagine* ourselves and the world in order to create such a world? Can it be that simple?

Mr Hicks has some more things to say about such possibilities:

'Today a young man realized that all matter is merely energy condensed to a slow vibration, that we are all One Consciousness experiencing itself subjectively, there is no such thing as death, life is only a dream, and we are the imagination of ourselves...'

So, come on ... let's put our imaginations to good use. No worries, no animosity, and definitely no phones ... just caring, sharing love and mutual consideration. Imagine that!

31

You Decide

By Stephen James Gray

This is not an ordinary story. You cannot read it from start to finish, but will instead be asked to make decisions at the end of each section. Once you have made your decision, you must head to the corresponding number. Just as in life, whatever path you take, the outcome will be affected by the choices you make along the way. All you need to play this game is an open mind. Please continue…

1

It is a warm summer's day and you are walking through town when you're approached by a man with a clipboard. Behind him is a minibus with a sign that reads 'Free Testing Here Today'. You recognise the bus as a PCR testing site, where members of the public are encouraged to take a nasal swab to ensure they are free of a new virus the Government has been warning about. The man stops you and asks if you'd like to take the test.

Do you agree? Turn to section 17.
If you refuse, turn to section 7.

2

Putting on your mask, you enter the supermarket. The aisles are filled with others just like you—those who are comforted by the belief that the cloth that covers their faces will prevent the microscopic organisms in the air from entering their bodies.

'Would you like to use the self-service?' a young girl asks, when you're ready to pay.

You notice that more self-service tills are now in use, and fewer people are employed each year to serve customers. One day maybe places like this will become fully automated. Already there are shoppers that walk around with scanners, pricing up their items before they reach the tills. How long before supermarkets everywhere are run entirely by machines, or until everyone shops exclusively online, you wonder?

Do you use the self-service tills? Turn to section 18.
Or the traditional ones instead? Turn to section 9.

3

You agree wholeheartedly with the demonstrators' message and wish to help spread awareness of what is being planned. *'This is no more than a tax on the poor,'* you think, *'and the council is using "climate change" as an excuse to implement it.'*

You admire the demonstrators for standing up to what you perceive as corruption, and hope the protest will achieve its aim of preventing the unnecessary measures.

Soon, you are pulled back to mundane reality, and head to the supermarket to buy some essential items. When you are finished, you proceed to the checkout area.

Do you choose self-service? Go to section 18.

Or the traditional method? Go to section 9.

4

You take a seat and sit down, feeling a little sad that so many companies refuse to accept physical money these days. 'Ah well,' you think, *what can anyone really do about it?'* On your phone there's a text from your GP. The message says that you haven't booked an appointment for the new vaccine that's been introduced to help combat the latest airborne virus.

Do you book an appointment? Go to section 22.
Or delete the message? Go to section 20.

5

You nod and agree to sign the petition. You found it strange when the 5G towers appeared out of nowhere after the nation was locked down for several months during the most recent virus scare, and you've heard unsettling stories about the risk to health if they're switched on. Whether or not these stories are true, it seems reasonable to be cautious. *'Is there really a need for 5G at all?'* you wonder.

The man thanks you and asks if you'd be interested in helping him deliver leaflets about the 5G towers and the potential danger they pose. You consider this question for a moment, before agreeing to help him and a group of other concerned citizens. Before you leave, you arrange to meet at a later date and the man seems impressed that you still carry an old 2G phone. 'It's all I need,' you say. And the man smiles.

Please turn to section 19.

6

You leave the bank and walk past a group of people gathered in the town square. The group are protesting against the local council who are about to trial something called a 'Fifteen Minute City', saying this will help reduce carbon emissions by preventing people from driving outside the immediate area. Those who do, will be forced to pay a fine. A counter protest group who are in favour of the trial has formed close by, and in order to keep the peace, the police are out in force.

Do you approach the demonstrators? Go to section 14.
Or join the counter protest group? Go to section 8.

7

You shake your head. 'No thanks,' you say, and continue with your journey. You are surprised to notice the man glaring at you over his clipboard. It seems he is not used to people refusing his test, and his reaction unnerves you slightly. To take your mind off this encounter, you enter a café, order a coffee and get out your wallet/purse to pay.

'We're no longer accepting cash,' says the barista. 'It's card only I'm afraid.'

Do you take out your debit/credit card? Go to section 4.
Or do you refuse? Go to section 11.

8

You approach the counter protest group who wear dark uniforms resembling those of a paramilitary organisation. Though many of them are masked, you speak to a young girl standing on the fringes and ask her why the group is there. 'We're here to express our right to free speech,' she says, 'and to defend the environment.'

'But aren't the demonstrators only worried about being able to drive to work?' you ask. 'Surely the idea of 15-minute cities is just another way to tax the poor?'

Before she can answer you, however, the group begins to

chant and the call of 'Fascist! Fascist!' goes up. You walk away, confused by the counter protesters' message.

'Oh well,' you think. '*What can be done about it?*'

You enter a supermarket but are stopped at the entrance by a security guard who asks you to put on your mask. 'It's to help stop the spread of the new virus,' he says, 'and it's store policy for customers to wear one.'

Do you comply with his request? Turn to section 2.
Or do you refuse? Turn to section 16.

9

At the checkouts, you smile at the assistant and pay for your groceries. You are glad to still have the choice to use cash here, and hope your decision to do so will help to keep physical money in circulation and staff in employment. It's not possible to make conversation with machines, after all.

Before leaving, you thank the checkout girl for her assistance.

Whilst heading home, you meet a man who asks if you would be kind enough to sign his petition. When you enquire as to the reason for it, he points towards a new 5G tower which is being erected. 'It's about those,' he says. 'Not only are they an eye-sore, but we don't know for certain how safe they are.'

You've heard of the potential dangers associated with the towers, and it's certainly true that they're an eye-sore.

Do you sign the petition? Turn to section 5.
Or refuse and walk away? Turn to section 12.

10

A dark future is the reward for the decisions that have been made. It's now ten years later and the world in which you exist is one where nobody is truly free, and people are monitored by a surveillance grid twenty-four hours a day, seven days a week. High rise buildings blight the landscape for as far as the eye can see—Pod Towers into which thousands are crammed. The residents who dwell here receive a Universal Basic Income which enables them to afford the meagre rations of insect protein the media insists is good for them. Everything from the food you eat, to the places you go, to the people you see, is recorded and kept on file by a ruling class that no longer has any concern for your rights. You gave those away a long time ago, swapping freedom for security and losing both along the way. If you step out of line in this world—buy the wrong thing, or utter a perceived grievance against those in charge—points are deducted from your credit rating and your quality of life will fall further than it already has. If that is even possible.

No one would have planned to take the path that brought *you* here. It is a series of poor choices and apathy that has done that, and, of course, a plot that has been in preparation for generations, concocted by those who think they know what is best for you. Here, at the end, you will own nothing, but do not worry, those in charge assure you that everyone will be happy…

11

Shaking your head, you apologise and tell the barista you cannot support a business that refuses cash payments. 'Cash is freedom', you say, and, to your surprise, he agrees. 'I know what you mean,' he replies. 'I don't like these rules either, but it's store policy. I hope I can change things.'

You wish him luck and go on your way.

Further down the street, you go into a bank. Upon entry you are met by a member of staff who reminds you that this branch will soon be closing its doors permanently. 'Don't worry, though,' she says, 'you can access all our services with the online banking app. Would you like me to show you how to set it up?'

Do you agree? Go to section 15.
Or do you refuse? Go to section 21.

12

'What's the point?' you think. *'Those towers will be erected whether I like it or not. What can any of us really do? And besides, perhaps the reception on my phone will be better once the signals are switched on.'*

At home, you turn on your heating using your Smart meter—the one the energy company said would be to your benefit, but which doesn't appear to have done your savings any favours. You then use your Smart phone to make an on-line purchase before you sit down to watch television. There is depressing news about another war that no one quite understands the reasons for, but which has nevertheless brought problems to your own country's door in the form of food shortages (amongst other things). The growing tensions that have arisen because of your government's willingness to provide arms to one of the warring nations, has given you reason to be worried, but what can you really do about it, you ask yourself?

You go to bed but cannot sleep. *'What a strange day,'* you think. So many things have changed in such a short time, and today, for some reason, you noticed as though for the first time. *'Still,'* you sigh, *'what can I do? I am but one person, after all, and if things continue to change for the worse, it won't affect me for many years to come, if at all.'*

But the years go by so very quickly, and issues that once seemed so trivial soon converge to become something much more.

Please turn to section 10.

13

You quickly delete the message. You have no wish to take a vaccine that you don't believe has had time to be adequately tested. Besides, you've heard rumours that many who've taken the inoculations have suffered problems that were not previously foreseen, and on which the media appears to be reluctant to report.

You leave the café and head to the local supermarket. Once you've gathered the items you require, you walk to the tills.

Do you choose self-service? Turn to section 18.
Or the traditional ones? Turn to section 9.

14

You walk over to a young man and ask to know more about the demonstration. 'The council wants to introduce passes to allow people to drive through town,' he tells you. 'They say it's to help make the air cleaner by reducing emissions, but this means we'll only be able to drive through twice a week. Any more than that and we'll be fined.'

You ask how the council will be able to police such a scheme. 'Look around you,' says the man, pointing to all the surveillance cameras that have been installed. 'They'll pick up our licence plates and we'll have no choice but to pay. It's not only here, either. If this plan is successful, they'll no doubt try to implement it nationwide.'

Across the square, the counter protesters carry banners with derogatory slogans and have started to chant at the demonstrators. This confuses you. Surely this scheme will affect the poorest in society who have to drive through town for work. How can it be wrong to decry this scheme?

Do you speak to the counter protesters? Go to section 8.
Or stay with the demonstrators? Go to section 3.

15

You allow the girl at the bank to help you set up a new online account, and are pleased when she tells you how easy it is to use their new app. 'It's much simpler than I thought it'd be,' you say. 'Maybe soon there won't be a need for real money at all!' The girl smiles an awkward smile as you leave.

Turn to section 6.

16

You refuse to comply with the man's request, and instead tell him that you don't believe a mask will prevent microscopic viruses from entering your respiratory system. To your surprise he is sympathetic, and agrees to allow you in as long as you have an exemption certificate.

'The cameras are watching me too,' he says, 'and I have to be seen to be doing my job.'

You pull out a blank piece of paper and show him. He nods and lets you pass.

When you have finished your shopping, you head to the tills to pay.

Go to section 9.

17

You step onto the bus and a nurse asks you to take a seat. Sitting down, you notice that a group of people has gathered outside, all waiting to take the same test that you are about to receive. The nurse produces a swab which makes you feel uneasy, and for a brief moment you wonder why you are there—you don't feel ill, after all.

'All done,' says the nurse when it's finished.

'How long until I receive the result?' you ask and are told that it should arrive within 24 hours.

The next day, you are sitting in a café when a text message is sent to your phone telling you that you tested 'positive.' *'Strange,'* you think, *'I do not feel ill in the slightest.'* Not long after, you get another message reminding you of the positive test result you have only just received, and letting you know that it would be in your best interests to book an appointment with your GP to get the new vaccine. This has been introduced to help combat the most recent airborne virus that the media never seems to tire of talking about.

Do you book the appointment? Go to section 22.
Or delete the message? Go to section 13.

18

When you reach the self-service area, you find that the few that still accept cash are not working today, and instead you have no choice but to use those which only accept card payments. You find this concerning because you like to have a choice when it comes to how you pay, and if that choice is taken away it could lead to all kinds of problems in future.

'Oh well,' you think, as you put your card into the machine. *'What can any of us really do about it?'*

Later, as you head home, you meet a man who asks if you'd like to sign his petition. When you enquire as to what the petition is for, the man points towards a 5G tower. 'It's about those,' he says. 'Not only are they an eye-sore, but we can't be certain if they're safe.'

Will you sign the petition? Turn to section 5.

Or refuse? Turn to section 12.

19

At home, later on, you consider the events of the day. You think about the man with the petition and wonder if there is more you could do to help. There is a growing sense of unease within you that started some time ago and refuses to go away. You see corruption all around you and do not wish to sit idle while the world is thrust towards a digital future in which the freedoms of ordinary citizens are taken by those who would seize power for themselves. The things you are able to do now may seem small in the grand scheme of things, but they are also vitally important.

Please turn to section 23.

20

You immediately delete the message. You've heard some terrible accounts of people who have taken the vaccine and you don't wish to be injected with something that you do not believe has been adequately tested. Besides, you eat a healthy diet, trust your body's immune system to prevent you from becoming ill, and don't feel unwell anyway.

You enter a bank and are met by a staff member who reminds you that this branch will soon be closing permanently. 'Don't worry, though,' she says, 'you can access all our services with the online banking app. Would you like me to show you how to set it up?'

Do you agree? Go to section 15.
Or do you refuse? Go to section 21.

21

You politely tell the assistant that you do not like to use internet banking and would much prefer to continue using the branch while it's still possible, as you cannot be certain your account is safe online. Sadly, as this branch is about to close, you will have to travel to the one on the other side of town in future, but at least you may be able to help keep that one open, and those who work there in employment.

You leave the bank and walk past a group of people who are gathered in the town centre. It appears the group are protesting against the local council who are about to begin a trial of something called a 'Fifteen Minute City'. The council says this will help reduce carbon emissions by preventing people from driving outside the immediate area. Those who do, will be forced to pay a fine. Another group has started to form not far away—counter protesters who seem to be in favour of the trial—and in order to keep the peace, the police are out in force.

Do you speak to the demonstrators? Go to section 14.
Or the counter protest group? Go to section 8.

22

You book an appointment with your GP and are surprised when you're asked to come in the next day. *'Strange,'* you think. Most people say it's difficult to get GP appointments nowadays, but for you it seems to have gone quite smoothly.

The following day you arrive at the surgery to receive your vaccine. Once it's done you feel a sense of relief that you have been afforded at least *some* protection from the new virus (one of many over the last few years) and will not have to worry about contracting it now. You are only mildly concerned when the nurse tells you that you will have to come back for a 'booster jab' in three months' time, and every three months after that for the foreseeable future.

'Oh well,' you think, *'it's just the way things are these days. The*

"new normal", as they say.'

The stories of excess deaths and increased health problems that are rumoured to be associated with the vaccines do not overly concern you.

At a supermarket later on, a security guard asks you to wear your mask. 'It's store policy,' he says, 'to help prevent the spread of the virus.'

Do you comply? Turn to section 2.
Or refuse? Turn to section 16.

23

It is one year later, and you have begun to get organised, helping to spread the word about the things you feel strongly about. To reach this point has required great courage and a determination to remain true to yourself. You are an independent thinker and not easily led. For you, the future is a bright one where freedoms remain intact, though many challenges still await you. Those who would steal away your rights are not yet defeated—unfortunately they may never be—but do not worry, you will forever be willing to rise to the challenge, teaching the next generation to be just as alert as you were to the threat posed by those who dwell in the shadows...

32

There Is Reason to Be Optimistic

By David Sheppard

If you desire change, do you change things from the inside or the outside?

As a sovereign individual I chose from the inside.

I work for a global corporation, in lockstep with World Economic Forum (WEF) ideology, and have seen clearly what is happening to our everyday lives, inside and outside of work, as global, centralised corporations work together to drive change for their own good and at your expense. You notice that the big corporations do not compete—all they desire is a monopoly. Market share amongst themselves, the big players, within an industry and a monopoly of smaller and medium sized businesses.

There is and never was any control from governments, or interference, because they are all part of the game and oversight is as mythical as COVID.

Around five years ago, capitalism...

1. Lifted more people out of poverty than ever before
2. People laughed and had fun
3. Competition in the energy industry was strong, prices

low
   4. Interest rates were low
   5. Employment was strong
   6. Food was plentiful, with a wide variety
   7. You could say what you believed without hindrance
   8. You could say ghastly things, you could take offence, but these were both inalienable rights

And, despite its inherent flaws, capitalism was as good as it could get.

What you need to know is that just like individuals, some people resent success, resent achievement, resent the happiness of others and desire chaos instead of order. I see this in a global corporation, the biggest barriers to positive change are individuals. This ironically happens when things are good, *not* bad.

Then a myth was sprung and named COVID.

A designed, beautifully executed economic and destructive scam, not medical, purely political and planned many years before. Behavioural 'nudge' units sent into action by Government on its own people, global corporations did it to their own staff to convince them of the righteous 'no other' WEF way. Lying, brainwashing and conniving its way through its crazy unrelenting madness, crushing free speech and personal liberty. Destroying the economy, small and medium sized businesses, pitching friend against friend, families against each other to keep themselves in check. Lines of good people having injections of something, not sure that they knew what, but they did not care. Inappropriate PCR tests giving false positive readings, masks having no scientific basis and people stepping up to be pious promotional tools for government, big pharma, technology and media 'propaganda' companies. Threats of fines and intimidation.

I have never owned a mobile phone nor am I on social media

of any kind. Inside a 'woke' company, I am careful with what I say but I say what I truly believe, in the most articulate way I can. I am not curtailed by another's point of view or ideology, and I have critiqued the company's culture as toxic, arrogant and under performing. I do not consume anyone's culture, but I do create new culture and take colleagues with me. People are drawn to these types of behaviour; they feel in their gut something is not right. So, recognise a positive vibe, take it with you. Leading a light through an illusionary tunnel of darkness.

I work with 'cloud based' technology.

In good hands useful to people, and in bad hands, restrictive, crafty and dangerous. This technology is mainstream now.

But there is reason to be optimistic.

There are more bright souls than dark. I have seen many such souls in business and there is a common denominator—they do not last and disappear. The ideology being pursued has never worked anywhere. The malevolence of the last few years is easing and more people are waking up. Change must come from you—be the change that you desire.

1. Trust and be your authentic self
2. Do not own or carry a mobile phone
3. Get off all social media
4. Be resilient with family and friends and have empathy
5. Involve yourself in an area where you feel uncomfortable and see if you can change it e.g. politics, technology, a topic that abhors you in order to test yourself. The myth of George and the Dragon has survived millennia because of the embedded wisdom. There is a pot of gold once the dragon is confronted and killed.
6. Be flexible and above all light-hearted in the face of chaos and malevolence
7. Educate yourself (none of this is new) and share wisdom

8. Do not let a point of view send you into chaos—create order from that chaos

9. Take control, people need you, 'there is no authority but yourself' as Crass said and continues to say!

The next few years will lead to political change and only then will a critical mass be reached to change the system for all, for human betterment. Things are changing.

How?

The sheer vitriol and poison against specific individuals with an alternative viewpoint, a contrary viewpoint, highlights to me their concerns and fears.

It is comforting on one level to feel like running and hiding away, to live on an island or on a barge, to stay outside the system. But are you truly happy if other human beings are being played?

If not, try introducing some of the points I highlight above. You will be surprised to find that life is for living, life itself is good, people are good and you can lead by example through this wrong-headed nonsense. Do not consume toxic culture, create yourself a healthy one.

All tyrannical dominators believe things are permanent—nothing is permanent.

33
Moving Forward

By a New Fan of Sophie Scholl

We humans are 'reflexive' readers. I mean that we can't help but read and/or hear short statements, quips, bumper-stickers, cliches, bromides, maxims, saws, billboards, ads, sayings, memes, etc. Even if we disagree with what we just read, we cannot 'unsee' it. We cannot 'unhear' it.

With great danger comes great opportunity. Or something along those lines. See? These past three years have been challenging but keeping active and wide open has been inspiring.

I hadn't heard of Sophie Scholl until this mess. I know about her now and I love the reigniting of her White Rose project and paradigm. I have a printer and oh, I print and distribute these sticker memes far and wide—by any memes necessary! I first learned of her in 2021, the 100th anniversary of her birth. She sacrificed her life, but her legacy is shining *bright*.

Control might come from the top down, for a time. But control from the top *never* wins in the long run. (Nick Hudson of 'PANDA') The criminals who sparked this psyop will never succeed. Some will escape justice (in this life), for sure. But no matter. They have catalysed a massive awakening. They opened an epic Pandora's box upon themselves that they will never be able to close. I could *never* predict how long this will take, but justice will eventually be served. (Nassim N. Taleb 'Antifragile: things that gain from disorder')

In chemistry, you only need a spark (catalyst or enzyme) to get a reaction, conflagration, going. The tipping point fuse was lit by the criminal cabal and though there is some online censorship and seeming 'digital slavery' about, I know exponentially more about science and nature than I did before this. I am grateful. There are innocent victims to this the world over. They were here on their own journey and may they rest in peace. But, with my actions, I honour them (and Sophie Scholl) by seeing what needs to be done to assist survivors and future generations.

There may be 'only' millions of us who see what's going on. But just like the use of the PCR test fraudulently to gin up 'cases', the bona-fide use of PCR is to amplify! If each of us reaches two and each of those two reaches two—this information will spread faster and faster, accelerating. And that is exactly what is happening. The last three years have been a slog, but the conflagration is *on*!

And when bad happens, comedians, cartoonists, satirists, jesters, cynics, creatives, geniuses, writers, illustrators, and social critics go into overdrive. These groups are the epitome of 'antifragile'. Also, leaderless groups are unstoppable (and 'antifragile'). 'The Starfish and The Spider'. Ori Brafman.

Communications between people is *not* stopped. On the contrary, the would-be controllers, who think they are God, have no idea what they've unleashed.

Truth is immortal. It can be battered, massaged, and abused, sure. Nature doesn't care at all if we know and are correct about how She operates. Proofs about 'cures' and 'preventatives' and even knowing that pathogenic viruses don't exist, makes no difference. She will do what she does and keep healthy those who rely on their communion with others, experience, intuition, and better judgement to get in line with Her.

I have met so many new people, have made hundreds of new friends, done so many new things, that my head spins. I have had so many paradigms that I once held dear, changed, and expanded. The world is so much more fascinating than I ever imagined. It's been difficult and demeaning at times. But going forward and moving towards much better is assured now, and unstoppable.

Early on, I learned of a video with Dr Thomas Cowan, 'The heart is not a pump'. This was a new concept to me, and Rudolph Steiner pointed it out over 100 years ago. It's revelatory and the implications are *profound*.

I have discovered a transformational speaker, Kyle Cease, who brings me great joy.

I have reread so many books. The second reading is like I had never read it before.

Genius biophysicist Gerald Pollack's 'The Fourth Phase of Water' should be read by all.

I had a consultation with Dr Andrew Kaufman of Medicamentum Authentica. Stellar.

I could go on and on and on. All of it, online. And even if the internet shuts down, I have good and many people near me in my community. I have a lifetime supply of books in my house to read and reread.

If somehow, we are stopped from obtaining food, water, gasoline, heat, we are *all* in this together.

I don't plan on leaving this life earlier than I would want to, but I am not in control of that. When it's my time—it is what it is. But for now, my actions (and thoughts) are to continue moving forward.

34

Digital Identity—The Final Lock Down in the Final Countdown

By Simon of the family Shields

A *Digital Identity (DID)* is an offer that many governments and corporations are packaging as a convenient way of verifying a person's identity and a way to avoid personal information being stolen. This offer, like the offer of the experimental mRNA poisonous jabs to end the *scamdemic*, is another 'Trojan horse', 'wolf in sheep's clothing' scam. The final step towards the New World Order (NWO) prison planet. Like many offers from scammers, at first glance the offer seems innocent and reasonable, but like all mouse traps, once triggered it will become impossible to reverse the entrapment.

The first action to take to resist the roll out of the NWO Digital Identity (DID), is to decline their offer. I have written an Affidavit template that anyone can download and use[51] to proclaim the truth regarding the claims made by alleged Australian authorities concerning the Digital Identity (DID).

---

51 See [file], <http://sssw.com.au:8082/commonlaw/affidavits/Affidavit-DirectorID.pdf>, accessed 4 May 2023.

One of the statements made in the Affidavit communicates that the DID is a contractual offer and alleged authorities have no legal or lawful authority to enforce compliance. I think it is important to ensure they are aware that their allegations of authority are not recognized and that, unless the proponents of the DID can provide proof that the benefits outweigh the risks or/and they have authority to enforce the DID, then you are at liberty and within your rights to abstain from participating in their New World Order (NWO) DID. If a large proportion of the population pushed back by declining the offer of obtaining a DID, via a three-step correspondence Affidavit process[52] to obtain proof via tacit acquiescence that their claims concerning the DID are fallacious, then people would have proof of their criminal attempt to financially enslave the people via coercion, intimidation and threats of menace to obtain a DID. Throughout most Western democracies that have a national constitution rooted in the UK's Magna Carta and/or have become signatories to the UN Charter of Civil and Political Human Rights[53], the people in

---

52 See [file], <http://sssw.com.au:8082/commonlaw/affidavits/CreatingLawWithAffidavits.pdf>, for details on how this is done in practice. Accessed 4 May 2023.

53 See Article 8 on Slavery from 'International Covenant on Civil and Political Rights', [file], <http://sssw.com.au:8082/downloads/ICCPR.pdf>, accessed 4 May 2023:
'Article 8: 1. No one shall be held in slavery; slavery and the slave-trade in all their forms shall be prohibited. 2. No one shall be held in servitude. 3. (a) No one shall be required to perform forced or compulsory labour; (b) Paragraph 3 (a) shall not be held to preclude, in countries where imprisonment with hard labour may be imposed as a punishment for a crime, the performance of hard labour in pursuance of a sentence to such punishment by a competent court; (c) For the purpose of this paragraph the term "forced or compulsory labour" shall not include: (i) Any work or service, not referred to in subparagraph (b), normally required of a person who is under detention in consequence of a lawful order of a court, or of a person during conditional release from such detention; (ii) Any service of a military character and, in countries where conscientious objection is recognized, any national service required by law of conscientious objectors; (iii) Any service exacted in cases of emergency or

these nations who use the Affidavit process discussed to obtain proof of criminal intent, would then have the evidence necessary to start legal challenges in the Courts. Such action can at least delay the onset of the NWO and at best ensure the implementation of a NWO DID could be made illegal or its effects could be seriously neutered.[54]

Australia's law courts have shown themselves to be biased towards leftist sensibilities and very susceptible to the influence of mainstream media. A case that demonstrates this assessment was the 2019 court actions brought against Australian Catholic Bishop Pell, which were found to be erroneous after an appeal launched in Victoria's Supreme Court[55]. Throughout this case the leftist media jumped on the opportunity to slander Bishop Pell and the courts initially ruled against Pell even though it was discovered through appeal that he was innocent of all charges and the original decision against Bishop Pell, was without substance, spurious and lacked any evidence to convict beyond reasonable doubt, clearly a miscarriage of justice.

The bias in the courts has been noticed by many Australians, especially when the COVID mandates were challenged. Even Section 51 XXIII(a) of the Australian Constitution was ignored by the Judges even though the section specifically states the illegality of medical mandates. *Australian Constitution 1901*[56].

Any court actions brought against the NWO DID would need to be tactical, with the understanding that any court action would have very little chance of succeeding in stopping

---

calamity threatening the life or well-being of the community; (iv) Any work or service which forms part of normal civil obligations.'

54 See [file], <https://youtu.be/ogYHWg13KCM>, accessed 4 May 2023.
55 See [file], <http://sssw.com.au:8082/downloads/GeorgePell-unfairconviction-GeorgeWeigel.pdf>, and [file],
<http://sssw.com.au:8082/downloads/GeorgePellFalselyConvicted-AndrewBolt.pdf>, both accessed 4 May 2023.

the roll out of the NWO DID, but could publicize the shortcomings to the general public and give businesses pause for thought.

For too long Australian's have been complacent in defending their rights. The price of freedom is vigilance. Australian's should stop trying to fix a system that is broken and proven to be a scam. They must seriously consider whether voting in State and Commonwealth elections is in their, and the Australian community's, best interests. By voting at these elections they are agreeing to the draconian rule that has resulted in the measures that have being implemented to bring in the NWO. They should also consider refusing to pay taxes, instead they could hold their taxes in escrow accounts pending proof of claims from alleged authority and guarantees that their taxes would be used in the best interests of the people. Australians need to understand that aiding and abetting a foreign takeover by paying a private non-entity, the Australian Taxation Office (ATO), with their sweat equity, when the ATO have admitted in Court to be neither part of the Australian Government nor a legal entity[57], is an act of treason.

We must stop feeding the beast with our energy.

I am in touch with a few groups attempting to break away from the *matrix* and form new Common Law Food Communities. The groups in the Ballarat region of Victoria, Australia that I am aware of, and have had some interaction with, are composed of ordinary Australians who have been shaken

---

56 See [file],
 <http://sssw.com.au:8082/commonlaw/docs/AustralianConstitution1901.pdf>
 and *Commonwealth Consolidated Acts* [website],
 <http://classic.austlii.edu.au/au/legis/cth/consol_act/coaca430/s51.html>, both accessed 4 May 2023.

57 See [file], <http://sssw.com.au:8082/downloads/ATO-HighCourtDeterminations.pdf>, and [file],
 <http://sssw.com.au:8082/downloads/ATO-Lawful-v-Unlawful.pdf>, both accessed 4 May 2023, and <https://youtu.be/ZuNBSrER6Z0>, no access anymore 4 May 2023.

out of their despondency due to the genocidal COVID mandates and draconian lock down measures experienced particularly by Victorians under the dictatorial Labour Premier Dan Andrews. Most of the people in these groups have not participated in the mRNA global medical experiment euphemistically referred to as COVID *vaccines*. I think as the NWO DID cage tightens its grip on fiscal resources these groups will provide their own bartering systems and money tokens that could be used to thrive outside of the matrix.

I have attempted through my website[58] to educate and motivate as many of these fearless free- thinking individuals as I can, to learn how to defend themselves using common law techniques such as *conditional acceptance affidavits, private settlement, knowledge of existing common law* so they can defend their property against extortive attempts by zealous brainwashed bureaucrats.

My experience in dealing with alleged government entities such as the Australian Electoral Commission[59] and Fines Victoria[60] has been that the bureaucrats dealing with the public, are at the lowest level in the chain of command and are clueless about the law, even the statutes they claim govern their behaviour. These people are only interested in earning an in-

---

58 See *Common Lore Resources* [website], <http://sssw.com.au:8082/commonlaw>, accessed 4 May 2023.
59 See [file], <http://sssw.com.au:8082/commonlaw/affidavits/SimonsAEC-SignedCertifiedAffidavitCopy.pdf> for my latest Affidavit which has been privately settled, respondent being in default and tacit agreement. An example of how to deal with their presentment fines using Acceptance for Value, [file], <http://sssw.com.au:8082/commonlaw/affidavits/SimonsAEC-A4V.JPG>, both accessed 4 May 2023.
60 See [file], <http://sssw.com.au:8082/commonlaw/affidavits/Speeding_Default-210912-221012-NialKing-signed.png>, my default notice to Constable Niall King agent for Fines Victoria noticing his tacit acquiescence agreement to my Affidavit statements that his claims are unsubstantiated in fact and law. My Affidavit on this matter: [file], <http://sssw.com.au:8082/commonlaw/affidavits/Affidavit-1-SShields-2BendigoCourtToQuashASpeedingFine.pdf>, both accessed 12 April 2023.

come and aren't conscientiously afflicted when harming their fellow Australians. They tend to be delusional cowards, who can be influenced using *Affidavits*[61] where they must respond with their own Affidavit rebutting the points made point for point under penalty of perjury and risking their own personal commercial liability. Once they realize they become personally commercially liable for the harm they may inflict upon their fellow men/women by their actions and cannot hide behind the corporation that employs them, they tend to go quiet and no longer wish to parley. They are not willing to sign their name to their actions because they know their actions are causing harm. They rationalize their behaviour by relying on the defence that they're only following orders, or that they must earn an income to support themselves and their families. These excuses won't save them from legal action.

Humanity will prevail, even though many will voluntarily accept their slavery as have done in the past and are doing by compromising their bodily integrity by participating in the COVID mRNA medical experiment, for the promise of safety and access to privileges. There are many that will freely exchange their God-given freedoms for corporate privileges, selling their God given freedoms for a handful of empty promises. These people will be victims and their life span will be seriously shortened due to their contract with the devil. Those resisting the tyranny will have the courage, entrepreneurial spirit, and innovative mindset to survive and thrive uninhibited by the timid, emotionally and morally compromised majority.

The world is getting a clean out, the wheat is being separated from the chaff, the enemy, in spite of themselves, always

---

61 See [file], <http://sssw.com.au:8082/commonlaw/affidavits/CreatingLawWithAffidavits.pdf>, accessed 12 April 2023.

end up doing God's Will. In the final analysis the meek will inherit the earth and God's Law, freedom, peace and prosperity will reign.

35

Time Traveller

By Ruth Reins

My name is James Johnson, and I am a time traveller. I have travelled to many different time zones and seen many things. My aim is to help mankind when and if it is possible, I do what I can, change the past and improve the future. Yes, I know I shouldn't mess with the past, but sometimes people need a nudge in the right direction.

Here I stand in the year 2023 and, by the looks of my surroundings, it is approaching spring, but alas, I can see already that all is not well. I see a young female, I must approach cautiously, I cannot reveal where I am from. The young girl looks to be in her teens. 'Hello there, what's your name?' She looks at me with fear in her eyes. 'It's okay' I said, 'I am afraid too.'

'Really?' She smiled.

'Yes, this is a bad time. I suppose everyone is scared. Tell me about it?' I enquired. 'You see I have lost my memory and I forget so much of what is going on today.'

'Oh dear,' she replied. 'You don't recall what the authorities have demanded? The poisonous vaccines they make us have? Those of us who refuse will not be allowed to have any food, because the vaccine will become mandatory. We will be required to carry a digital identification that states your vaccine status amongst other data. Hence, if we are not up to date with our toxic vaccines, which are given every three months, we are to be denied food. We could be arrested and put into camps as terrorists.'

'I see.' I thought a moment and replied. 'I know in my heart that you will survive. People will find a way to put an end to all this. Please be strong and do not fear.' She smiled and spoke.

'I hope so, sir, I really do.'

'Have faith, I must go now, bye my friend; chin up.'

I returned quickly to my Time Machine, I pondered on the thought that I know it works out because I am here and I exist! I thought for a while and I finally came to a decision to make sure this situation never occurs. I will travel back further to around the turn of the 21st century. Yes 2007 sounds perfect. I will see if I can affect the outcome.

I ventured outside into 2007 and all around me looked normal. Unlike the empty streets of 2023, this street was all hustle and bustle. A grand sight to my eyes indeed. Ah there is a sign, let me read it. 'Welcome to County Kent.' I read out loud. Yes, I thought, the garden of Eden or something like that if my memory serves me. I smiled and thought I do hope so. It will be, if I have anything to do with it. I see a young couple approaching in the distance. Soon they were close. 'Hello there, can you possibly help me?'

'What's the matter, mate?' The man replied.

'Can I trust you sir?' I asked calmly.

'It depends, are you on the run mate?'

'No, no.' I laughed 'but it's imperative you believe me, I'm really not mad although what I am about to tell you may seem mad, it is entirely the truth.' I took a long deep breath and said 'Here goes, I am a time traveller and I come from the future. I have come to warn you of the dangers you will have to face in your lifetime. It will begin in late 2019 and you will need a plan to thwart this looming danger, otherwise it will be the end of all freedom and possibly all humankind.' I related what the young girl had informed me in the year 2023 and, when I had finished my story, I could tell they were only half listening. 'Look' I said impatiently I can take you forward in time and you will see for yourselves. Then will you organise a resistance movement please?'

'Wow, oh wow, this is amazing, I guess I could,' he said voice trailing off with a look of total disbelief on his young face.

'Don't worry I will bring you back safe and sound.'

'I am definitely coming' said the young woman, 'I am a back bencher, an independent party MP and I am in a position to get a team to help me. If I can convince them, that is. My name is Sophie Cartwright-Brown and this is Tom Cartwright-Brown my husband.'

'My name is James Johnson. What are we waiting for? Let's go, it will be a little tight inside the machine, but it only takes a minute or so.'

We arrived at our destination - the year 2023. On stepping from the machine the couple observed their surroundings.

'Where is everyone?' they both chorused.

'I warned you times are much harder now. Look there is a police officer coming towards us, hurry let's move now.'

'Why, he may be able to help?'

'No, no they are a part of the establishment, I told you about the girl I met. We have to find someone we can talk to.'

'Look there's a school over there, lots of people waiting in cars.' Tom said whilst pointing across the road. Sophie headed across the road towards a couple of young women.

'Hello ladies how are you?' she began.

'How do you think we are?' one of them replied. 'I am totally sick to death of it all. Do you know they are all crazy these days trying to get our kids to change gender? It is totally confusing our poor kids, I'm going to take Jenny out of school. I will teach her myself.'

'Yes I agree' said another 'You know they're going to make all our kids have a mRNA vaccine. You know Kerry's child Elaine died after having one, so I won't let our Sam have one. Must go, the kids are coming.'

'Have you heard enough yet?' I asked.

'Oh, my yes, don't worry, I will put a stop to this. I have a good idea what to do and I promise I will do it. I have a contact. I will talk to him and we will formulate a plan of action. Thank you, James, can we go now please?'

I turned back the clock to 2007 and dropped the young couple back home. 'Can you stay and talk to some people I know?' asked Sophie.

'I am sorry,' I replied 'I have to go home, good luck with your conquest.' I smiled and said: 'I know you will win because I am from the future, farewell my friends.' With a wave of my hand I was gone.

36

Davos Speech Codes—The Grammar of Digital Slavery

By Dominic Berry

The World Economic Forum (WEF) is discussing a 'Great Reset' whereby, a range of global organizations intend to solve world problems which are 'too big for governments or private industry to solve on their own'. Between them, they hope to create global government, mass monitoring individual behaviour and regulating each of us toward global objectives. Opponents notice how centrally controlled these systems are, and the lack of any means of influencing them, or of holding controllers accountable if they abuse their powers. Accordingly, they refer to it by their own term, 'Digital Slavery'.

If your awareness of the world is taught by mainstream media, you might well wonder what to make of this. What you see on television and read in most newspapers is a pattern of struggles between one country and another or internal controversies between a liberal left and a conservative right. A world of nations and factions, so to speak. Very few people are aware there is an effort to create a global government. One might dismiss the whole thing as conspiracy theory, except that there is nothing really secret about it. Klaus Schwab, Chairman of the WEF, has published several books explaining strategies and tactics for such a transformation. Moreover, the WEF stages public talks at Davos in Switzerland, attended by Presidents of China and the USA, global organizations like the United Nations and the World Health Organization, and CEOs of global companies like Google and Goldman-Sachs. There, they nominate the most urgent problems of the world, such as global warming, epidemics, and terrorism. They propose a wide array of technological solutions which none of us have ever heard of; digital money, automated markets, 15-minute cities and so on. But when we look at the enormous lists of very rich, very powerful people attending and the sheer scope of their influence, it might be wise to pay attention to what the people at Davos are saying.

I do not know more than anybody else about technology or its effects on society. It has become fashionable for everyone on the internet to spontaneously become expert on geopolitics, and then a week later, decide they are analysts of international law, before suddenly deciding to specialize as epidemiologists. I do not. I am a humble English teacher who, like you, knows a little bit of all these issues, but probably not enough. Nevertheless, I do feel competent to say something, about a subtle, but very odd feature of the Davos talks which is deeply concerning to me: Their grammar.

Listening, I was struck by regulated patterns of grammar, adopted by all speakers on any of their various topics. It is easy to miss these patterns if you aren't looking for them, because everyone is speaking in polite English. Nevertheless, if we watch, these rules can be observed in almost all Davos speeches and discussions. In this essay, I will analyse their language, to discern implicit assumptions, worthy of explicit critique, before suggesting how we might respond.

To begin with, there are several grammatical tense formations which are not only absent, but harmfully neglected. To take one example, there is a minimal use of the conditional tense to consider what 'might', or 'could' happen. Every statement is given using confident, modal verbs, describing what we 'should do' or, what 'ought to happen', or indeed what we 'have to do' and 'what must happen' and then finally, the simple future tense, stating flatly 'what we are going to do' and 'what we will do'. Mr Schwab himself, artfully progresses from one tense to the other, so that the talk transforms, from a proposal to do something ('We have to combat terrorism',) into an unavoidable necessity ('We must prepare for an angrier world'), so that when we finally, hear him using the simple future tense, ('You will own nothing and be happy',) what had introduced itself as mere proposition has transformed into an expansive prophecy.

Besides the hypnotic way these suggestions become certainties, we should remember that future predictions normally involve several steps which this selective use of grammar removes from the talks. Let us consider these steps, in rough order: We ought to assess the range of our available choices; we should then consider the likely costs and benefits of each; we then might observe a principle for deciding among them. Only then do we decide what we ought to do. And even after that, we still must acknowledge that things might not go according to plan. Of course, there are no fixed rules in English that say we have to talk about the future this way, but people who say they are going to take radical action without saying why, aren't normally trusted, either in public or in private life. It isn't normal behaviour. Anyone who really wants to be trusted, will observe the kind of common-sense steps observed since the days of Aristotle.

Davos speakers don't do any of this: they describe a perceived problem. Then they insist that it absolutely must be solved; then they present a radical solution made possible by new technology; then the host thanks them and everybody claps. As I say, I'm not an expert in any of the crises they are discussing, nor the technologies they present, but I will say in perfect confidence as an English teacher, that such patterns of speech don't allow for much critical thinking.

To take oil pollution as one example, we have a wide range of options to respond to that. To pick a few, we could start substituting hemp for plastic, or encourage traditional craft methods or, (here's an idea,) we could find out who has bought up all the patents on substitutes for crude oil and hold them accountable.

To choose from among these, we could adopt the principle that those who have the most freedom to act, and those who would suffer the least, should be the first to make changes in their lifestyles. So, from the options listed, we ought to go to the patent offices and call time on the predatory patents, because by happy accident, those who have the greatest freedom to act are those global corporations who own those patents. And by happier accident, they are rich enough not to suffer very much by acting. And by even happier accident again, these are the very people gathering right there at Davos. So, one might hope they could sort this out between themselves in an afternoon.

But that is not the kind of solution or criteria they propose. No. They propose solutions like requiring everyone to live in '20-minute towns', where everything they need will be within twenty minutes' walking or cycling distance of their homes. And not own cars. Why this solution? Because anything else is destroying the ecology. And why are the other solutions not better? Why do the elites who attend Davos get to keep their cars and their yachts and their private jets and create a million times more carbon emissions than normal people do? I don't know. And neither do the Davos people, because they haven't discussed this. Maybe you can talk about that with your local '20-minute' town representative.

Funnily enough, all strategies suggested at Davos require surveillance of almost everyone in the world and demand a sacrifice of freedoms and resources by exactly those people who are least free and most poor, while placing no constraints on the kind of people who are inventing what they like to call, 'what we need'. And I think this explains the grammar of their solution making, because it removes logic or evidence from the conversation, as they explain the need for predetermined solutions.

It also draws attention to the consistent use of the first-person, 'we'. When people like the Presidents and Prime Ministers use 'we', they might be referring to the people of the world or their own countries. When leaders of global organizations like the UN say 'we' they might be referring to their stated mission as an NPO, or they might be empire building. When CEOs of banks and technology corporations use 'we', they probably aren't representing inhabitants of the Congo or the Amazon Basin. Effectively, it acts like the royal 'we' used by English monarchs. Whatever this 'we' might be, it creates a kind of lacuna, a blind spot in their communication, discretely hiding away exactly those aspects of their plans which would concern the wider population the most, which is who is likely to benefit from these changes and who is likely to suffer. The grammar of Davos speech evaporates these kinds of question.

It accepts as unspoken terms of parlance, that all solutions arrived at will involve the richest and most powerful people having more money and more power.

But there are other sections of analysis which are conspicuously absent: a refusal to examine causes. In Davos talks, the present is described in terms of our pervasive danger and uncertainty. Mr. Schwab refers to 'our disintegrated world', as if it had been much more integrated in the past and urgently needs to be re-integrated. The future, by contrast, is described as a place of reassuring order, where all our problems will be solved by the deployment of new technologies. Many, if not most of the problems they hope to solve; epidemics, pollution, or global warming, are the unexpected side effects of technology and globalization. So, it's a little odd that the only solutions they are presenting are globally deployed technologies. As I say, I'm just an English teacher, and maybe I lack some special insight, but as I watch them, I start to feel I'm witnessing very polite, very professional people, describing how they are going to extinguish lots of fires using petrol. But this unwillingness to examine the causes of problems leans on another grammatical curiosity in play: the absence of the past tense.

Davos speakers seem constrained to talk in the present tense, when they describe problems and the future tense, when they describe solutions. But if we look at similar conferences like TED Talks or the US Congress, or addresses to the Oxford Union, we people are using all kinds of past tenses; past simple, past perfect or past continuous. We are, as it were, spoiled for choice. So why would Davos speakers want to embrace forgetfulness in their speech forms?

In a way, it might be necessary to their credibility, because they have a regular recent history of making very poor short-term predictions. Consider US Senator Al Gore, (a noted Davos speaker,) who declared in 2009 'a 75% chance that the entire north polar ice cap, during some of the summer months, could be completely ice-free within the next five to seven years.' 2014 and 2016 have come and gone, and not only is the ice cap still appreciably large and cold, but in Davos 2023, he is still making eloquent prophecies of doom. I am not a scientist, and I will happily allow that his logic and evidence were good, and we were all just very lucky, but I do believe scientific models should be adjusted when their predictions are disproven and that people like Mister Gore should acknowledge when they were wrong.

Going a little further back to my childhood fifty years ago, I distinctly remember worries about an impending ice age and the terrible effects that that might have. If the predictions have changed from cold to hot in fifty years, who knows what people will be predicting in another fifty years. Of course, climate change is hotly contested, and I am not a climatologist, so I don't ask anyone to abandon their belief in global warming. I only wish we could all notice what people are saying, and compare it with what they said in the past, before we accept them as reliable oracles of the future.

But we can see that the amnesia of Davos is actually much more acute than this, when we compare one talk with another. One talk says that in the developing countries, people aren't having enough children, and they anticipate a demographic time bomb. They propose a borderless world, where anyone can live anywhere. In the next talk, we hear that there are too many people on the planet, and we need to control our carbon footprint to reduce greenhouse gasses. They propose we constrain movement radically with vaccine passports and, yes, 20-minute towns. In the next talk after that, we hear we have to monitor and control everybody's movement with vaccine passports to stop any epidemic ever happening again. Quite besides the 'Henny Penny' unreliability of their analyses, and the impossible 'King Canute' manner of their solutions, I keep thinking things like, 'How are we going to let immigration solve demographic problems, without creating the perfect conditions of an epidemic?' and 'If the epidemics don't sort out the population problem, surely the demographic time bomb will finish the job?'. Each problem seems to be a solution for one of the other problems. I never see this kind of reflection happening among the speakers. They have technology and they do not want their bright future plans to lose their lustre under the shadow of the past.

But there is a more general problem with their disdain for the use of past tense formations. It demonstrates they would much rather decide what they want and how they are going to get it, than learn from history what is wise or good. And so, for all their bold words about 'progress', 'democracy', or 'the rule of law', we can see in rules of their underlying grammar, that they do not want to find the best answers, they are only trying to rationalize decisions which they have already made. If the lessons of history helped their case, I expect they would be using them, and as they are not using them, it is fair to surmise that they have not found any lessons from history which actually do encourage them. This is what makes the absence of a past tense truly ominous.

Inasmuch as conditional tenses and modal verbs help us to observe, compare and prioritize our freedoms, past tenses allow us to learn from our mistakes and to analyse our problems, not just as accidental facts, but as the results of ongoing events. Questions like 'What used to happen?' 'What has been happening?' and 'What is always happening?', collectively compel us to recognize what we ought to know should never happen again, and that life is often messy, and that sometimes, even very good plans go horribly wrong and especially, that if we do not learn from history, we will likely have to learn its terrible lessons again.

Those of us who do not attend Davos have no problem with past tenses. I can certainly talk to my family or friends about the world in the present tense which are fairly critical: 'Replacing the nation state with global government? That might be complicated. All my legal rights, democratic rights and human rights are provided to me by a nation state. None of them are provided by corporations. I think the biggest threat to these rights is those global corporations. I'm rather worried about their influence on our governments through lobby funding. Are any of the Davos speakers speaking about that?'.

So, it is definitely possible to think critically in the present tense. But from experience, we can say much more interesting things using past tense. My father, who always read more history than I do, might say, 'What you're describing is an over-arching government, and it's entering into competition for power with separate national governments and their own ventures?' and I would say, 'Yes, something like that. It's as if there is an emerging competition for power between the national scale and power at the global scale', and he might say, 'Well we had something like that when the Protestants wanted to break free from the Catholic Roman Church', and I might ask, 'What was the result of that? Wasn't that when the Spanish Inquisition and all the witch burnings happened?', and he might say, 'Oh yes, but it was a bit more than that. It was all over Christendom. Thirty years of warfare. Catholics and Protestants massacring each other by turns in tens of thousands. And it was all dressed up in religious language, killing each other in the name of 'God, goodness and everything we hold dear'. And it was very ungodly. Trust me, you really might want to keep an eye on this'.

And so finally, I think I should ask: What would be a better solution to all the world's problems than a Great Reset? And what should we do to prevent the Digital Slavery which might be the horrible result of all these Davos devised 'solutions'? As I say, I am a humble English teacher, and I do not know the answers to all the world's problems, nor do I know very much about the technologies being vaunted by Davos to solve them. But I am always happy to give advice on grammar. I recommend the use of conditional tense formations, as in 'what might be happening', to recognise both the many possibilities around us and our possible ignorance of the whole story. These not only protect our sanity, but they reveal the full range of our freedoms in responding to the challenges and opportunities we meet. I recommend a cautious understanding of the first-person 'we' when the person speaking has arrived in a private jet and is recommending we give up cars and stick to bicycles from now on. And we ought to pay particular attention to how people remember the past, before we listen to their predictions of the future. These little tricks will help you live a safer, happier life and might be all that you need to protect you from Davos.

37

Where We Are and How to Resist and Fight Back

By David Lawrenson

Today, many respected senior scientists, including professors of medicine, epidemiology, physics and from other disciplines are *still* banned from talking openly, engaging in debate and are frequently de-platformed and threatened with unemployment if they dare discuss the actual real science on Covid 'lockdowns' or the trail of destruction of the experimental gene therapies, (cleverly branded as 'vaccines'). The same goes for the real science around new hobgoblins such as 'global warming'. For these banned experts, censorship is very much *not over*.

One such expert who remains targeted and banned from many mainstream and online media is leading statistics expert, Professor Norman Fenton[62]. Others include leading oncologist Professor Angus Dalgleish and Professor of Medicine, Jay Bhattacharya.

This censorship worries me, and I feel it ought to worry other people. Indeed, the banning of free speech in many countries, is even being legislated for. In the EU it already has been via their Digital Services Act. The EU are effectively saying, 'So, if Elon Musk won't do it, we will instead legislate to ban free speech or any so called "disinformation" we don't like'. The UK had similar plans to ban free speech via the Online Harms Bill, as do many other jurisdictions.

But as if that was not bad enough, I must then point out this is about far more than 'just Covid', which is why I believe *the purpose* behind what was clearly a lab-generated pathogen *was always much deeper—and had two main objectives*:

The first objective

The first objective was to see if the propaganda techniques first used by the Nazis and the Soviets could be used on an even grander scale.

---

62 David Marks, 'Forum Conversation: Norman Fenton, On The Revelations of Pandemic Data', 21 November 2022, *Robert W Malone MD, MS* [website], <https://rwmalonemd.substack.com/p/forum-conversation-norman-fenton>, accessed 8 April 2023. This links to an interview with Professor Norman Fenton, one of the UK's leading statisticians and risk management experts, published in Nov 2021. It shows, using detailed statistical analysis, that
a) the injected are getting Covid more often than the non-injected and
b) the injected are suffering a higher death and hospitalisation rate too.
He uses UK and German data to show this. Data from Germany is especially useful because
a) the data is high quality and
b) in Germany, the eastern states had a far lower rate of 'vaccine' take-up than western states.
The analysis shows the lowly injected eastern states also had a far lower rate of Covid infection, hospitalisation, death, but also fewer excess deaths from all diseases in general over the last two years since the 'vaccination' roll out started.

So, what came under the heading of this first objective? And what did those controlling this want to test and to see?

They wanted to look at a number of things.

They wanted to see if people could really be coerced by enough wall-to-wall mass 'news' and panic-spreading psy-op techniques to get them to agree to be injected multiple times to 'protect themselves' against what for most people amounted to nothing more than a bad cold or seasonal flu. (Stanford University estimated across 32 studies, the median infection fatality rate of COVID-19 was 0.035% for people aged 0-59 years. 95% of those who succumbed had multiple existing co-morbidities.[63])

Could people really be persuaded to take a risky experimental gene therapy treatment in exchange for being allowed to carry on with their 'normal life'? Of course, it was kept quiet from people that the makers of the gene therapies/'vaccines' refuse to pay for any damages resulting from that treatment, out of the massive profits generated for them by tens of billions of pounds of free taxpayer-funded marketing. I wonder why this important aspect was kept so quiet from the public.

Could people really be persuaded to ignore the 1.5million (as of October 2022) cases of Covid 'vaccine' injuries, reported by 460,000 people that have already been listed on the UK government's Yellow Card scheme? And then there is the small matter of the 2,600 deaths? (These figures are thought

---

[63] 'Age-stratified infection fatality rate of COVID-19 in the non-elderly informed from pre-vaccination national seroprevalence studies', *medRxiv* [website], <https://medrxiv.org/content/10.1101/2022.10.11.22280963v1>, accessed 8 April 2023. Imperial College and Professor Neil Ferguson estimated the infection fatalist rate (IFR) at 0.9% in March 2020, giving 510k U.K. deaths and 2.2m US deaths. This was discredited as nonsense and a massive over-statement as early as April 2020. More recently, Professor Jon Ioannidis et al of Stanford University estimated across 32 studies, the median IFR of COVID-19 was 0.035% for people aged 0-59 years and 0.501% for those aged 60-69.

to be between 1% and 10% of the true casualty rates based on surveys in the US and Japan where similar reporting systems are in place).

Could people later be persuaded to ignore the Covid 'vaccines' role in suppressing peoples' immune systems which has led to excess deaths from all causes currently running at between 15% and 30% above the five-year average in the most 'vaccinated' countries?

Could people be persuaded to ignore the significant falls in the birth rate ever since the 'vaccines' were first rolled out? Or the rises in miscarriages?

The answer to all these questions was 'Yes'. With enough wall-to-wall propaganda and monies spent, this could all be done.

None of this should be a surprise because these sorts of psy-op techniques were investigated fully in the conformity and obedience experiments conducted in the 1960s by Asch and Milgram respectively. Their work was an attempt to see if the mind control used by the Nazis and Soviets could be understood and explained in a test setting. They showed how easily people could be persuaded to conform and to obey authority figures. These studies should be familiar to anyone who has studied GCSE level psychology, though sadly many seem to be unaware when these techniques were being practiced on them, as they were starting in March 2020.

The second and main objectives

The second and main objectives were more long term and more insidious still, which is why the 'Covid is over' narrative is so misplaced.

The main longer-term objective is to massively increase digital surveillance to the same level that's now the 'New Normal' in China.

And so, Covid restrictions and the 'vaccines' were both

used as a tool to get populations familiar with accepting surveillance through the widespread use of things like QR codes and health passports to either admit (or refuse) entry to restaurants, bars, concerts, hospitals, and other places, at the whim of governments. This is because the QR codes and test and trace systems used in Covid restrictions are fully intended to form the basis for this more extended digital surveillance.

To fully implement surveillance though would require the roll out of something called central bank digital currencies (CBDCs). These allow governments to control and monitor what people spend their money on and where they spend it. Even more powerful.

So, I predict the next step in this process will be the stated 'need' to control people's carbon footprint. This, in itself, is a product of the scare of the 'climate-aggeddon' hobgoblin—which is that climate warming is supposedly caused mostly by carbon dioxide increases and hence mostly the fault of humans.

I expect the central bank digital currencies will initially be offered to the poor in exchange for debt relief and/or as a condition of receiving things like universal credit.

Later, it will be offered more widely to other income groups at such time as the next accidental (or planned) financial crisis occurs. The message here will be: 'Sorry that your building society has gone bust, but here is a new CBDC account with the same amount in it'. As of November 2022, ten countries have already got CBDCs live.

The difference with the CBDCs and a normal bank account is that with CBDCs credits can be awarded to control people by rewarding low carbon spends and applying penalties for high carbon spends.

For the poor, credits might be set so they can be used only on certain items and be limited in time (thus also controlling the level of aggregate demand in the economy in real time). Banning the use of credits for items like alcohol, cigarettes, fast food and gambling would find favour with those not on benefits who think all the poor are scroungers and will be sold heavily as a 'useful feature'.

But there are other uses too. So, some examples:

➢ Too much meat consumption will mean your digital account will prevent you buying any more.
➢ Too much travelling in your car and your digital account will prevent you from buying petrol, or if you have a connected-up electric car, it just won't start.
➢ Too much foreign travel and you won't be able to buy any more flights.

But it goes further still:

➢ Publish something deemed to be 'misinformation' online in breach of the Online Harms Act (or its successors) and you can expect a fine on your CBDC account as well as your social media account possibly being closed.
➢ Attend a rally that the ruling powers don't like under new laws and you could be fined via your CBDC account or have your movement curtailed. (This has already happened in Canada).
➢ Finally, on the health front, credits on CBDC accounts will be given for 'grade A' people who keep their injections up to date and penalties for those who don't.

If this all sounds far-fetched or a 'conspiracy theory', then I would direct people to consider that a lot of what has happened already since March 2020 was very much predicted in the book, *The Great Reset*, by the leader of the World Economic Forum and intellectual guru of the global elite, Klaus Schwab. Indeed, what has happened in the last three years would, back in January 2020, be surely described by any sane person as a 'conspiracy theory'.

The future sequence of events I have described here is also covered and predicted in the same book in great detail. Mr. Schwab thinks this digital prison world is a perfect world, in which 'people will own nothing, but they will be happy'. That is one of his key quotes. This ought to beg the question, if the masses own nothing, then who will own things in Mr. Schwab's brave new world?

Klaus Schwab regularly meets the world's government leaders at all the key summits, including most recently at an evening event just after the recent G20.

We should all ask, 'Why is he there and why does he matter so much to the world's leaders?' Herr Schwab has openly boasted about his penetration of the world's governments many times, including most stridently in a speech in 2017.[64]

If people are sceptical of what I have stated here, I would plead with them to read Mr. Schwab's books or at least read the reviews.

We need to wake up—and very fast.

So, what can be done?

➢ We need to do our own research, (not on the controlled Google please, you won't find much there—you could try the 'Brave' search engine). Or ask already 'awake' people where they go to get the real science from proper senior scientists, economists, engineers, and medics.

➢ We need to stop complying with obviously pointless man-

---

[64] HAF, 'Klaus Schwab Brags About Controlling Western Governments', *Humans Are Free* [website], <https://humansbefree.com/2022/01/klaus-schwab-brags-about-controlling-western-governments.html>, accessed 8 April 2023.

dates like face nappy rules and the myriad dumb strictures that are still in place restricting freedom.

➢ We need to actively campaign for changes to break up the unaccountable and undemocratic global control systems that exist in health in which, for example the regulatory body for drugs in the UK, the MHRA, is 86% funded by drug manufacturers and staffed entirely by former senior employees of the same, via a revolving door.

➢ We need to change the World Health Organisation so it is no longer funded by Big Pharma. (Currently their third biggest funder is not a country, it is an individual—'vaccine' investor, Bill Gates). The solutions to the problems of the poor in the world lie much more in better food, clean water and sanitation, not failed drugs and vaccines.

➢ We need to demand that social media firms be forced to allow free speech and payment system organisations be banned from cutting off payment mechanisms or censoring people just because they don't like their validly held opinions. If it is legal to say something in the real world, it should be legal to say it online too, even if it is wrong and even if it is offensive.

➢ The activities of Newsguard and the British Board of Film Censors, wherein they choke off advertising revenue to any site that fights against the globalist agenda by labelling them as 'disinformation' or 'adult sites' must be stopped. By doing this, they stop commercial companies advertising with the likes of free speech sites like GB News, TCW Defending Freedom and Daily Sceptics. Both Newsguard and BBFC have, like FullFact, FactCheck, Wikipedia and Facebook, all got shady globalist agenda parentage and backers.

➢ We must demand a proper investigation of the harms done by the so-called non-pharmaceutical interventions such as Stay at Home orders and face nappy mandates. We must demand a full and open investigation of the harms done to both adults and children by Covid 'vaccines' and by the mandates for these 'vaccines'. We must not allow the events to be 'memory holed', (to borrow from Orwell's 1984), and we must absolutely refuse to 'just move on' as though nothing happened.

➢ We must demand that every health worker, every care worker and every other worker in the UK (and worldwide) who was forced or coerced out of their job because they refused to get the so called 'vaccine' is compensated in full for lost earnings and hurt.

➢ We must stop complying with all testing and tracing systems and get back to real science and basic, old-fashioned knowledge which is, if you are ill, you stay home and don't see old people. If you are well, you get on with your life.

➢ We need to start using cash more, we need to only trade with organisations that accept cash and refuse to give our money to those that don't.

If we don't do all these things, we really are heading straight to the digital slavery system that Schwab and his ilk want.

38

Box Clever

By U Canrun

We are all being led into a world we didn't ask for in the name of health, climate, safety and so on.

At some point you will have to reject aspects of this 'evolving' world and in the process you stand to lose functionality.

For example: Banks and ATMs are disappearing so you can't just pop down to access your money so easily anymore and now to log into some banks on a PC it's impossible without pressing and holding your thumb on your phone. A secret password hidden in your head is not enough anymore. Two step identification and device authorisation lead into further control, all in the name of protection.

This is to protect you from fraud of course. Meanwhile you are being forced onto your phone more and more. Soon your phone will be you ... and you will be no-one without it.

As well as control brought in by corporate banks and businesses your freedom of movement will eventually be trimmed down or controlled.

Each step is carefully planned so the net closes around you.

I will be very surprised if this 'great-reset' with financial reset, health-pass/digital-ID and climate lockdown malarkey doesn't happen.

Armed with this realisation, what will you do if you reject dodgy vaccines, reject a digital-ID, geofencing and CBDC and all the other new things on the horizon?

If you accept you are going to make a stand and reject these things you never asked for then you can move on to making your plans.

You can start by throwing your television in the skip, along with your satellite dish or whatever else you use to connect to your TV. Like it or not, TV pollutes your mind and is one of the biggest tools of control.

Do not wear a smart watch and never put pods in your ears again.

Run all devices through a VPN [virtual private network].

You have to cut the surveillance feed off for great chunks of the day and night.

Spend as much time of the day as you can in airplane mode, when you are about to meet friends switch wifi, data and bluetooth off. Ask them to do the same if they want to talk about personal matters. Or simply say you can't talk about it now. Remember it's all feed, key-words and associations, who you were with and where you were.

Same at night and definitelywhen you sleep, switch it off.

Pull the router out the wall at night and even odd times through the day.

Tape your camera on your devices.

Try to understand that nothing is private if you have devices around you, including your friends' device, even in a crowd.

Go for walks when you need to discuss family matters or financial stuff; don't take any devices and walk on roads without surveillance and street light poles.

I don't live in UK anymore but was there in December

2022 again and saw the frightening reality of these new street poles going in everywhere, even in remote Wales. Governments are spending a lot of money to eventually control your movement and use of the vehicle you bought on the roads you paid for in the name of carbon emissions. There are many other measures that can be implemented to make for a healthier environment, and we were doing very well with implementing these over the last few years.

The ultimate solution, if you have no faith in your fellow people anymore, is to sell-up or rent and move to a developing country. Even if only temporarily. With places like UK and EU and most Westernised countries you are likely not to win. The governments of these countries probably don't want you anyway as you are defiant and may one day stand in the way of their totalitarian goals.

The country I've moved to has global goals too but the government is so utterly useless at anything but stealing. Who would have wanted to live in a country like that three years ago?! Now it's a great selling point. Plus, the people are mistrusting of their own government and the banks, they accept the value of cash but prefer presenting their wealth in cattle and goats.

Running is not cool but having good plans in place is, at the end of the day true survival is down to the individual. Remember that we are likely in a window on movement that could be closing soon.

In reality, you want to be a real prepper with rural land to hand and an arsenal of weapons to defend your family and community against hungry mobs. That's a worst case scenario but those of us who reject deceitful change are being pushed into a corner. Everyone has their breaking point and while this whole operation is no-doubt being controlled and steered you and I have no real idea of where we are being led and if it fails you could be left a little stranded, and in a position where you would need to be more self-reliant. Being a little prepared for that wouldn't hurt.

George Orwell's book *1984* is worth another read, with what's supposedly going on in Ukraine, EU asylum seekers, our schools, MSM news and even our distant history, all is not what it seems and basically now is a time for taking stock and being clever.

To me the old way of life (accumulation and acquisition) with work and so on are now no longer so important. Most of it just feeds the beast. Having talks with close ones and putting markers out like forced acceptance of vaccines, digital-ID, geofencing, CBDC etc. as triggers for action are now the important issues.

It's a strange war we're in. It is all very confusing as the attack is personal with psyop-driven choices, consequences, and freedom curtailment on top of lies while always keeping the real enemy in the dark and confusing us. We have grown too reliant on a tax-paid-untrustworthy-representative to take care of our safety for us. This is a big thing to change and seeing it all through is the challenge.

Best of luck for the days ahead and keep making the right choices.

39

Steps Towards a Brighter Future

By Alan Kay

While Plato's allegory of the cave[65] is cited as an eternal story of the human condition, it's set to become a whole lot less relevant to the human story because of the trauma experienced by the human collective in the past three years. Within it there are two types of people, 'cave dwellers' and 'cave leavers'. In short, the dwellers stubbornly refuse to give a fair hearing to the leavers' claims of a big bright beautiful world outside the confines of the cave. In recent times, this divide could be seen between many of those complying with the digital enslavement agenda and those resistant to it. Despite a myriad of approaches being employed by the resisters, including rallies, postcard campaigns, speaking truth here there and everywhere and more, most of the compliers did not find the resisters messages and actions compelling.

---

[65] The Allegory of the Cave, or Plato's Cave, is an allegory presented by the Greek philosopher Plato in his work *Republic* (514a–520a) about the nature of reality and how our perceptions can deceive us. It's main message is that knowledge gained through the senses is not necessarily true knowledge, and that true knowledge can only be attained through philosophical reasoning.

However, there's something very powerful about trauma, because it can forever change you. And as the collective endures trauma together, it is set to be transformed collectively.

Since 2020, many resisters have processed the agenda with a whole host of negative emotions, particularly anger. On the surface that may seem like a negative aspect, however, anger can help people move away from complacency and arm them with courage to take the next step. As the threat of digital enslavement looms over us all, it is crunch time for us humans. Can we unify and preserve our freedom? Well, if we are to remain human, we are going to have to. And in a way, we all know what the next steps are. We have to unify with other resisters, and reach the hearts and minds of the resisters.

With human freedom at risk of being replaced by the illusion of safety there is so much to be negative about. Digital ID, if accepted, could pave the way for CBDCs and before long most people will be trapped into a system they may never break free from. However, the anti-human agenda we all face now, can provide us with the trauma we need, to get angry enough, to take decisive action to co-create a better tomorrow, where our freedoms are protected from the prying eyes of bad actors.

Plato's allegory of the cave offered little hope for humanity. But now there is hope, because the resisters must change the story forever. In Plato's allegory the cave dwellers turned a blind eye to the truth. Similarly, today, the compliers have turned away from truth. And that's despite being exposed to a barrage of memes, video clips, comments and more online and various actions taken offline, from the resisters.

It is easy to view the digital enslavement agenda through a depressing lens, one where hope is all but lost in terms of preventing it from taking shape. But that need not be the story, because the resisters powerfully possess tools that in actuality make succeeding, a likely outcome. Of significance, smartphones, and instant messaging apps enable everyone involved to share the evolving story in real time like never before in human history. So too, computers enable resisters in particular to make memes and movies as well as create materials to focus minds on actions that will make the difference.

In the story of David and Goliath, many people focus on the sheer size of Goliath compared to David and how surprising it was that David was victorious. But for a few, their reading of the story differs in that it was always a foregone conclusion in David's favour because Goliath was cited as being half-blind as well as clumsy. So, while David in terms of size paled in comparison to Goliath, it was the latter who was most vulnerable. Right now, both the resisters and the compliers may seem vulnerable to the digital enslavement agenda, but in actuality it is the bad actors pushing this anti-human agenda who are most vulnerable. The collective stands on the precipice of ending the so-called eternal story of the human condition, where one group of humanity turns away from truth and the other towards it.

We are living through transformational times, but the threat of digital enslavement need not be viewed as something that could break us. Instead, it can be the making of us. We can create a new eternal story of the human condition, and it can be fuelled by the trauma we are all experiencing now and will experience. We can do it; we can use our collective anger to take the steps towards a brighter future. Let's resist digital enslavement as one and put the anti-human bad actors pushing it to the sword once and for all.

40

God Knew

A True Story
By Lily

A smallholding in the country, a place to hide Christians, an underground church, a small home-educating co-op, a community of people working together towards a common vision. Many people have thought about doing this since the events in March 2020 played out, but God whispered them into my heart more than a year before.

It was in 2017 that my husband and I decided to take our large family from the suburbs to the hidden beauty of the English countryside. It was another two years before we got there. During that two years God enlarged my vision. At first, we just wanted a big house in the country for our children to spread their wings, but as time progressed God showed us a specific property; it was there that the vision took hold. On that first visit I didn't just see empty barns and fields left to go to seed, I saw people working together, children learning together, areas for animals and vegetable gardens. At first, I thought I just had a vivid imagination but then God stepped in and showered us with signs, signs that showed us that this was the house He had planned for us. Miraculously, the owners of the property held the house whilst we waited for our home to sell. They turned down offer after offer, continually telling us they thought we were the right people for the house and they would wait. It was nearly a year and a half before we found a buyer. During that time, we met people hundreds of miles away who had just visited the tiny hamlet we would be moving to. We met people who were friends with the church elder at the church we planned to attend. We were given items that could only be used for that specific house. Each sign was a constant reminder that we were to wait and trust. To some they may have been coincidences, but to us they were crumbs of bread leading us home.

Over a year later we finally found a buyer and moved into our smallholding. We had no idea what we were doing but God sent us numerous experts to start us off on our journey. He sent us hen houses, pig arcs, 12 chickens, a pregnant cow and three pigs, all without us even asking. We were constantly amazed and yet had conviction that we must say yes and prepare this place, for what, we did not yet know.

March 2020 came round and lockdowns hit. The pieces of the puzzle started to fall into place. We saw the need for our cow, as we offered milk to all our neighbours. We had eggs to sell at the bottom of the drive and sausages in the freezer to sell to friends when they visited to buy 'essential food'. We had an ever-growing vegetable garden where we were able to gather for outdoor learning, God had thought of everything. We had already found a group of sceptical home-educating friends and it was with them that we worshipped God each Sunday.

Our children often reminded me during those lockdown days that we were simply living out all that God had prepared us for. Lockdowns as we all know, were awful. I was constantly banging the drum on social media that this wasn't right, only to be shouted down by family who thought they knew better. On the other hand, lockdowns were amazing because it was then that we saw what God was doing. He was calling us to share all that He had given us, to feed those in need, be a refuge for the lonely and offer hope that God was in control.

I say all this, not to boast that we were ready, but to help us all remember that God knew. Long before the World Economic Forum were planning Agenda 2030, God was planning our lives, He was preparing us to do the work He had planned for us. He always positions each of us perfectly in order that we might be His hands, His feet and His voice.

My family are here to provide hospitality and love because that's what God has called us to do. Others provide their voices, voices which rise up above the lies to speak truth. Some are encouragers, some organisers, some prayer warriors, some builders, some gardeners, everyone has a purpose.

The future isn't something to be afraid of, it's something to be excited about, because God is already there. He has a plan and it's always for our good and His glory. Our job is to trust Him, to listen for His voice and to follow Him wherever he leads. Whatever God is calling you to do to fight the evil we see, do it all and do it for the glory of God.

Written with a prayer that each reader may know the hope of Christ and live for Him.

41

Human Flourishing in a Digital World

By Dylan Roberts

A positive account of human flourishing would clarify the costs and risks of dependence on digital technology; provide a convincing alternative to digital experiences; and point towards actual benefits that technological development could be aimed at.

A global digital infrastructure is well under way: digital ID, central bank digital currencies, pervasive optical surveillance, on-line censorship, social credit systems, 15-minute cities and so on. There is little doubt about what this infrastructure puts at risk, politically and socially. It is presented as enhancing safety, convenience, and economic efficiency, but seems designed for totalitarian surveillance and social control. If events do not go well, then reading articles about digital tyranny would be at best pointless; at worst it would be a seditious, punishable thought-crime. It is difficult to see that as a world worth living in.

Events going well would mean political and personal freedoms are preserved, or even enhanced. Events going well is usually presented as popular knowledge of what is happening; political defence of what is at risk; and political and legal safeguards and improved technology. The desired outcome being less repressive economic and political arrangements. However, economic activity and political freedom are not the only things in life. An account is required of the damage done by digitisation to everyday psychological experience; and of positive alternatives that complement a resistance based in political fear and outrage.

Degraded personal experience is politically useful

Digital technology is very effective at hollowing out the quality of human life, both individually and communally. It's not hard to come up with examples:

➤ Anyone with a content streaming service is familiar with the feeling of being daunted, bored, and somehow diminished by the amount of material to choose between.
➤ Some pre-teen girls have no escape from schoolyard harassment and ostracism, even at home, due to social media.
➤ Limitless pornography alters the reward centres of the brain. Hook-up apps, catfish filters and cost-free pornography skew young people's expectations of sex and relationships; this, plausibly, undermines development of the skills of actually forming relationships.
➤ New types of dysfunctional behaviours become possible: 'Women on internet forums are constantly encouraging one another to escalate small or non-existent misdeeds into existential relationship threats. It's incredibly toxic'; 'women are being psychologically destroyed by social media and there's basically zero upside. It's their porn' (comment found on Twitter).

> A more diffuse example is the replacement of music made on physical instruments with digitally produced music. Making music has been crucial throughout history for knitting together the social fabric. Digitally produced music has much less of the rich social meanings of music-making on physical instruments.

This hollowing out suits those who profit from the manipulation of economies. Since the Enlightenment, the public narratives justifying western societies have been based in a humanistic account; roughly, that human lives are the ultimate source of value, and are the ultimate good the societies exist to advance and protect. These narratives are rather at odds with historical events, which suggest that the revealed value of actual human lives is low; and that an instrumental, utilitarian account of monetised human assets is closer to the actual animating principles. The more individual everyday experience is hollowed out, the easier it is for population to be reduced to masses, interchangeable, monetised and disposable. For example, Yuval Noah Harari, asked what will useless eaters do without labour to structure their time: '*With all these useless people, I don't think we have an economic model. For that my best guess ... is that food will not be a problem. With that kind of technology you will be able to produce food to feed everybody. The problem is more boredom, and what to do with them. How will they find some sense of meaning in life, when they are basically meaningless, worthless? My best guess at present is a combination of drugs and computer games.*'

The character of the current digital infrastructure reflects this attitude, although presented otherwise. However, much of the rhetoric opposed to digital tyranny is within the paradigm of oppositional politics: the political threat is located in oppressive external institutions and forces; political activity is designed to destroy these institutions and replace them with virtuous ones. This is to accept the paradigm of the digital infrastructure. A kinder, gentler global digital infrastructure would not address the digital hollowing out.

Technological change is not spontaneous and inevitable, and not morally neutral

Most accounts of technological change present it as inevitable, as the only practical choice and say it should therefore be embraced without reserve. This entirely leaves out the morality implicit in the development of the technology. For example, social media was initially presented as morally-neutral places where people could post content and connect with others. In reality, it was designed, with careful psychological research, to capture data and guide attention.

Also, this is why human-digital interfaces are being pursued so vigorously: as science fiction has been wondering about for the last century, it would eventually erase all differences between biological and digital experiences. Human meaning is inseparable from human biology; that is, primate, mammal biology. Advocates for transhumanism say that once biology is replaced with technology, a new and distinctive morality will emerge. Again, this is presented as somehow inevitable and utopian, although there are obvious risks. For example, if a person is dependent on proprietary technology, what rights do they have to it? Would the real-world equivalent of Blade Runner's Tyrrell Corporation own the new and distinctive morality?

There are no convincing accounts of what is so deficient in human biology that it has to be replaced. Rather, everyday experience shows that ordinary human biology, as fallible as it is, is perfectly sufficient for people to lead meaningful lives.

Non-digital human flourishing will be useful whether

things go well or not, which is just as well. Most people will have no influence on how the global digital infrastructure develops, or the legal and political structures around it. They will just have to make the best of the conditions they find themselves in, as they always have. It makes sense to focus on making the most of what agency is possible, and how digital technology undermines this.

The language of non-digital human flourishing needs to develop

There is nothing mysterious about non-digital human flourishing: it is anything that enables living more fully, with more agency, in the evolved bodies and minds we have, in a digitally-controlled environment. For example, there is no shortage of science-fiction in which beleaguered protagonists struggle in a technocratic dystopia. Roughly, everything these protagonists do to maintain a life worth living are the same activities with which people have pursued meaningful lives throughout history. It is explicitly based in its biological foundations and in long established practices. A positive account of it would clarify the costs and risks of dependence on digital technology, provide a convincing alternative to digital experiences, and point towards actual benefits that technological development could be aimed at.

It would be good to have a concise descriptive term, as the language around human virtues in a digital environment has yet to evolve. None of the current terms is exactly right: 'The offline world' is like journalistic jargon, and analogue (rather than digital) sounds like a technology issue; 'the material world' and 'the physical world' sound like geology or physics; 'evolutionary biology space' and 'the biological world' is like natural history; 'the world of living and dying' sounds something like Buddhism; 'Meat space' is reductive and slightly revolting; and 'real life' and 'human life' are vague and not descriptive.

A useful term would include the relevant aspects of all of these, but focus on the material, biological and psychological basis of non-digital human flourishing. It might also be useful to have neologisms for entities such as 'a digital experience that is worse than a real-world experience it replaces'; 'the crushing of an illusion of a fulfilling on-line life by real-world poverty.', 'the final, total replacement of a biological or real world option by a commercially-owned technological option', and so on. The last century of science fiction could well be a source of these situations and ideas.

Working against the negative effects of the digital infrastructure would benefit from being as psychologically sophisticated as the creators of social media. Knowing that other approaches have been proven to work provides a stronger basis for resisting digital social control. An independent person with agency in their own lives is a much stronger refutation of the 'useless eater' characterisation than someone dependent on digital technology and state services.

Practical approaches

It is difficult to make practical suggestions that are appropriate to everyone: suggesting someone gets more exercise, spends more time outside and more time with people they care about sounds rather lame. However, there are a few approaches that act as a place to start:

➢ Notice the thinness of digital experiences, and the richness of real world experiences.

For all their power and convenience, digital experiences do not engage all aspects of the human animal. They are thin or hollow in comparison with real world experiences. For example, watching sports on TV rather than being at the match, or listening to a symphony on headphones compared to being next to the orchestra; or conversations on Zoom. Traditional sources are more meaningful. A place to start is to pay attention to prosaic activities that are psychologically richer than their digital equivalents. For example, why is reading paper books nicer than an e-reader?

➢ Be clear about the damage done by, and the hidden costs of, digital experiences.

Digital infrastructure is sold as convenience, but there are plenty of hidden costs: surveillance and collection of personal data; use of surveillance data for social control, general or targeted; edging out of physical world options; centralised control of functions essential to modern life. Being able to express these costs and risks succinctly makes it easier to avoid them, and convince other people.

➢ Replace passive entertainments with more active, cognitively challenging pursuits.

Passive technology-based entertainments are cognitively cheap but ultimately unfulfilling. An analogy is with drugs that give a fantasy of an interesting life, but no actual meaningful experiences to look back on. More demanding activities are harder but provide actual meaningful life. For example, it might be a challenge to knit booties for someone else's baby, but is guaranteed to be more meaningful and memorable than the same time watching TV dramas. Jordan Peterson's most convincing position was (roughly) that modern life was hollowed out by consumerism and neoliberal politics; and that anyone could re-moralise their own life with character and virtue, and by pursuing fulfilment and achievement over pleasure and status.

➢ Keep alive the experience of individual and social life outside of digital control.

Currently there are people who can remember a world without the internet, who are in a good position to see what is being lost. This will be different for subsequent generations. It will only take a couple of decades until there is no-one alive who can remember life before the internet. It is experience to hang onto. For example, old novels, old films give a vicarious experience of a world not controlled by technology. It is worth developing and passing on the skills and wisdom of a life not controlled by technology.

Human flourishing in a digital world is a big subject, although it is more important to focus on actual practices than to compose a magnificent conceptual structure. In previous times, it might have been worth suggesting a university department for studying it. However, scholars and institutions have little defence against control by larger interests. The infrastructure for decentralised dissemination of information exists, so it probably makes sense to look to individuals, Youtubers, citizen journalists, civic activists, and small media entrepreneurs rather than institutions to generate wisdom in this area.

It is hard to imagine a future world without a pervasive digital infrastructure. Perhaps a utopian aspiration would be for everyone to be able to participate fully in the power and convenience of the digital world, and also to have a life completely outside of it.

42

Region One

By Stephen James Gray

The following is a transcript of a letter that was received five years ago by the writer of an online blog known as 'Truth Space'. The blog, which had been active for some time and dealt mostly with issues surrounding the direction in which the writer believed society was heading, has since gone quiet and the whereabouts of the site's owner is unknown. What became of the young woman who wrote the letter, remains a mystery...

'My name is Sarah Lewis, I am nineteen years old and today I was arrested for speaking in public, warning those who cared to listen of the catastrophe that awaits. I told them of my life in the broken country of my ancestors and of the city in which I lived that became known as Region One—its true name having been lost long ago. I wish to tell of my experience in the grey city and of my daily routine, watched at all times by those who'd indoctrinated us all into accepting our lives there as natural and good.

I recount this tale because I do not wish for the same harsh fate to befall you. If your freedoms are slowly lost, as ours were, then a similar future awaits you too.

A typical morning in that bleak place involved leaving the Pod Block that housed the "Lows" in their thousands, and walking towards the waiting transport. I don't know why I remember this period between leaving home and boarding the bus? Perhaps it was because it was the only time in which I did not feel completely hemmed in and crushed against others, as was the case in almost every other area of life for me at that time. The shuttle bus was entirely driverless and the vehicle programmed to take passengers to their destination after waiting a maximum of three minutes at each stop along the way. If those wishing to catch the bus were not on time, they were forced to wait for the next shuttle which came along thirty minutes later. To miss this second bus, meant we'd be late for work and a punishment would be issued in the form of points being deducted from our credit scores. Since the introduction of the Social Credit System, those who lived in the city were closely monitored and even minor indiscretions were punishable by points being reduced. Should a citizen's points have fallen to zero, they were sent to the "Clinics" where their lives were also reduced to zero so that they'd no longer be a burden upon the society they were unfortunate enough to have been born into. The so-called "doctors" who performed these procedures had long ago forgotten the oaths their forebears had once held in such high esteem.

Once on the bus, we would scan our phones against a panel which bleeped to indicate payment had been accepted, before taking our seats, cash having long ago been abolished. The other passengers, all of them heading to the same vast warehouse, would all sit with their heads down, eyes staring into the screens of their phones, getting the latest important news that came straight from the official state broadcaster—the EBC, or Elite Broadcasting Corporation—that pumped out its propaganda twenty four hours a day, seven days a week. It mattered little whether the population tuned into the news or the entertainment channels, both were peppered with the constant barrage of messages which proclaimed that life in the "modern paradise" of Region One was better than it had ever been at any time in history, and that the population had the phones they carried to thank for that. The faces of the passengers were covered by the ever-present masks which hid their features and made it difficult to tell what they were saying, if they ever bothered to speak at all. It was best to keep to oneself in Region One, lest you said the wrong thing and were punished accordingly. There were times when I would adjust my own mask, pulling it above my nose and mouth, nervous in case it had slipped down and the cameras had spotted the indiscretion. Points could be lost by the dozen if germs were allowed to spread and the finger of blame could be pointed at a potential culprit. Not only that, but I did not wish to be seen as different. Difference was frowned upon in Region One, and was viewed as having the potential to encourage subversive behaviour in others. If a person was judged to have ignited the spark of rebellion, it was punishable by a trip to the "Clinic" and those who made that trip were never heard from again.

    Often, I would look out the window at the grey buildings that flew past as the shuttle moved on towards its destination, noticing the people shuffling by outside, stepping carefully lest any one of the million cameras that monitored their every move was to catch them doing something they shouldn't have been doing. What this thing was, however—this mysterious "crime" that they were afraid of committing—was not known. I suppose it could have been any number of things, thought up on a whim by those who carried out the will of the mysterious Elite who appeared to change their minds at the drop of a hat, always ready to keep the population on their feet and on the edge of a nervous breakdown.

All for the common good, of course.

"Where would we be without the EBC to remind us that the Elite have our best interests at heart?" screamed the posters on every street corner and in every corridor, canteen and toilet cubicle at work. Those same break areas that served the insect protein and which required a scan of the phone, both upon entry and when leaving, to reassure the system that an employee had not gone over their allotted period of rest. If they were to do so, of course, points would be deducted and the associated punishments incurred.

I remember once receiving a message reminding me that I'd got to make an appointment for the monthly inoculation before the end of the week, and I quickly replied. Failure to do so would have meant a loss of two points from my credit score and I'd have been two steps closer to visiting the Clinic. From birth, all Lows are allocated a credit score of one thousand points, but minor indiscretions by those below the age of eighteen are usually ignored and put down to youthful naivety. Once adulthood is finally reached, however, all indiscretions are noted automatically and the credit score quickly begins to fall if not carefully monitored by all "considerate" citizens. I booked the appointment via an app on my phone and remember rubbing my arm at the memory of the pain caused by the dozens of other inoculations I'd received over the years. What these injections were really for, or what they protected the population against, was anybody's guess. The EHS or Elite Health Service, which never seemed to be used by the Elite themselves, did not bother to explain the reasons for the inoculations and simply called for the population to receive them each month and every month, or face the prospect of losing points.

"I suppose it provides jobs," I remember thinking, as the bus pulled up at the gates of the huge complex that was my place of work. "And keeps us safe and healthy, or course," I added, genuinely believing what I'd been conditioned to accept. We'd scan our phones against the gate and enter the building, glad to be on time again. I was late once and the panic that rose inside my stomach as points were docked automatically from my credit score, made me vow to never miss the first bus again. We'd press our phones against our lockers so we could store our belongings away, not forgetting to use our phones once more to order groceries to be delivered to the Pods for the following day. Everything was bought this way in Region One. Everything from food to clothing anyway, which is all anyone really needed. Personal possessions were not required by the populace and many books were outright banned due to the potential for them to spread subversive ideas. Most books were read on phones anyway, and could be deleted or updated as and when the Elite felt it necessary to do so. No, clothes and food were all anyone needed in Region One, and only two outfits were required at that—one for work and one for recreation. The one for work being the most important, as that was where people spent most of their time. The twelve-hour days we were instructed to work needed practical and sturdy clothing, whereas the other outfit was only required for the one day off the workforce was granted per week. This secondary outfit was mainly worn when the population assembled at one of the Gathering Points to give thanks to the Elites of the past who were represented by statues in the old park—those who'd first ushered in the protective vaccines and the power of the phones and the towers, without which no one would be able to buy food or clothing or check on their all-important credit score. At the Gathering Points, the assembled stood two meters apart at every moment and were watched over by the EPUs—the Elite Police Units which carried out the will of the Elite, making sure the rules were enforced and credit losses amongst those gathered had no reason to occur.

At work, we'd stand at our posts, watching items we did not recognise go by on a conveyor belt. These were destined for the homes of the Elite who lived beyond the walls of the city on their expansive estates. From there the chosen few watched over the populace of Region One, making sure they were taken care of—or so the messages that regularly flashed up on the peoples' phones told them. In reality, none had ever met a member of the Elite. How could they? No one was allowed out of the city, and that was generally accepted as a good thing. Only the Elite had the physical strength and mental dexterity to deal with the things that lay beyond the walls, we were told. "Always thinking of the people and how best to serve us," I thought. "What would we do without the Elite?"

I remember once looking over at my workmates, all of whom wore masks as it was forbidden not to, and seeing a foreman screaming at two other drones—cogs in the machine that were easily replaceable if their scores dropped to zero—who'd committed the sin of conversing whilst standing too close together. The two separated immediately, all too aware that points were about to be deducted. In the canteen at break time, the bugs would always be on offer, in fact they were the only things that had ever been on offer. I'd heard that there'd once been a choice between them and a miserable looking form of synthetic meat, but to choose the "synth" too often was viewed as unhealthy and could lead to a substantial loss of points on the credit score. It was difficult to determine how much synth could be consumed before an employee's credit rating was affected, or just how many points would be deducted if it was. Everything seemed to be determined on a whim in Region One, and so, as a result, most opted to dine on the tasteless insect matter as it was easier to do so than to risk incurring the wrath of the system, and be forced to accept the inevitable punishment.

How long these rules and regulations had been in place in Region One, I had no idea, but at some point in the not-so distant past, a generation indifferent to the changes that were happening around them had grown into adulthood and become fixated with the new technology which they held in the palms of their hands. A technology that would eventually help lead their descendants into a form of slavery that most would come to view as "normal". In those far off days, as laws were introduced to prevent large numbers of people from gathering together, those who realised the potential consequences of these new rules were criminalized when they tried to speak out against them, and mocked by the apathetic majority who thought them to be nothing more than cranks, trouble makers and conspiracy theorists. Of course, the laws were brought in quietly, ostensibly to put an end to protests conducted by extremist activists and pressure groups, many of whom, in reality, were acting on behalf of the Governments they claimed to despise whether they realised it or not, and the repercussions of their actions were far reaching and terrible.

After a long and demanding shift, I'd disembark from the bus which dropped me off outside the Pod complex where I'd use my phone to enter the building, and once again when I reached my personal Pod. When I entered, I'd bump into the middle-aged lady who shared the Pod with me, and say goodbye as she headed out for her own shift at the same warehouse. We'd literally have to squeeze past one another in the cramped one room apartment. Like most of the population of Region One, we were expected to share our living space with others who worked at a different time of day. "At least the Elites have been considerate enough to place me with someone who is not at home whilst I am asleep," I used to think, believing that they had our best interests at heart. Work was difficult, but it was better than the alternative. For the majority who received the Universal Basic Income, the days were long and meaningless—soul destroying. Creativity was not encouraged and so many found themselves becoming depressed, finding solace only at the end of a bottle. Health suffered and no plans were put in place to reverse the trend.

After a tasteless insect meal, I would sit for a while watching the EBC news report. I remember seeing a bulletin once that told of a large country somewhere far away which had attacked another, smaller country, and somehow, I knew that this would affect relations with my own as the Elite inevitably decided to send arms to the smaller country. This, they always seemed to do, regardless of what had actually caused the violence to erupt in the first place. Perhaps the large country will restrict food or fuel again, I would think, all the while knowing that the restrictions would not affect the Elite.

If I felt cold, I would turn on the Smart meter installed in all pods, which never seemed to improve the situation. The cost of heating was high, but all bills were taken automatically from our wages and so there was no choice but to pay it. Afterwards I would climb into bed at the correctly allotted time, the lights would go out on cue, and I knew that nothing would change tomorrow—every day the same dull grey as it always was. I knew I would wake up at the same time and eat the same insect infused breakfast, owning nothing and being happy, though never truly feeling it. Sometimes, before I went to sleep, a tear would run down the side of my cheek, and I would begin to cry, although I did not know why. "I am happy," I would whisper, to no one in particular, repeating the words we were all encouraged to say, as though to reassure myself of the truth behind the words, before I'd go quiet and pull the covers over my head.

Always I was afraid to speak the words that I knew to be my own. The ones that came from the real me that had been buried somewhere deep inside. The phone on the bedside table was always listening, always waiting for the wrong thing to be said—a single word or phrase that might upset the algorithm, and cause the points on the credit score to come tumbling down, falling towards the ever-nearing destination of zero...'

It is still unclear where the city described by Sarah Lewis as 'Region One' is located, but many have speculated that it exists somewhere beyond the Sorrows—that barren waste whose leaders forbid the leaking of information to foreign countries on pain of death. If this is the case, it is with great sadness that we must accept that little can be done to change her situation at the present time, though her story, perhaps unbeknownst to her, has had much affect upon our own. Whatever fate befell Sarah Lewis afterwards, it appears from her writing that at some point she was able to escape the grey city, and made a seemingly unsuccessful attempt to warn others (perhaps in a neighbouring country) against following the same path, before being taken into custody. It is most fortunate, then, that she was able to get her message out to the Truth Space blog before this occurred.

After the letter was uploaded, it soon went viral throughout the nations that were still allowed to receive non-government approved information, and the affect upon those who read it was both life changing and immediate. Appeals were made to governing bodies to refrain from replacing physical money with digital currency—a plan which had been touted by some MPs for a long time beforehand. The argument was made that to lose cash would be to lose the freedom to remain private, and the voices that rallied behind this call to keep the old system in place proved too numerous for those in power to resist.

People that had never before taken much interest in how

things were run, began to question everything, and viewed anything that was being sold to them on the pretext of being good for their well-being, or for the well-being of the planet, with suspicion. Aware that unpleasant truths are sometimes hidden behind pleasant lies, they began to look deeper into what was really being said and the potential consequences of blindly putting their trust in those who'd been elected to govern them. The media, too, sensing that the mood of the nation had changed, began to delve deeper into the stories they came across, holding to account politicians and anyone else whose unscrupulous methods may have led to the suffering of millions. Those journalists who'd previously been in the employ of those who were prepared to pay the most money, were weeded out and ejected from the industry, leaving an unbiased media which reported the news objectively, and which the citizens were proud to celebrate.

Notions that politicians had harboured over the introduction of ID cards and a Universal Basic Income were quickly scrapped, along with plans they'd drawn up for cities whose borders the populace would have been unable to travel far beyond. The citizens had collectively opened their eyes and a nation that was willing to take the necessary steps in order to prevent itself from becoming a country of slaves, was a nation which those in charge knew better than to disrespect. Transparency was demanded in all areas of life. When a mystery disease was announced to the public as being a serious health risk, scientists and medical professionals did their best to convey the truth of the situation, offering advice where it was required, and turning down the monetary incentives that had been offered to them to remain quiet. The oaths they had taken were regarded as sacrosanct and their duty to their patients was of far greater importance to them than any financial reward could ever hope to be. Business owners who'd read of life in the grey city refused to rely on machines when a human being could do the job just as well, if not better, and many refused to accept anything other than physical money. Opposing political factions, too, from all Parties and systems of belief, found common ground in their shock at Sarah Lewis's account and disavowed the corruption that had been allowed to fester in her country of origin. There was a coming together, a general consensus that what had happened in Region One was not acceptable and that the policies which had led to such a state of affairs should never be allowed to occur at home.

All of this began five years ago, and today things continue to improve. Our nation, that was on the brink of a disaster equal to the one that befell Region One, managed to prevent itself from falling over that edge by the actions of one young woman and by those who trusted her story enough to believe her...

Hope Amidst a Tsunami of Evil—Exposing the Great Lies. Veronica Finch, September 2022, 250 pages.

Evidence, facts, essays, testimonies, letters and reflections.

The White Rose—Defending Freedom. Veronica Finch, November 2021, 102 pages.

All about the White Rose UK, including English translations of flyers from the German underground resistance.

Freedom!—An Anthology of Poems, Short Stories and Essays. Various authors, March 2021, 147 pages.

Composed by 36 authors questioning Covid restrictions and lockdowns.

The Big Bad Wolf and the Syringe—A Fairy Tale. Connie Lamb, December 2022, 35 pages.

Can the hens of Henton trust Wolf's 'miracle cure'?

Stop Them!—Together We Will End World Control, and This Is How! Propositions from 81 authors, June 2023, 50 pages. Free download.

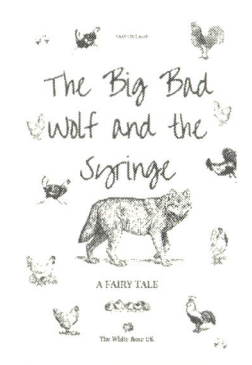

➢ Order more books online: thewhiterose.uk/white-rose-products
➢ Visit thewhiterose.uk to view over 1,500 articles for free.
➢ Sign up to our free weekly newsletter: thewhiterose.uk/newsletter

Made in the USA
Columbia, SC
08 August 2023

cdbf5cc9-eb30-4763-b7bc-df691d30b1ebR01